DAVID'S HARP

The captured vessels of the Jerusalem Temple, with the sacred silver trumpets. Relief from the Arch of Titus, Rome

Alfred Sendrey
&
Mildred Norton

DAVID'S HARP

The Story of Music in Biblical Times

Sponsored by the Jewish Heritage Foundation

AN NAL-WORLD BOOK

PUBLISHED BY THE NEW AMERICAN LIBRARY

In writing this book, we were privileged to have had the encouragement and counsel of Dr. Joseph Gaer, Director of the Jewish Heritage Foundation, who has given generously of his time and wisdom.

A. S.
M. N.

FIRST PRINTING
Published by The New American Library of World Literature, Inc.
501 Madison Avenue, New York, New York 10022

Published simultaneously in Canada by General Publishing Company, Ltd.

Library of Congress Catalog Card Number: 64-24526
Printed in the United States of America

Contents

1
IN THE DAYS OF THE PATRIARCHS

Abraham heads west . . . Music's legendary beginnings . . .
Songs of the Patriarchs . . . Moses' use of music . . . The
Red Sea song . . . Dance around the golden calf . . . The

2
THE PROMISED LAND

Canaan, a highway of commerce . . . Musical instruments of
neighboring peoples . . . Some musical customs of antiquity
. . . The struggle against pagan influence . . . The Well-

3
MUSIC DURING THE COMMONWEALTH

Settling in Canaan . . . Hannah prays for a son . . . Samuel
is born . . . Saul anointed king . . . The first lay academy of
music . . . Sons of the Prophets . . . Saul's melancholy

4
THE STAR OF DAVID

A magnetic new personality . . . David slays Goliath . . .
The women hail him in song . . . Saul plots to kill him . . .
David flees to Samuel . . . Musical instruments at the acad-
emy . . . Saul pursues David . . . David joins the Philistines
. . . Saul and Jonathan are slain . . . The Song of the

5

THE ARK COMES TO JERUSALEM

David is made king . . . Music as a folk expression . . . Religion as yet uncentralized . . . A singing host goes to reclaim the Ark . . . An ominous mishap . . . A formal musical escort . . . David dances before the Ark . . . Inaugurates the sacred musical service

6

THE TEMPLE OF SOLOMON

Music's new role in the cult ritual . . . David in later days . . . He counsels young Solomon . . . He appoints hereditary cult musicians . . . Solomon builds the Temple . . . It is dedicated with music

7

ORGANIZATION OF TEMPLE MUSIC

A royal musical dowry . . . New musical instruments appear . . . Duties of the Temple singers . . . Rehearsals . . . Conducting technique . . . Length of apprenticeship . . . Women may have belonged to the sacred choir also

8

THE SACRED PSALMS

Who wrote the Psalms? . . . Some reasonable conjectures . . . Possible folk sources . . . Egyptian and Babylonian influence . . . Pre-Psalter collections . . . Ancient authorship was largely anonymous . . . Traditional authors of certain psalms . . . Jeduthun, a nonexistent singer

9

THE CHARACTER OF HEBREW MUSIC

How were the Psalms sung? . . . A basic error of scholarship . . . An overlooked clue . . . Hebrew music was Oriental . . . An enlightening stone slab . . . The makam principle . . . The character of Oriental song . . . Meter in Hebrew

10
THE ENIGMA OF THE PSALM HEADINGS

11
MUSIC AND THE HARVEST FESTIVALS

12
MUSIC IN SECULAR LIFE

• 13
THE MUSICAL INSTRUMENTS OF ANCIENT ISRAEL

18

A MUSICAL RENAISSANCE IN JUDAH

19

WOMEN'S ROLE IN ANCIENT
HEBREW MUSIC

20

MUSIC AND SUPERSTITION

21

THE DANCE IN ANCIENT ISRAEL

1

IN THE DAYS OF THE PATRIARCHS

THE MUSIC OF ancient Israel, like the story of Israel itself, begins with Abraham, who nearly 4,000 years ago left his native city, Ur of the Chaldees, to seek for something.

What that something was, Abraham did not know. He knew only that the time had come for him to leave that ancient metropolis near the Euphrates delta where Nannar, the moon god, ruled the city's fortune. Nannar was no worse—in some ways perhaps a shade better—than the patron deities of neighboring cities, but for all that his reputation was not reassuring. In the already long annals of Ur it was told that upon a king's death his attendants and court musicians were traditionally slain and buried with him, while on the mound above his burial chamber some hapless boy or girl was ritually sacrificed to the moon god.

Abraham as yet had no children, but the outlook for their future in that land must have struck him as needlessly uncertain. As men would do later when a local situation looked unpromising, Abraham pulled up stakes and headed west, not incidentally setting in motion one of the great epic sagas of the world.

Taking a circuitous northerly route to skirt first the hot Syrian desert and then the mountains of Lebanon, met now by hostile native tribes and now by the threat of famine, Abraham and his band of kinfolk had to abandon their hope of settling down in the green valleys of Canaan and make their way south into Egypt. Here the granaries were full and the people too prosperous to resent the intrusion of yet another band of westering nomads and their cluster of goathair tents.

Abraham's stay in Egypt was short, but when he returned to Canaan he was a rich man. When the children of Israel, his grandson, went again into Egypt their stay was less happy and it lasted 400 years. But when they returned to Canaan they were a People.

Music is a gift of every people and in every age, but for the children of Israel, whose religion forbade their making "any graven image" of their deity, music took on a deeper meaning. It united them as a congregation chorusing its faith in a God who, if he was not visible in wood or stone like other deities of the time, was at least within earshot. It united them, too, in one of the oldest and deepest impulses of the human spirit: to give songful expression to a sense of awe before the terror and the glory of creation.

Man's devotional impulse was joined with music in the unrecorded ages of prehistory. In a cave drawing of Magdalenian times a primitive shaman dances with his flute. Faced with the need to conciliate forces beyond his reach or knowing, primitive man wooed them with his body in the dance, but more significantly in the sphere uniquely contingent to his human status, that of speech. His earliest vocal overtures may have been no more than a rhythmic chanting, whose hypnotic repetition in the ritual combined with heightened emotion to evolve a kind of speech-melody, out of which simple patterns knitted themselves into rudimentary short "tunes" of a few easily sung notes, repeated without variation.

Over the course of ages other kinds of song evolved: some from the physical rhythms of daily work, some from the chants by which the tribal elders passed on to younger members the lore and teachings of the clan. Personal passions, too, came to be expressed in song. The oldest Hebrew song of which a fragment remains is attributed to the biblical patriarch Lamech in a legendary age before the Flood:

> Adah and Zillah, hear my voice;
>   You wives of Lamech, hearken to what I say:
> I have slain a man for wounding me,
>   A young man for striking me.
> If Cain is avenged sevenfold,
>   Truly Lamech seventy-sevenfold.

Following the nomadic pattern of the ancient Near East, the early Hebrew shepherds made for themselves the simple musical instruments used by all primitive herdsmen. They knew that a reed with holes drilled in it could produce a succession of agreeable tones, and that a ram's horn with the tip cut away could be used to rally the flock together or to signal the whereabouts of a lonely shepherd on some far hillside. A hollow gourd and a bit of sheep gut provided a crude stringed instrument to reinforce their song. Animal skin stretched over a hollow tree trunk, concussion sticks, dried gourds filled with seeds or pebbles—a variety of percussive devices was readily at hand to furnish rhythmic accent.

According to biblical lore, Lamech's son Jubal "was the father of all those who play the lyre and pipe," while Jubal's older brother, Jabal, "was the father of those who dwell in tents and have cattle." If we pronounce the J like Y—as many languages do—we see how similar Jubal and Jabal are to *yobel*, the Hebrew word for "horn" or "ram." By extension we may thus speculate that long before Abraham left Ur, Jabal was a tent-dwelling shepherd on the edge of the Arabian desert with a thriving trade in hides and livestock, while his musician brother, Jubal, pursued his own profitable sideline of converting the animals' horns into rustic trumpets.

Eventually this trumpet of animal horn acquired the name *shofar*, from the Assyrian word for "wild goat." The instrument itself was to have a long association with the Hebrew people. The ritual blasts blown on the shofar in today's Jewish synagogues hark back nearly 4,000 years to the voice of the primitive shofar that hung from Abraham's saddlebag on the long trip west.

By that time, however, music itself had come a long way. In leaving Ur, Abraham also left behind him that city's richly developed musical life. We do not know if he carried any features of this with him; but when his grandson, Jacob (Israel), returned to visit kinfolk who had dropped out of the westering caravan along the upper Euphrates, he found them observing well-established musical customs of a strong social character. We learn this from Jacob's father-in-law, Laban, when Jacob after twenty years departed without leave-taking:

> Why did you flee secretly . . . and did not tell me, so that I might have sent you away with mirth and songs, with tambourine and lyre?

Between the age of Lamech's vengeful chant and this pretty custom of escorting a departing friend with music, much time and cultural evolution had been spanned. Music brightened the long summer of the patriarchs, as it would cheer the winters of their children in bondage. The Hebrews entered Egypt with a great but unformed gift for music. For 400 years they submitted this, along with themselves, to the most rigorously organized culture of the antique world. The result was a heightened intensity of musical feeling by which song was enabled to traverse the widest areas of the Hebrew spirit. Throughout their early years of prosperity and their later years of oppression under the pharaohs this shared emotional outlet defined their tribal solidarity "in a strange land" and cemented it ever more firmly. By the time the Israelites left Egypt they were a people given uniquely to song.

The man who fired them with a sense of purpose, led them, scolded them, and taught them was, according to the story, Moses. According to this account also, he was the adopted son of a pharaoh's daughter, in which case he would quite possibly have been educated for the Egyptian priesthood, and may even have functioned as a priest himself. Inasmuch as music was a part of all ancient religious ritual, Moses would have been as well versed in this as in other arts and sciences of the time. In Islamic tradition he is looked upon as the patron of pipers, and the legend, like all legends, may contain a kernel of historic truth.

Throughout forty years of desert wandering, at any rate, Moses appears to have made active use of music as a means for teaching his people to preserve the intellectual heritage, the songs and proverbs, and the musical instruments they had brought with them from

Egypt. Thus in addition to being priest, judge, and prophet, Moses may perhaps also be regarded as the first music teacher of the Hebrews.

Above all else, however, Moses was a symbol of man's never-ending search for truth. Historically he stands for an organizing force that was to gather and codify the laws deriving from a new kind of God—and one not to be found in heathen idols or the animal-headed deities of Egypt.

For Abraham, nearly eight centuries before, had found what he was seeking—a God who would not tolerate the ritual sacrifice of human beings. The name of this new God was Yahweh. He was jealous and exacting, but he could be reasoned with. And to do him homage the children of Israel turned the full force of their creative passion into praising him with music, with dance, with poetry, and with song.

Few areas of their life, in fact, remained untouched by music. In the frightening vastness of the wilderness they drew communal strength from the unifying power of song. The singer might be one of the folk bards, who already had a store of heroic tales from still further back in history—about the Flood, perhaps, or the creation of the world, as these had traveled down the ages from a still older people, the Sumerians. Or a song learned during the long stay in Egypt might be adapted to the occasion. Song at times welled up spontaneously, spilling over when some extraordinary event swelled emotions past containing. Then a leader had only to strike up a tune for all the rest to join in. Often this would spring to life as a kind of free prose-poetry that found its fullest expression in song.

Such was the song that Moses and the children of Israel offered in thanksgiving after safely crossing the Red Sea, which had drowned the pursuing horsemen of the pharaoh:

> I will sing to the Lord, for he has triumphed gloriously;
> The horse and his rider he has thrown into the sea.
> The Lord is my strength and my song.

In the biblical account the song is probably longer than it was originally. For many generations its preservation depended on folk bards who, like all performers, were not loath to build up their part. But because of them we are today able to picture the magnificent old prophet leading the triumphal ode beside the white seabanks, as the other men repeated after him words exalted into high poetry by the intensity of the hour.

The women, too, took an active part. Moses' sister, Miriam, who seems to have shared the family's natural bent for leadership, took a timbrel in her hand and led all the women in a dance of joy, caroling to one another after the custom of the time the verses that the men sang with Moses. The celebration continued far into the night, while the sparks from a thousand campfires mounted upward with the singing.

Even at this early stage a consciousness of incipient nationhood shines in the verses of the Red Sea song, but for all its religious coloring it was not a ritual song in the strict sense. True liturgical song did not develop for the Israelites until they became the chosen people of Yahweh through the covenant on Mount Sinai. From that time on Israel, as a theocracy that took its laws directly from God, would have its own form of religious cult, which eventually was to invest both ritual and music with an ethical force unprecedented in history.

Like any religion, however, it was not established overnight. Throughout their early history there would be many times when the Hebrews had recourse to pagan ritual. Even as Moses was receiving the Ten Commandments on Mount Sinai, the people, restive at his long absence, tossed their gold ornaments into a melting pot and made a golden calf to worship after the Egyptian fashion.

When Moses, bearing the Testimony on two stone tablets, came down from the mountain, he heard the people singing from a long way off. It sounded disturbingly like the rude chanting that went on at rural nature orgies in Egypt. Hurrying to camp, he pushed his way past faces too inflamed by the sensual revelry to recognize their leader. Above the din of hoarse cries and incantations pipes shrilled suggestively and drums urged the pounding pulses to ever faster tempo.

The biblical account of the orgy is terse, but we can imagine the scene that must have met his eyes. Stark against the leaping flames of the altar, half-clad men and women staggered drunkenly in an obscene dance around the golden calf, "for Aaron had made them naked unto their shame." Couples, heedlessly embracing, dotted the shadowy hollows in the lewd abandon of pagan fertility rites.

Moses pressed on to the altar. His eyes ablaze with more than mortal anger, he broke the stone tablets with their holy message to a people that was unworthy. Before the golden idol he stood with arms upraised, a figure of majesty, terrible in his wrath.

The drums and the shrilling pipes fell silent. The revelers, recalled to sanity, began to whimper. Furtively they tried to smooth their torn garments over their nakedness. Eyes seeking the ground, they waited to learn their punishment. This was prompt and not without a certain poetic quality. Moses melted the golden idol in the fire, ground it to powder, strewed it upon the brackish desert water, and made the people drink of it. Then he had all who had taken part in the orgy put to the sword.

But after his anger had cooled, Moses was thoughtful. He called the remainder of the people together.

"It is the wish of Yahweh," said Moses, "that you build an Ark to house his spirit when he chooses to visit you." And he described precisely how this should be built.

"It is the wish of Yahweh," said Moses, "that my brother Aaron and his descendants form a perpetual priesthood for the sacred service." And he described the duties and privileges of the office, and the garments they should wear.

"It is the wish of Yahweh," said Moses, "that my own tribe, the Levites, assist the priests in the tabernacle that you shall build to house the Ark."

As soon as he left off speaking, the people set to work. It kept them out of mischief for more than a year. Their jewels and gold now went to adorn the sanctuary of Yahweh. Their silver trappings they hammered into a pair of matched trumpets, resembling those that Moses had seen in Egyptian temples. The Israelites consecrated their trumpets to the Lord, and only the priesthood, the "sons of Aaron," would ever be allowed to sound them.

One blast summoned the tribal leaders to the general tent; two blasts assembled the congregation. Other signals would start the various camps on their way. From now on the sound of the silver trumpets, blown before every battle, would stouten the heart of Israel's fighting host against all adversaries.

No longer were they a straggling band of fraternally linked tribes fleeing from an oppressor. Now they were organized as a cult and governed by a code of laws. Slowly and with innumerable setbacks they pressed forward to the land of Canaan—an army on the march.

Each dawn the silver trumpets sounded the call to break camp. In the forefront went the standard of Judah; then, ringed protectively by the other companies, the Levites set out, bearing upon their shoulders the Ark of the Covenant. The lifting of the sacred burden was an awesome moment. As it rose, Moses and the people sang:

> Arise, O Lord, and let thy enemies be scattered;
> And let them that hate thee flee before thee.

When at nightfall the Ark came to rest, they sang:

> Return, O Lord, to the ten thousand thousands of Israel.

On the long trek north to Canaan and during the years of fighting its resistant tribes, the Ark was carried like a banner in the midst of the marching host.

2

THE PROMISED LAND

WHAT WAS IT like, the land to which they marched, the Promised
Land that was to be their inheritance?

Canaan was the highway between the two great civilizations of
antiquity, Egypt and Babylonia. One might suppose that under
such circumstances it would itself have had a high order of civilization. Instead, it was separated into small quarreling city-states,
each worshiping one or another nature god, or Baal, with pagan
rites and songs.

For thousands of years caravans had passed through it with a
steady flow of merchandise from a dozen lands: rubies and coral,
honey and wine, ebony and ivory, purple dyestuffs from Phoenicia,
tall cedars from the forests of Lebanon, mirrors of polished copper
from Egypt, spices from southern Arabia.

Rulers exchanged gifts of fragrant balms and jewels and con-
cubines. Soldiers, ambassadors, merchants, and nomads crisscrossed
the fertile floor of Canaan on a thousand errands, and carried
home with them many of the luxuries and customs of other lands.
In time the people of the various countries showed almost as many

points of similarity in their culture as of difference, and one of these was their musical instruments.

All peoples borrow from one another so constantly that after a while it is not easy to tell where a particular article or custom originally came from. This is the case with the musical instruments of antiquity, and especially with those of the ancient Hebrews. Because their religion forbade them to make any graven images, they left no pictured records of their own musical customs. The Old Testament, which gives us such a vivid account of their history, mentions various instruments used by them, but it offers no clue as to what these looked like or even, in some cases, whether they were stringed instruments, drums, or woodwinds.

Fortunately, other peoples left many such pictures. On the walls of Egyptian tombs and temples, and on Babylonian and Assyrian monuments, we find reproductions of instrumental types that were common to all countries of the ancient Near East: harps of various shapes and sizes, sundry kinds of lyres, the long-necked lute, the double oboe, clarinet, and trumpet, as well as drums, cymbals, and other percussion instruments. (Ill. 4)

Such pictures help us determine what kind of instrument is meant when the Bible mentions a timbrel or a psaltery, or any one of a dozen other instruments whose early names were already obscure by the second century B.C., when the first translation of the Hebrew Bible was made. Stone carvings have one great advantage over the written word. After 3,000 years a picture of a harp carved on a wall or monument can still be identified as a harp. But the original word for harp will have undergone so many changes that even scholars cannot easily tell what it once meant.

Discoveries of archeologists during the past century have told us something also about the musical customs of the peoples neighboring Canaan, as well as about those of an even older people to whom all of them, including the ancient Hebrews, owed much.

The Sumerians, who built a great civilization on Abraham's native soil many centuries before the Semites arrived, had a vigorous musical culture. Singers and musicians entertained the court and the nobility. On the famous "Standard of Ur," a mosaic panel inlaid with lapis lazuli and white shells (c. 2700 B.C.) we see royal banqueters after a victory being entertained by a female

singer who is accompanied by a man playing a lyre. This, supported by a strap over his shoulders, appears to have eleven
strings and is adorned with a carven bull's head.

The lyre, in fact, seems to have been the most popular instrument in both the religious and secular life of Sumeria. Elaborately
decorated lyres, often several together, have been found, along
with various harps, in the royal graves of Ur. The famous Harp
of Ur, more properly called the King's Lyre, is also surmounted by
a bull's head and has a front panel inlaid with ivory depicting
scenes from Sumerian mythology. (Ill. 1) A silver lyre shaped like
a tiny high-prowed boat and ornamented with a silver stag (c. 3000
B.C.) was being played in Ur 1,000 years before the time of Abraham.

In Sumerian temples instruments of all categories appear to have
been used. Singers were accompanied by the harp, the lute—a
long-necked variety with two strings—and a seven-stringed lyre,
while the double pipe and an oboelike single pipe were among
the woodwinds. Drums and horn blasts accompanied the sacred
libations, which took place in the outer courts.

The predominance of stringed instruments suggests that, like
the sacred music the Hebrews would evolve, music in Sumerian
temples had restraint and dignity. A psalmist led the divided choral
groups in liturgical chants and performed the daily rites. Singers of
both sexes, trained in schools attached to the larger temples, had
their own guilds and formed an educated class that studied and
edited the sacred liturgy.

When in time conquerors invaded Sumeria and took the in-
habitants captive, the laments, composed on this occasion and addressed to the city deities, were curiously similar to those the Hebrew psalmists would write in times of national disaster.

Along with their general culture the musical tradition of the
Sumerians was adopted by successive intruders and subsequently
passed on to the Babylonians and Assyrians—peoples so closely
allied culturally that their musical customs were virtually identical.
Babylonian priests took over the Sumerian liturgy, singing its
hymns in the venerated Sumerian tongue. The liturgist was assisted
by professional singers who were accompanied by oboelike pipes
and sometimes by lyres. In Assyria the hymns and chants were sung
antiphonally by the priests and congregation, or by alternating

choral groups. All liturgical offices were hereditary. Student priests were taught in the temple schools, the larger ones of which maintained well-stocked libraries of clay tablets, which served as a source of knowledge for future priests and priestly musicians.

Southwest of Canaan, meanwhile, the land of Egypt, thousands of years old and rich in sciences and arts, was keeping for us pictured records of its own musical culture. These murals and bas-reliefs, preserved in great number, show a wide inventory of musical instruments in both the Old Kingdom and the New.

Harps, dating from 3000 B.C., were among the earliest Egyptian instruments of which we have record. Among the many varieties developed were portable, angular harps with either vertical or horizontal strings, a high, vertically arched harp that was played in a kneeling position, and a smaller "footed" harp whose vertical sounding board continued downward to form a bulky base.

About the time the Israelites entered Egypt, presumably around the sixteenth century B.C., a remarkable increase seems to have occurred in the number and variety of Egyptian musical instruments. These appear to have come from the Near East, borne westward as part of a general migration of Semitic peoples from the Euphrates basin and the Arabian desert. When the Israelites arrived, they found the harp already in Egypt, but they may have brought with them a gift that the Egyptians were to like even better.

This was the lyre, which in the New Kingdom (1580 B.C) became a favorite not only among the common people but also in fashionable circles, where ladies embraced a small five-stringed variety. A Theban wall painting (c. 1420 B.C.) shows an "all-girl orchestra" entertaining at a banquet with an ensemble composed of a seven-stringed lyre that had a square sounding board and asymmetrically curved arms, a long, thin double oboe, and a standing harp with eleven strings whose sounding board appears to be covered with leopard skin.

The lute, carried west from Babylonia about the same time, also became an overnight favorite, especially with women. Part of the tribute exacted from Southwest Asian countries included dancing girls, who brought the lute as part of their equipment, looping it from their shoulders with bright ribbons and decking with gay tassels the thongs that secured its strings. These early lutes were long-necked, with fretted fingerboards and two to four strings. Unlike the more unwieldy harp and lyre, which for every note had to have a separate "open" string, the lute, because of its "frets" (movable loops tied along its neck), could produce any number of tones with only a few strings by pressing (or stopping) these at given points.

Among Egyptian wind instruments we find the double clarinet (with parallel pipes), the double oboe (with pipes diverging), and a kind of short oboe. Metal trumpets were also used in popular life and as military signal instruments. (Such signals, sounded by pharaoh's captains in the field, were familiar to Moses and may have done equal service in the Hebrew armies.)

The Egyptians also had a great variety of percussive and shaken instruments. On various tomb murals are depicted entire families of drums, large and small cymbals, castanetlike rattles, and any number of sistrums, or small horseshoe-shaped metal rattles popularly identified by the Egyptians with the goddess Isis.

Wealthy families maintained permanent instrumental ensembles for their own pleasure as well as for entertaining at their many elaborate feasts. Soloists and choral groups, always accompanied, performed at court and for the nobles. But we have little knowledge whether music, particularly vocal music, ever played the intimate role among the common people that it was to play for the Hebrews.

With Egypt's conquest of Syria (c. 1550 B.C.) music changed markedly, assuming a more sensuous Asiatic character. Even the staid temple music was forced to modify its ancient sobriety to keep pace with the changing times. Women of noble families now participated as singers and musicians, particularly in rites associated with Isis, who was the patron of sacred music. In organization, however, this continued to follow the general pattern of the age, being performed by a hereditary caste of temple musicians who transmitted their songs orally from father to son.

For the Egyptians, whose influence upon the early Hebrews can hardly be overestimated, sacred music was a magic gateway to the ear of the gods, and in its noblest period was part of a hushed and solemn rite performed by priests and priestesses in the dim recesses of a temple hall.

Babylonia also was to share its rich Sumerian legacy with the Hebrews, whose sacred musical practice would remarkably reflect this. Like Egypt, Babylonia had behind it a noble literary tradition by which the thinking of its poets had refined its religious expression and consequently the music connected with religion.

All nations of antiquity, however, frequently put music to much darker ritual uses. In Phrygia and Lydia the priests of Cybele, aroused to bacchic frenzy by the shrilling of loud pipes, castrated themselves with stone knives, and dressed as women, surged through the streets chanting hymns in honor of their goddess.

In Syria the great fire festival of Ashteroth, the naked goddess of fertility, was celebrated every spring, during which wine-maddened dancers slashed themselves with knives and cruelly mutilated themselves to the orgiastic sound of drums, cymbals, and whining oboes. Syrian legend held that the temple housing these rites had been built by their first priest-king, Kinnyras, who in their mythology was the world's first musician. Kinnyras' "daughters," the Kinnyrades, formed the cult prostitutes at a similar temple on the neighboring island of Cyprus. They took their name from their use of the lyre, the Syrian word for which was *kinnor*.

In Phoenicia, while pipes and drums stirred up patriotic fervor, young virgins were sacrificed at the founding of any new colony or city. In times of epidemic or drought the most cherished child of a family, selected by public vote, was made to pass through the fire to the cruel god, Moloch. Every year boys of the noblest families had to be sacrificed in flames to the god; later, children were bought and specially fattened for this purpose. Once when several parents managed to conceal their children, three hundred boys of the noblest families were sacrificed together in expiation. Three hundred others, moreover, offered themselves voluntarily in atonement. During such sacrifices pipes and drums kept up a constant loud din "so that the cries of the wailing should not reach the ears of the people."

Temple prostitutes, calling attention to their trade with pipes or small triangular harps, thronged the streets of all major cities in the ancient Near East. Their earnings they turned over to the temple of the goddess Ashteroth and they also provided the music and singing at the sacrifices performed for her morning and evening.

Phoenicia and Syria flooded the Mediterranean basin with many thousands of these so-called flute girls, whose numbers at the larger temples sometimes ran to more than six thousand.

But if the religions of all countries had their shameful features, such evils paled beside the sensual depravities that were practiced in the religious rites of the Canaanite tribes. Into the troubled melting pot of Canaan dropped all the refuse of perversion and superstition from the most backward fringes of the major civilizations.

Belief in every kind of dark magic flourished side by side with a fertility cult that had degenerated into a ritual orgy of sexual excesses carried out under the official sanction of the priests of Baal. The chief Baal was the Canaanite god of rain, and in that arid country his power was supreme.

One of his three sister-wives was the goddess Ashteroth, whose power over the fertility of field and flock made her the center of a cult that ritually encouraged the indulgence of every sensual appetite. Another wife was the war goddess Anath, who "waded up to her neck in blood" and whose votive rites included hideous acts of sadism.

Into this welter of savage cults stepped the young Israelite people, untested and with their only guide a set of laws that they had not yet learned to live by. That they were able to adjust the foreign elements they now met to their own conception of culture and ethics and to amalgamate the contrary forces into a homogeneous national idea reveals a gift for organization that older and more powerful nations might have envied.

Against the debased social and religious customs of the age the Hebrews opposed the rigorous moral code of Moses. But from every people they took whatever features of its culture, including its music, might serve the new concept of human dignity they had been painfully evolving ever since Abraham.

For all this, it was a two-edged struggle in which they were engaged. The "iron chariots" of the Canaanites were swift and terrible, but they were less dangerous than the fascination their stone gods held for a migrant people not yet consolidated into a cult.

Moses had warned of this in the song he wrote and sang to the congregation in the closing days of his life:

Do you thus requite the Lord,
O foolish people and unwise?

Moses not only wrote it down with care, but he taught it to the people and made them sing it. He further made sure that their children would learn and remember it and be counseled by it when in a time of greater prosperity they would be led to worship strange gods. It must have resounded often in the hills and valleys of Canaan.

But despite Moses' warning, more than once the name of some pagan deity was substituted for that of Yahweh in the songs lifted up in praise. The music of the Canaanites struggled for supremacy in the places of worship as their captains did in the field. It was a confused and turbulent age, noisy with the clash of sword against sword and the clamor of voices raised in triumph or in penitence.

Whether the music of the Canaanite cults was similar to that of the bordering Phoenicians, or whether it had its own features, can only be surmised. But in the years of contesting for the land the music of the original tenants joined with many native customs to influence the young newcomers. Yahweh was often worshiped with pagan ceremonies, consequently with pagan songs. The "high places" so often mentioned in the Scriptures were the sites of such ceremonies, and these remained, tacitly condoned, throughout a great part of Israel's early history.

Song was yet a long way from becoming an art form. For the early Hebrews it was a practical tool, used as the common people have always used it, to lighten the day's work, to commemorate a cherished event, to heighten the gaiety of a feast, to nudge the ear of God, or to lament the dead. Custom and need evolved their own musical ceremonies, entering into every phase of daily life.

Digging a desert well was a solemn event for the Hebrews, as for any nomad people, and was attended by appropriate ceremonies and songs. Such a song perhaps as the Israelites sang along a barren stretch by the Red Sea after wetting their parched throats with the sweet, cool water that bubbled up from the rocky soil:

Spring up, O well! Sing to it!
The well which the princes dug,

Which the nobles of the people delved,
With the scepter and with their staves.

Songs of welcome met the returning army whenever the Israelites scored a victory, the women dancing to the rhythm of their
small hand drums (*tuppim*) and singing to one another, chorus
answering chorus, about the triumphant event.

From such an occasion rose the song that Deborah, the prophetess, sang with Barak, the Hebrew general, after his victory over the
Canaanite chieftain, Sisera, who for twenty years had refused to let
the Israelites set foot on the king's highway, forcing them to keep
to the thorn-grown desert byways. We do not know how Deborah
and Barak sang it, but the imagery, after three millennia, is still
powerful:

The stars in their courses fought against Sisera.
. . . O my soul, thou hast trodden down strength.

Doubtless the people joined in, for they were encouraged to take
part in all rejoicings of a national character. These always had a
strong religious cast, for the feasts of victory were calculated to
strengthen religious sentiment as well as to promote a feeling of
national solidarity.

Some of these songs were preserved by folk bards, who in those
heroic times were at once poets, composers, and performers. A later
generation of bards would recite at banquets the ancient tales of
heroism and daring—the exodus from Egypt and the struggle to
wrest a homeland from a perilous and hostile country.

3

MUSIC DURING THE
COMMONWEALTH

ONCE THE ISRAELITES were settled in their homeland, music spread swiftly into every area of their new life. Work songs sprang up as the people gradually settled into the cities and fields, the vineyards and olive groves once held by the many tribes of Canaan.

The ploughman, the weaver, the stonemason, the winepressers, the threshing crew at harvest—all had their songs, cadenced to the rhythm of the task.

> The men . . . went out into the fields and gathered the grapes from their vineyards, and trod them, and held festival . . .

The days were busy and fruitful; the Promised Land hummed with life.

Israel then was a commonwealth, composed of the twelve Hebrew tribes grouped into an easy federation called Israel in the north and Judah in the south. As the largest, Israel would give its name historically to the entire nation, which during the commonwealth was governed by a succession of military leaders, called judges, who kept its boundaries secure and administered its laws.

One such judge earned a place in Hebrew history for his many services to his country. His greatest service, though, seems to have struck the chroniclers as nothing more than the agreeable hobby of an old man quietly passing his latter days in scholarly retirement.

This is the way it was:

In Ramah, not far from Shiloh, there lived a man named Elkanah with a wife he dearly loved named Hannah. But although they had been happily married for several years, Hannah's heart was sad because she had borne no children.

Every year, as the custom was, Elkanah and his wife went up to worship and to sacrifice at the feast of the Lord in Shiloh, where the Ark then rested. After the feast, at which she had been too unhappy to do more than nibble at her food, Hannah went into the sanctuary to pray. And while she was there she vowed a silent vow: "O Lord, if thou wilt give unto me a man child, then I will dedicate him to thee all the days of his life."

Now it was not the custom to pray silently in the sanctuary. Prayers were supposed to be chanted loudly enough for God to hear. Eli the priest, who was sitting beside the doorpost, observed Hannah's lips moving silently and supposed that she had drunk too much wine at the feast.

"Is that any way to behave in the Lord's house?" said Eli. "For shame, woman, put away the wine. You have had too much already."

"No, my lord," replied Hannah with dignity. "I am a woman sorely troubled. I have drunk neither wine nor strong drink, but have been pouring out my soul before the Lord."

"In that case," said Eli, somewhat abashed, "go in peace. And may the God of Israel grant you what you have asked."

Elkanah and his wife returned home, and in due course Hannah gave birth to a son, whom she named Samuel, meaning "asked of God." As soon as he was weaned she took him back to show Eli and to dedicate him to the Lord as she had promised. And this time she sang out loud and clear:

> My heart exults in the Lord;
> My strength is exalted in the Lord . . .

Little Samuel grew up helping Eli and the other priests with the sanctuary chores, and by the time he was grown everybody from Dan to Beersheba, as the saying went, knew that young Samuel was destined to be a prophet of the Lord.

A prophet, it should be noted, was not the same as a soothsayer or a necromancer. These had long before been outlawed by Moses, even though they would flourish under cover for many centuries. The Hebrew prophets of Samuel's time were religious scholars who under the proper conditions were thought to be filled with the word of God. Music was the prime means for achieving the state of transport in which they received and communicated the divine message.

Samuel turned out to be a good prophet and served Israel long and well. When the Ark was captured by the Philistines it was Samuel who urged the people to repentance, that they might recover it. After that for many years he served as a circuit judge, riding on his sturdy gray mule around the three cities neighboring his own. But at last he grew old and retired to his home in Ramah.

It was there the elders of Israel visited him when they felt the time had come for them to have a king. Samuel himself was too old for the job, and he did not hold with monarchy in any case. At their urging, however, he chose for them a strapping young farmer named Saul, who stood head and shoulders taller than anyone around.

Saul looked the way a king ought to look, but he was never very easy in his mind, and he was particularly dubious about his qualifications for being king. That, Samuel assured him, could be taken care of. He explained that as Saul drew near the city he would meet a company of prophets coming down from the high place with a harp, a hand drum, a pipe, and a lyre before them.

"And they shall prophesy," said Samuel. "And the spirit of the Lord will come upon you, and you shall prophesy with them, and be turned into another man."

Saul did as he was bidden, and before long he was prophesying too.

What was this procession that wound its way down the hill, "prophesying" to a musical accompaniment? And how could Samuel have known that it would be coming along at just that time?

That is where his greatest service comes in.

Samuel had first thought of the idea during his boyhood years of assisting Eli in the sanctuary. It seemed to him that learning should not be confined to a special caste jealously performing dry rituals, but that it ought to be spread freely among all the people.

Now that his political life was over, Samuel decided to devote his remaining years to bringing the arts of cultivation, which then meant music and poetry, to as many people as possible. But first he would have to train a capable staff of teachers to carry on the work after he was gone.

To do this, Samuel founded a school, or academy, designed to prepare men not belonging to the priestly caste for the great educational task. Heretofore all education had been wholly in the hands of the priesthood, but Samuel wielded enough power, both in the hierarchy and in political life, to override the priests' natural reluctance to share any part of their authority.

Around him Samuel gathered a group of men of all ages, married and single, who shared his ideals and were prepared to devote their lives to carrying them out. Before long in other cities more such schools sprang up, modeled after his. The teachers were holy men, that is, men inspired with the spirit of God, who were called fathers. From their ranks were to come such great prophets as Elijah and Elisha.

The students were called Sons of the Prophets. They lived together with their teachers and led a frugal life, building for themselves simple wooden huts, which in time clustered into small villages. (It is this community of huts that we must think of when envisioning such an academy of ancient times; universities of brick and steel were still several millennia in the future.) The students came from all social levels and from every tribe of Israel. Even women were not refused. The sole condition was the wish and the aptitude for learning, submission to the common discipline, and devotion to the religious and national ideals of Israel.

They were instructed in the Law and the Scriptures, and in psalmody. Special attention was paid to music, and those who showed an aptitude were probably taught some instrument. Singing, however, was doubtless taught to everyone, since group singing, accompanied, was a regular feature of their gatherings and processions.

Since teaching in those days was entirely oral, they learned by reciting or chanting proverbs and parables, and by singing sacred and secular poems. The inherited lore of bardic songs, legends, and ancient poems, which at that time were still preserved from heroic times, were an important part of their studies. The art of writing such poetry was also taught, with special emphasis, perhaps, on its rhythmic construction and the technique of setting it to music.

Thus the way was paved for the nation's great hymnic poets, the psalmists. In fact, such a revolutionary educational step was to have a profound and far-reaching influence upon the religious and moral development of the Hebrews. This influence would still be making itself felt centuries later in the teachings of Israel's great literary prophets, Isaiah, Jeremiah, and those who came after.

Samuel's own school was located in a settlement called Naioth, meaning "huts," a little way outside of Ramah. From their hut dwellings the Sons of the Prophets every morning and evening filed in solemn procession to a high place, a "hill of God," where an altar had been erected, and there they performed sacred ceremonies. Samuel had built the altar upon his retirement from public life; it was maintained by the sons as a place of devotion and prayer, but it was also a place of pilgrimage for the people.

Samuel had no intention of thrusting a raw, untutored boy upon Israel as its king. He had labored too hard in his country's interests, and it grieved him that his own sons had proved unworthy. When he told Saul that he would meet a company of prophets and learn to prophesy with them, Samuel meant that Saul was to join the students at the academy, where Samuel himself would instruct him in the art and ethics of governing.

Saul made a better king than history gives him credit for being, but he was always at odds with the powerful priesthood. As he grew older, Saul became subject to fits of melancholy, and people began to whisper that the king was troubled by an evil spirit.

This was bad for the country's morale, and pretty soon his advisors said to him, "Let us seek out a man who is skillful in playing the lyre, that he may cheer you out of your melancholy."

The king agreed that this might be a good idea.

"Find such a man," he said, "and bring him to me."

"I have seen a son of Jesse, the Bethlehemite," said one, "that is a skillful player, and prudent and comely, and the Lord is with him."

Saul sent messengers to fetch the boy. They found him sitting on a green hillside, idly fingering a small rustic lyre. It sounded thin against the noisy bleating of the sheep. As they approached, he rose to greet them, a ruddy-faced stripling with a tangle of bright hair.

His name was David, and he was destined to bring the music of ancient Israel to its golden age.

4

THE STAR OF DAVID

DAVID ROSE ON the horizon of ancient Israel like a young sun god, spreading the warmth of his vitality across a land fast ripening to its own young maturity. From the moment he arrived at court David won the hearts of everyone, high and low, old and young. He generated some personal magnetism that made people feel more alive just to be near him.

It made Saul feel better, too. The dark moods went away when David would sit at the king's feet and strum for a thoughtful moment or two on the strings, then begin to play with a command and power that searched out the dark places in Saul's soul and washed them clean with the healing radiance of music. Saul loved the boy. And David, in return, gave the unhappy king his complete boyish devotion.

Saul's worries were not wholly in his mind. All too real were the Philistines, the bellicose people between Judah and the Mediterranean, who kept him very often in the battlefield. Soon Saul made David his armorbearer so the boy could go along, in case the black moods should overtake the king during sleepless nights and the sweet sound of the lyre have to be invoked to drive away the demons of the mind.

Once when the two armies faced each other across a narrow valley, the Philistine champion, Goliath of Gath, taunted the Israelites for forty days with his offer to decide the battle by meeting one of them in single combat. Since Goliath stood close to ten feet tall and looked even taller in his plumed brass helmet and gleaming armor, the absence of any takers was fast demoralizing the Israelite camp.

David pleaded to try his skill and Saul reluctantly consented, pressing upon the boy his own stout sword and armor. David thanked him and gravely took the armor off again. All his life he did things in his own way. He took his shepherd's staff and his sling, and picked out five smooth stones from the brook. Then he walked across the open field toward the enemy, whirling the rustic weapon above his head. With his first shot he cracked Goliath's bull-like brow and measured the length of the giant of Gath in the dust of the valley floor.

After that the star of David was blazingly ascendant. When David stood to receive his sovereign's thanks, the king's own brave son, Jonathan, was beside his father. And as David spoke, "the soul of Jonathan was knit with the soul of David, and Jonathan loved him as his own soul." The lads made a covenant of eternal friendship, and when David went again into the field, this time as a captain over thousands, it was with the gift of Jonathan's own sword and bow that he consolidated his claim to valor.

Overnight David became a national hero. To the people he embodied the qualities of sensitivity and physical courage informing that most romantic figure of every age, the soldier-poet. His name shuttled the length and breadth of Israel like a song—and it was a song that nearly proved his undoing.

When the army returned from routing the Philistines, the women gathered along the roadsides to cheer the dusty marchers. Singing and dancing, they greeted Saul and David, beating their little hand drums and shaking shiny three-pronged rattles (*shali-shim*), whose tiny metal discs set up a bright silvery clatter. As they danced they sang to one another:

Saul has slain his thousands,
and David his ten thousands.

Saul was enraged and frightened. "They credit me only with thousands," he said, "but David they credit with ten thousands. What more can he have now but my very kingdom?" And he eyed David with no love.

The next day Saul fell into one of his blackest moods. David as usual brought his lyre to the king's feet and ran his fingers over the soothing strings. But this time his playing had no effect. As the music flowed innocently forth, Saul darkly fingered a javelin. Then, rising suddenly to his feet, he hurled it at David with all his might. David dodged the blow but he retuned his strings with unsteady fingers as the courtiers sought to calm the king. Again David undertook to play for him, but again Saul hurled the spear, its point biting deep into the wall, scant inches from David's head.

It seemed imperative to remove him from Saul's presence, so David was sent off to his military duties. The court missed him, but the one who missed him most sorely was Saul's younger daughter, Michal, who had fallen in love with the handsome youth. Saul learned of this, and in his ailing mind a scheme was born.

He promised David his daughter in marriage if the lad were successful in bringing off a particularly dangerous coup against the Philistines. David agreed, but instead of falling in battle as Saul had planned, he returned to claim his bride, who promptly took the part of her husband against her royal sire.

When the maddened king sent men to David's house one night to kill him, Michal let David down by a rope through a window. While Saul fumed in helpless rage, David fled through the night to the one place he knew he would find sanctuary—to Ramah, where the spiritual leader of Israel was still living. Into Samuel's sympathetic ear David poured the whole story, and the next morning he and the wiry old prophet went to stay at Samuel's music academy in Naioth.

It is not known how long David remained there, but it may well have been several months. We may suppose that he took his place as one of the student prophets, studying the Law and the Scriptures, learning the art of psalmody and of psalm-writing, and taking part in the group singing that formed so important a feature of the daily processions to the altar on the "hill of God."

As a poet-musician he found all of it absorbing, but what especially interested him were the musical instruments. As a shepherd boy on the outskirts of Bethlehem, David had fashioned his own tuneful lyre and had found the mechanics of instrument-making intriguing. And in the field with Saul he had seen the twin silver trumpets (*hatsotserot*) with which the priests authorized the army to set out, and the common shofar, or ram's horn, with which the captains signaled their men in battle.

But here at Naioth he found still other instruments. The harp (*nebel*), for instance, which had strings like a lyre and like it could be played from both sides with the bare fingers. Some harps, as David would later learn, stood as high as a man and were narrow and curved like a hunting bow. But those used at Naioth were angular and portable, and were hung from a thong around the shoulders to make marching easier. Unlike the lyre, their sounding board, wrapped with goatskin, was vertical and at right angles to the crossbar holding the strings.

David, however, still preferred the softer-toned lyre, nor was he alone in this. The lyre was one of the earliest and most popular of Hebrew instruments. Later ages would refer to it as "David's harp," but it was not a true member of the harp family since its sounding board was always at the bottom, whereas that of the harp, rising from the string holder, was rounded and completely covered with a skin. The small, primitive lyre that David perhaps found at Naioth may have been shaped something like the traditional Jewish candelabrum, the menorah, the parallel arms of which curve upward in a half circle. In playing it the Sons of the Prophets held it slanting against the left arm with the front, or top, away from the body. (Ill. 9)

Woodwinds or pipes also played an important part in the academy's musical life. These were rather like a primitive oboe, the commoner ones made of reed or animal bones. The latter may have been preferred by the student prophets, since their shriller, more exciting tones might more quickly generate the state of transport needful for the act of prophesying.

Hand drums (tuppim), more commonly identified with women, were also used by the students to furnish rhythmic stimulus for the dancing that further hastened the state of prophetic transport.

Samuel himself presided over the sessions, and it was the canny old statesman's dedication and wisdom of heart that crystallized the genius of David into a lifelong testimony of faith in the Lord. David had arrived at Naioth as an untutored youth, his talent for greatness still unshaped. In the daily devotions before his God and in discussions far into the night with Samuel, David conceived a vision of what he meant to do. And he plunged into his studies with doubled purpose.

Saul, however, finally learned where David was staying and sent messengers to seize him. But when they arrived and beheld the assembled scholars in a state of exaltation, singing the love of God to the sound of instruments and led by the venerable Samuel, the messengers were so caught up in the spirit of the occasion that they joined the company then and there.

When Saul learned of this he sent other messengers, and the same thing happened, and yet a third time. When the last group failed to return, Saul himself set out, but by the time he reached the settlement at Naioth, David, forewarned, had once more fled for his life.

Jonathan's loyal efforts to set things right between his friend and his father were unsuccessful. During the next three years David was forced to seek shelter in first one and then another province of Judah, until finally the only solution seemed for him to join the Philistines, where the hand of Saul could not reach him.

For more than a year David served in the Philistine army, maneuvering always, his biographers assure us, to keep from having to fight against his own people. The official account is that while he was off settling a border skirmish somewhere, the main Philistine host engaged the armies of Israel. It turned into a rout of the Hebrew forces, and both Saul and Jonathan were among the slain.

When David learned of this he rent his garments and wept for Saul, and for Jonathan his friend, and for the house of Israel. He lamented them in an elegy called the Song of the Bow, which he ordered be taught the sons of Judah, that they might mourn with him the death of kings:

The beauty of Israel is slain upon thy high places:
   How are the mighty fallen! . . .

The bow of Jonathan turned not back,
   And the sword of Saul returned not empty.
Saul and Jonathan were lovely and pleasant in their lives,
   And in their death they were not divided . . .

I am distressed for thee, my brother Jonathan . . .
   Thy love to me was wonderful, passing the love of
      women . . .

It is the first time we hear the voice of David the poet.

5

THE ARK
COMES TO JERUSALEM

WITH SAUL GONE, the tribe of Judah lost no time in anointing David king, and after a little military skirmishing Israel followed suit. When he came to the throne of Judah David was just thirty years old. To celebrate his new status he captured the thousand-year-old stronghold of Zion, Jerusalem, and established it as the City of David, the capital of his double kingdom. To welcome his new royal neighbor, Hiram, the young king of Tyre, sent cedar trees and carpenters to build David a fitting palace.

Jerusalem sat on a promontory jutting prowlike above two deep gorges. Off the main route of travel and on high ground, it was easily defensible. It quickly became the focal point for a nation that was eager to trade its years of strife-torn wandering and border warfare for a peaceful tilling of the soil and the development of a national culture.

Music until now had been largely of a folk character. The goatherd on his hillside, the farmer in his field, the weaver and the artisan in the many towns, the women at their special tasks—all shared a broad community of songs and dances, and many were proficient on the simpler musical instruments of the time. More elaborate ones were likely to be made of woods or metals not found locally, and had to be imported at prices beyond the reach of the common people.

But the rustic forms general to all cultures: the drums and rattles, the pastoral pipes of reed or bone, and the lyre, whose frame was suggested to any shepherd by the skull and horns of the wild goat—all these were readily at hand to enhance the hours of merriment or of relaxation after the day's work. The people's love of music and song, characteristic of the Hebrews from their beginning, had flowered during the time of the judges into a rich and fertile musical culture.

Music, however, had no formal status. No provisions had been made in the Mosaic Law for music in the service of the Lord. The two silver trumpets that formed part of the holy vessels merely adapted to Hebrew ritual usage similar trumpets used by the Egyptians in the worship of Osiris. In neither case did they serve a musical purpose. They were sounded to rouse the attention of the deity, to signalize some ritual act, or to commemorate some sacred event.

Unlike its older neighboring civilizations, Israel had no official schools attached to its sanctuaries to train men for the priesthood or in any musical rites connected with this. Priests and Levites alike passed their jealously guarded lore directly from father to son. The schools of prophets had not been designed to fill any priestly need. For all their religious basis they were secular institutions, and their concern was with the common people.

Neither was there any central religious authority, nor any officially consecrated altar to which the people might make pilgrimages. Several cities had their own altar where religious rites were performed, but in such provincial settings it was all too easy for Canaanite practices to creep into those ordained by Moses.

The tabernacle of the Lord, which Moses had made in the wilderness, along with its sacrificial altar, were on a hill, a "high place," in Gibeon. This came closest to an official site of worship, being the place to which Saul and other leaders repaired from time to time. But the Ark of the Covenant, since its return by the Philistines in the younger days of Samuel, had reposed on a remote hill in Judah several miles southwest of Jerusalem.

Many changes had taken place in the land since Yahweh had been carried in his golden sanctuary from camp to camp on the shoulders of young Israel. The character of Yahweh was also changing, from the God of a simple nomad people to the God of a settled agrarian nation sleek with the yield of grove and flock.

There was yet to be much fighting throughout the forty years of David's reign, but the people were able to enjoy at least an occasional respite from the interminable warfare that had disrupted the preceding two hundred years. They had learned much from their intercourse, peaceful and otherwise, with the surrounding nations. Slowly an autonomous culture was beginning to take shape. Once again the nation needed focus and a sense of purpose, as it had known in the days of Moses.

The time had come, it seemed, to bring to birth the Great Idea.

David called together the leaders of his host. "If it seems good to you," he said, "let us send for our brethren throughout the land to gather together here, and let us bring again the Ark of our God to us."

The trip to reclaim the Ark was the most festive occasion that Israel had ever known. The people traveled by mule and donkey, by oxcart and on foot, a hundred thousand singing pilgrims dressed in their gayest attire. Spilling over the narrow roadways onto the sandy dunes, a sea of moving colors, scarlet and purple and yellow and blue, surged slowly like a long unbroken wave from the City of David halfway to the gates of Gath.

When they reached the place where the Ark had rested for so many years, they lifted it reverently onto a new cart, specially built for the occasion, and pulled by a team of oxen decked with flowers and necklaced with jingling bells. As the cart wound its way slowly over the uneven ground,

> David and all Israel were making merry before God with all their might, with song and lyres and harps and tambourines and cymbals and trumpets.

Those with musical training perhaps formed instrumental groups spotted among the people, as military bands do in a modern parade. The musicians from the schools of prophets in a dozen cities would have proved invaluable, grouping into units bearing portable harps while other groups strummed the lighter weight Semitic lyre. Here and there might be found cymbal players, setting up a bright golden clangor with their gleaming brass discs.

The professionally trained, of course, formed only a small segment, but a people so musical as the Israelites could furnish plenty of natural talent. Swelling the more formal musical units were thousands of ordinary people performing on whatever kind of instrument best suited them.

Pipes of reed, metal, or thighbone lent their shriller tones to the sound of a hundred plectrums twanged across a thousand strings. Drums of a dozen shapes and sizes tattooed a rhythmic accent, from the maidens' dancing tabrets gaily aflutter with bright ribbons, to the fat, bongolike drums tied around a man's waist and beaten at both ends. The women, who always provided a lively part in any general merrymaking, showered the air with tinkling cascades from the tiny metal discs on their various sistrums, or metal rattles.

There was no lack of instrumental accompaniment to the songs of rejoicing that poured from thousands of throats. But it was a secular outpouring, unsanctified by priestly ritual and, among the common people at least, comprised as much of natural high spirits on holiday as of reverence.

And now a mishap occurred that all but wrecked the ardent hopes of David. More significantly for us today, it nearly blighted at the very outset the future of Western liturgical music as it was to flower through the next three thousand years.

As the cart with its sacred burden reached the threshing floor of a prosperous farmer, the oxen stumbled, jolting the Ark badly. In attempting to right it the lad driving the cart was killed.

This struck the assembled host as a formidably bad omen. David, afraid now to take the Ark on to Jerusalem, had it carried into the nearby dwelling of a man named Obed-Edom, where it would remain for the next three months. Then the king and a sobered multitude made their way back to Jerusalem.

During the following weeks David gave the matter a great deal of thought, while waiting to see how Obed-Edom fared with so uncomfortably potent an object as part of his household furniture. Obed-Edom was clearly prospering. Gradually David satisfied himself as to why his own well-meant effort had displeased the Lord.

One thing seemed clear. He had acted on impulse and without

due reverence. He had not taken care to prepare a suitable shelter for the Ark. At once he ordered that a handsome tent be set up. Next, he decided that none but the Levites were worthy to handle the holy object, for had not the Lord chosen them to carry it in the wilderness and to minister to him forever?

Once again David gathered all Israel together at Jerusalem. This time he ordered the priests and Levites to sanctify themselves for the sacred task, "For because you did not carry the Ark the first time, the Lord broke forth upon us."

Then David had the chief Levites appoint certain of their kinsmen as official singers, "to raise sounds of joy" in songs accompanied by harps, lyres, and cymbals. The chiefs selected three young singers, Heman, Asaph, and Ethan, to be the principal soloists. Each had a fine voice and a good musical background, but equally important was the fact that each was directly descended from Jacob's third son, Levi, who had founded the tribe of Levites.

Heman, Asaph, and Ethan (who will hereafter be called Jeduthun for reasons more easily explained later) were also appointed to provide the signal for the singing to begin. This they would do with a sharp clash of brass cymbals, and it amounted to quite an honor since the act was also designed to call Yahweh's attention to the devotional proceedings.

From secondary kinsmen the chiefs selected eight singers to accompany themselves on psalteries, or harps, "according to *alamoth*." The meaning of this term is still in doubt, but it may have meant certain harps tuned to an alto or soprano register and designed to lead the vocal melody by doubling it in either of these ranges.

Six other Levites were appointed to lead the melody with lyres "according to the *sheminith*." If we continue the above reasoning, this could mean a lyre set to a lower range. Seven priests were appointed to blow the sacred silver trumpets before the Ark, and the entire musical forces were to be directed by the chief Levitical musician, Chenaniah, because of his skill and experience in choral direction.

David this time was leaving nothing to chance. On the previous occasion he had been prompted as much by the wish to focus his people's political allegiance as by his own devotion to the God of his fathers. Now he had gained new respect for this God who could be approached only on his own terms, and the host of Israel had learned new respect also.

It was with a carefully organized procession, led by priests and Levitical musicians, that David with the tribal elders and the captains now went to fetch the Ark from the house of Obed-Edom. This time the Levites bore it upon their shoulders by its golden staves, as Moses had ordained. And to forestall any mishaps David made a sacrificial offering before setting out.

The official party was clothed in robes of finest linen, David and the priests, the Levites and the singers and the conductor, Chenaniah. It was a reverent procession but a joyful one as well. For the Hebrews, as for all ancient cultures, "making merry" with song and dance was a time-honored way of paying homage to their God, and the people felt that to give less than their utmost in either was to stint the deity of his rightful due. Thus it was with much joyful shouting that Israel at last carried the sacred Ark of the Covenant up the rocky slopes to the citadel of Zion, bearing it triumphantly through the city gates while the cheers of the greeting multitude swelled the jubilant noise of harps and lyres, of cymbals and pipes, of timbrels and horns and trumpets.

None was more exuberant than the king. David, fired by a religious transport, stripped his lean body of all but its linen ephod and "danced before the Lord with all his might." But as the procession moved through the streets, Michal, the daughter of Saul, looked from her window and saw her husband leaping and dancing like any common shepherd lad. And her heart was hot with scorn.

In the tent that David had arranged, the priests installed the Ark and made peace offerings before Yahweh. Then David blessed everyone and gave to each bread, meat, and a flagon of wine. Feasting, they rested from their dusty journey and the weary singers caught their breath.

But there was still much to do. David had not created a special musical corps merely to dissolve it. Certain priests and Levites who had led the musical escort he stationed permanently before the Ark, some to keep records, others to thank and praise the Lord continually with song and incense.

Of the three soloists, Heman, Asaph, and Jeduthun (Ethan), Asaph must somehow have distinguished himself, for he now emerged as chief, although each was to found a hereditary line of

Temple singers. Stationed next to Asaph before the Ark were now eight singers headed by Zechariah, with another Levite, Jeiel, set to lead the accompanying harps and lyres. Heman and Jeduthun continued to share with Asaph the honor of signalizing the start of the sacred songs with the brazen accents of the cymbal, while several priests, rotating in pairs, were appointed to sound the silver trumpets in perpetuity before the Ark.

Then, to mark the official start of the new musical service, David delivered to Asaph and his brethren a psalm of thanksgiving. Since we are given to understand that they sang it on the spot, we must assume that there had been a few behind-the-scenes rehearsals. However, we are told only that they performed it, as the first psalm credited to David by the court chroniclers:

> Sing unto the Lord, all the earth . . .
> Let the heavens be glad, and let the earth rejoice:
> And let men say among the nations, the Lord reigneth . . .

To this the congregation appended, "Amen." Then, leaving Asaph and his colleagues to minister perpetually before the Ark according to a daily set order, David and all the people returned home, well pleased with the way things had gone.

But when David reached his own house, Michal met him with a sneer: "How glorious was the king of Israel today, uncovering himself before the eyes of the maidservants like any vain and shameless fellow!"

To which David, with equal heat, replied, "It was before the Lord, who chose me above your father and all his house to rule over Israel. Therefore will I make merry before him. And I will abase myself still further; and the maidservants of whom you speak will honor me for it!"

No carping by a jealous wife could dim the triumph of that day for David. Long before, he had proved himself a soldier and a poet. Now he had also proved himself a ruler with a keen sense of the nation's temper.

Nothing could have so impressed upon his people the fact that they had an eternal covenant with their God as this double pilgrimage to bring the Ark of that covenant to their capital city. Nothing could have so effectively united the two provinces of Israel and

Judah as this dramatic reminder that, surrounded as they were by alien faiths and cultures, they shared a common God and a common destiny.

David's plan had been triply successful. The Ark was home, the people were united as never before, and the powerful agency of the priesthood was now solidly behind the king. The transfer of the Ark of the Lord to the City of David was the birth hour of an organized temple music that would last a thousand years. It was also a stroke of statesmanship without recorded parallel.

6

THE TEMPLE OF
SOLOMON

WITH THE APPOINTMENT of a musical staff to minister continually before the Ark, David put into effect the dream born years before at Naioth: the introduction of music as an essential element into the Hebrew sacred service.

This was an idea that he must often have discussed with Samuel in quiet hours after the daily devotions. We can imagine the two men, the one rich in years and wisdom, the other fired with young initiative, laying the theoretical groundwork for music in the service of the Lord, well enough organized to survive the centuries and with the spiritual force to create a lofty tradition.

It would not, of course, be the first such use of music. Older civilizations, as we have seen, had long made it part of their religious ritual. But again, as with everything they adopted from other cultures, the Hebrews would translate it in terms of their own ethics and philosophy. From their earliest memories as a theocratic people, song had been their way of exalting the single force they recognized as all mighty. But as a spontaneous expression of faith this had been too immediate and genuine to constitute a ritual formula as in other cults.

As David and Samuel saw it, therefore, music must be something more than a stereotyped tonal background. It must be an integral part of the divine service, coordinate and equal with the other sacred actions. For the ancient Hebrews, as for other peoples of antiquity, the focal point of their religious ceremony was the sacrifice. But as the Hebrews over the centuries gradually refined the purpose of sacrifice, it came to be regarded not only as a propitiatory rite, but as a spiritual offering, affirming man's devotion to his creator.

Music, then, was to be associated inseparably with the sacrifice. It was, in effect, to become itself a form of tonal sacrifice, exalting the Most High with dedicated songs accompanied by instruments. This was a revolutionary concept. The elevation of liturgical music to an equal plane with all other ritual ceremonies was the most important development in the history of Hebrew music.

We do not know whether the plan originated with Samuel or with David, but it is likely that Samuel's tireless mind had long cherished some such idea and that it came to focus only after his meeting with the younger man. At any rate, David, with the energy peculiar to him, was the right man to put it into action.

The pattern for organization was already present. The school of prophets at Naioth was its actual prototype. Samuel's system of instruction and the host of teachers he had trained had done much to foster a lay knowledge of music among the common people. But even more important for cult purposes, there had also been a long tradition of musical activity among the Levites. As functionaries in the cult ritual they constituted a special class, which assumed the cultivation of music as one of many privileges. Once David had established the sacred musical routine, he could safely leave it to the Levites to carry on, for their profession had the discipline of many generations behind it.

It was well that this was so, for during the next several years David was busy extending the kingdom he would leave to his son, Solomon.

The Lord prospered David, and the modest court that he had built from the tall cedars of Lebanon was bright with silken hangings and gay with the songs of trained musicians—singing girls, and players upon the lute and psaltery, dancers, and choral groups of men and women.

David's early interest in instrument-making never left him. As king, he found little time to pursue the hobby, but he gave the art his full royal encouragement, seeing to it that the Levitical musicians had whatever they needed of stringed and woodwind instruments and that these were the finest available at that time. Certain ones made from rare woods not found in Israel he ordered specially built by the expert craftsmen of Sidon and other cities famed for music.

Not until fairly late in his reign did David find leisure to become again the poet-musician. There was time, then, for occasional quiet moments when he would take out his lyre—now a kingly instrument inlaid with pearls and lapis lazuli—and thoughtfully begin to compose a psalm to his God.

Sometimes this would be a song of thanksgiving, sometimes a paean of praise. Often he prayed in song for help against his enemies and the ungodly leanings of his people. Once from the depths of illness he howled, "O Lord, heal me, for my bones are vexed!" Sometimes he complained that God was too slow in acting; he exhorted the Almighty to do better. But always from the lyre there breathed the simple trust of a poet who had spent his boyhood years among the pastured flocks: "The Lord is my shepherd; I shall not want."

Much as David had wished, he had not found time to build the Temple he saw in his mind's eye as a fitting place to house the Ark and the holy trappings of the house of God. But the vessels of gold and silver and brass, the jewels and the golden shields that were among the spoils of war—all these he brought to Jerusalem and dedicated to the Lord.

As yet, however, there was nothing better to house them than the tent David had erected for the Ark years before. Handsome at first, it was beginning to look a trifle worn.

Finally, in his closing years, David bought the threshing floor of a prosperous wheat farmer on the high eastern prow of a promontory overlooking the royal city. Here, he decided, was a fitting place for the permanent abode of Yahweh. Rounding up the local remnants of sundry conquered peoples, he set them to work in the stone quarries.

Then he assembled his chieftains and called to him his son,

Solomon, a lad still in his teens. "Take heed now," said David to the boy, "for the Lord has chosen you to build a house for the sanctuary; be strong, and do it." He cautioned Solomon especially to observe "the divisions of the priests and the Levites for all the service of the house of God."

Next, with the thoroughness of an experienced ruler, David took steps to ensure the continuation of the sacred musical service. He took a census of the Levites, from thirty years and upward, since this was the age at which, according to Mosaic Law, they became eligible to serve in the sanctuary. Of the 38,000 turned up by the survey, 4,000 proved accomplished enough musically to merit the privilege of singing in the house of the Lord.

In Oriental tradition the sanctuary's three original soloists, Asaph, Heman, and Jeduthun (Ethan), had trained their sons—perhaps their daughters as well—in their own profession. Inasmuch as service in the cult was hereditary, it was scarcely coincidence that these should have headed the final list of singers appointed to praise the Lord with the harps, lyres, and other instruments that David had ordered made and consecrated for the purpose.

Each of the sons was placed as leader over a group of twelve singers composed of his own kinsmen. Since Asaph had four sons, Jeduthun six, and Heman fourteen, their number amounted to twenty-four, thus bringing the total musical forces to 288 singers. To forestall any disputes or jealousy, their order of sequence was established by casting lots, group against group, the elder sons equally with the younger.

Thus democratically started off, the Temple singers from this time on constituted a guild with its own rules and precepts, the members of which, united by a strong class consciousness, jealously guarded their special privileges. Within the guild, which was organized rather like a trade union, there were no preferments and no priorities of experience or tenure. The singers who were admitted were uniformly considered masters, and as such they shared the same prerogatives and the same obligations.

According to Mosaic Law, the Temple musicians were supported by the congregation, receiving their portion of the tithes earmarked for the priests and other Levites. As a further source of revenue, they possessed their own hereditary villages and farming lands.

Thus throughout the existence of the state of Israel the Levitical

musicians were free from any economic concern. As befitted their
sacred office they represented a prominent and privileged class.
They remained, as they had been from the first, a select professional group, enjoying great esteem and gradually acquiring considerable power.

Solomon began building the Temple in the fourth year of his
reign. He wrote to his father's old friend, King Hiram of Tyre,
"Behold, I build a house to the name of the Lord my God, to dedicate it to him and to burn before him sweet incense. Send me
therefore a man cunning to work in gold, and in brass, and in iron.
Prepare me timber in abundance, for the house which I am about
to build shall be wonderful great."

The aging Hiram, delighted that his friend's young son was
showing the good sense to continue a commercial tie that had
profited both countries for forty years, promptly dispatched to
Solomon a gifted young artisan named Huramabi, a widow's son
who was carrying on his father's trade of metal worker.

Hiram also floated heavy timbers of cedar and cypress down the
Mediterranean, along with carpenters to plane and shape them, for
the great shipbuilding trade of the Phoenicians had made their
woodworkers famous throughout the ancient world. Solomon re-
paid him in wheat and olive oil, and sent 30,000 laborers to help
fell timber.

In the mountains of Judea the stone quarries rang with the
picks of 80,000 workmen hewing and polishing the great white
stones that would fit into place "without the noise of hammer or
axe or any tool of iron" violating the structure's sanctity. In the
white clay of the Jordan plains, Phoenician artisans cast and
molded heavy sacrificial vessels out of the bright brass helmets and
shields garnered by David as the spoils of war.

The Temple was seven years in building. By the architectural
standards of the Babylonians and Egyptians it was not large, but
it had an advantage possible to neither. It stood on an eminence,
lofty, remote, mysterious, crowned by the purple mountains of
Judea.

A dazzling amount of gold work lit it up within and without.
Thirty feet wide and 100 feet long, on a platform built of great
slabs of white limestone, it faced the rising sun, which kindled into

gaudy glory the gilded flowers and cherubim carved on the massive doors. Enclosing it, a protective stone wall formed a large court-yard, divided into smaller ones by terraces. Surrounding and but-tressing the building were three stories of small chambers for the use of the priests and Levites.

Everywhere it bore the stamp of its Phoenician designers, who were themselves indebted to Egypt. Its interior, after the Egyptian fashion, was divided into three areas of increasing holiness: a thirty-foot porch flanked by two commanding pillars of burnished bronze; a central nave where a clerestory light filtered dimly upon the cere-monies; and past a short flight of steps, the Holy of Holies itself, windowless and cubical, containing the Ark of the Covenant.

Only those priests and Levites who had been ritually sanctified were permitted within the central chamber. Behind its gem-encrusted double doors, gilded flowers and gourds were carved into the heavy panels of cedarwood lining walls and ceiling. On the table holding the shewbread gleamed bowls and censers of beaten gold. Before the Holy of Holies a golden altar stood to receive the priests' offering of incense, framed by ten golden candlesticks bearing a perpetual flame. The gilded doors of this inner sanctum were opened only once a year, on the Day of Atonement, when none but the high priest might enter.

Within the Ark reposed the Ten Commandments carved on the two tablets of stone that Moses had placed there nearly 500 years before. For the simpler people of the Exodus it may have been heartening to believe that Yahweh also dwelt therein, but Solomon was the child of a more enlightened age. The Temple had been built to honor God, not to contain him, as Solomon was careful to point out in his dedicatory prayer:

> "Behold, heaven and the highest heaven cannot contain thee; how much less this house which I have built!"

Nothing like the dedication of the Temple had ever before been seen in Israel. The knees of the people were weak with awe in the presence of such magnificence. Looped from the capitals of the tall bronze pillars were golden chains strung with golden pomegranates. Rising fifteen feet before the central door, a brazen altar thirty feet square darted blinding shafts of sunlight across the great court of the sacrifices. Beside the east gate stood a raised pool cast in gleaming bronze, fifteen feet across and supported by twelve bronze oxen, facing outward beneath the broad rim carved with lilies. Here the priests and singers made their ablutions before entering the sacred precincts.

At the east end of the huge central altar the singers solemnly ranked themselves for the dedicatory service, while up the long ramp stretching to the south gravely filed the white-robed priests bearing the sacred utensils of their craft. It must have been an impressive moment, not only for the thousands who had toiled in the quarries and the plains, but for other thousands who, from far below in the suburbs around Jerusalem, had watched the huge white stones rise tier upon tier against the close blue sky. Now the Temple was ready to be consecrated.

Arrayed in fine linen like the priests, the twenty-four choral groups under Asaph, Heman, and Jeduthun stood with harps and lyres, ready to burst into song at the signal clash of the cymbal. Opposite them for an occasion that could never again be duplicated in the history of Israel were 120 priests ready to sound the sacred silver trumpets.

The musicians had rehearsed for months, perhaps for years, in preparation for this hour. To them, as to the rest of the worshipers, it was far more than a musical performance; it was a consecration of their faith in the God who had brought them, after centuries of toil and hazard, to an age of peace and to this modest hill, ringed by other modest hills, where they had built an altar to his name in gratitude and love.

All the factors were right to ensure a performance worthy of being written into the record of time. And, in fact, it was—set down by an anonymous chronicler inspired beyond his task of mere reporting to indite the first music criticism known to history:

> It came even to pass, as the trumpeters and singers were as one, to make one sound to be heard in praising and thanking the Lord; and when they lifted up their voice with the trumpets and cymbals and instruments of musick, and praised the Lord, saying 'For he is good; for his mercy endureth forever;' that then the house was filled with a cloud, even the house of the Lord; so that the priests could not stand to minister by

reason of the cloud: for the glory of the Lord had filled the
house of God.

For seven days the king and all Israel observed dedicatory ceremonies within the Temple and without, the accompanying psalms
sung to the instruments that David had ordered made and hallowed to the Lord's service. Punctuated as it was by the fanfare of
the priestly trumpeters in their snowy robes, the unfolding of the
ritual must have had an effect almost apocalyptic upon the dazzled
worshipers.

Then for another seven days they celebrated with a great feast.
Now it was the people's turn to express their joy in song. Those
lucky enough to crowd within the great courtyard celebrated in
full sight of the holy edifice. Outside the walls, the stubbled grain
of the ancient wheatfield was trampled by the dancing feet of the
multitude, holding festival to the music of psalteries and pipes and
timbrels.

At the end of the second week Solomon blessed them and sent
them away to their homes "joyful and glad of heart for the good-
ness that the Lord had shown to David and to Solomon and to
Israel his people."

The Temple of Solomon would last for nearly 400 years, a site of
investiture for Israel's kings, a shrine of yearly pilgrimage for its
people, and the home of a musical liturgy that would outlast the
gilded cherubim by thirty centuries.

The Temple became and remained what David had wanted it to
be: the spiritual focus of the people's faith, the symbol of their
covenant with the God of Abraham. Despite the many periods of
apostasy under kings who abandoned Yahweh to follow alien gods,
it was the Temple that always provided a rallying point when the
people were again wooed back to the ways of David's God.

7

ORGANIZATION
OF TEMPLE MUSIC

THE PEACEFUL REIGN his father had assured him gave Solomon an
opportunity David had not had to explore the styles and customs
of other countries. Solomon liked their Oriental opulence, and he
liked their women. Nor was he displeased by the lavish dowries
that accompanied his numerous wives.

When the king of Egypt gave him his daughter to wife, the caravan of wedding gifts packed overland by mule and camel included
a thousand musical instruments, indicating that Israel's cultivation
of music had already won the respect of her most distinguished
neighbor. These must have materially enriched not only the royal
court orchestra but the store of Temple instruments as well.

Since the music of Egypt had continued its trend to a more Asiatic character, it is likely that along with the traditional strings went
such provocative instruments as nose flutes, double oboes, fretted
lutes, zithers, tall slender harps that were played standing, and any
number of exotic percussion and shaken instruments.

The religious strictures of the Hebrews forbade the intrusion of
sensuous or exciting timbres into the sacred service, but there was
nothing to keep the king and his companions from enjoying the

agile melodies played on silver flutes and love songs sung to the long-necked lute by the singers of the royal court. The new royal bride may herself have been musically trained, for highborn Egyptian women of the time took an active part in music, both in Egyptian temples and in social life.

Solomon's interests, however, were not confined to music. His father had taken pleasure in building more efficient instruments. Solomon now had done a bit of building on his own and had found he liked it. He, however, thought of building in more elaborate terms. Although he had inherited much of his father's musical talent, architecture for Solomon would be the commanding passion that music had been for David.

No sooner was the Temple finished than Solomon began building a new royal palace. As against the Temple's seven years, it took thirteen to build the kingly residence with its huge reception hall and the throne room in which six steps, flanked each by a pair of lions, led up to the gilded ivory throne with its golden footstool.

Solomon liked things to be showy, but to give him his due, it was as much a matter of statecraft as of vanity. David had been first of all a man of God. Solomon was first of all a monarch. No one, even visiting royalty, might be permitted to gaze upon the full splendors of the sacred Temple. But the magnificence of the royal palace was calculated to send foreign visitors away with impressive tales of the kingly might of the Hebrew monarch whose sway extended from the borders of Egypt to the Euphrates in the land of his ancestors.

Solomon's royal neighbors were quick to get the point. Back came caravans of kingly tribute to swell the state coffers and cram to bursting the treasure chambers of the Temple. With part of the income Solomon had the Phoenicians build and man him a navy to sail down the Red Sea as far as the Horn of Africa. Along with the returning cargo of precious stones came red-barked trees of fragrant sandalwood. Today we think that these more probably were cypress, but they had the charm of the exotic and Solomon had them made into harps and lyres for the Temple singers of a splendor and workmanship never before seen in the land.

Solomon also managed to combine his concern for the Temple singers with his passion for building. For years one of the hand-

somer wedding gifts of his pharaoh father-in-law had been awaiting the touch of the royal architects, ". . . for Pharaoh had gone
up and taken Gezar, and burnt it with fire, and slain the Canaanites that dwelt in the city, and given it for a present unto his
daughter."

Solomon had such fun restoring Gezar that he went on to rebuild a score of other cities that had been leveled in the wars of
Saul and David. Next, he founded a score of other cities, many
of which he presented to the Temple priests and Levites, along
with the adjacent farming lands.

This was a political gesture worthy of his father. Such royal
grants placed the influential priesthood ever more firmly behind
the king. More important for the future of the cult, it freed it from
complete dependency on the bounty of the congregation, and
insured the service of Yahweh against the pandering and degeneracy that were beginning to dissipate the cults of older nations.

As his father had wished, Solomon perpetuated a regular service of sacred observances, following the order of rotation that
David had arranged for the priests and singers. On the large
brazen altar before the Temple, offerings were made to Yahweh
thrice daily and on the Sabbaths, with special observances at the
times of the new moon and the three great yearly festivals.

Mosaic Law required that sacrifices be made at the regular
morning and evening services. But now in addition a stream of
congregants filed daily up the rocky hillside bearing personal offerings for the altar. These might be to thank Yahweh for some past
favor or to petition for a future one; sometimes they were offered
to expiate some personal sin or merely to remind the deity of the
donor's continuing devotion. Their number and diversity made it
impossible to schedule them at the regular ceremonies, so a special
noontime sacrificial service was created to accommodate them.

Like the others, this required the participation of the singers.
Since David had ordained that all offerings must be accompanied
by song, the people quickly came to believe that only thus would
a sacrifice be acceptable to Yahweh. The twenty-four choral
groups, therefore, had to be prepared for three different musical
services a day.

One group of twelve choristers was always present to provide music for each of these. On the Sabbath two groups may have participated in each service, thus utilizing the talents of all twenty-four throughout the week. At the three festival seasons the number of groups for each service must have been considerably increased.

How did they share the responsibility for the many and varied services? An obscure reference in the Chronicles suggests that, like the priests and gatekeepers, they rotated weekly. But this would have left each group, after one week's duty, inactive for nearly half a year. It would have been impossible to maintain the high artistic level for which the Temple singers became famous if they had participated so rarely in the sacred service. Not only did they need to remain familiar with the complicated ritual, but they needed regular performances before an audience to keep professionally trim.

Alternating the groups after each service would have been equally impractical. The three daily rituals differed considerably, both as to prayers and music. For the noontime sacrifices the music had to be adapted to various offerings. Moreover, on different days the Levites sang different psalms.

It seems more likely that the choir groups rotated on a three weeks' basis, the three daily services being provided by the same group, with two further groups jointly taking care of Sabbath ceremonies. Thus over a three weeks' period all twenty-four groups would have taken part, after which the cycle could begin again, starting possibly with a different group.

Throughout the year this would give the singers enough public workouts to keep them on their toes. It would also give them time to attend rehearsals, to teach their art to the younger generation, and to spend a certain time overseeing their fields. So continuously active, in any case, was their schedule when on duty that they were exempted from all other tasks, "for they were employed in their work day and night."

Artistry of a high professional gloss was assured by the strict discipline of the Levitical guild and zealously maintained by constant rehearsals. For these, special chambers were allotted the singers beside the Temple's north gate, which came to be called the Gate of Singing.

Inasmuch as everything had to be taught orally, rehearsals must have proceeded much as today in the case of choral groups that are unable to read music, such as workmen's choruses or "community sings," i.e., by painstaking vocal drills. These were perhaps made easier by the freedom and flexibility of Oriental melodies, but even so the end result must have depended greatly on the skill and application of the twenty-four choirmaster sons of Asaph, Heman, and Jeduthun, and their eventual successors.

Nor would their work have been confined to rehearsing the vocal melodies and their instrumental accompaniment. They also must have played an essential part in the actual "composing" of the musical numbers, although perhaps not in the way we think of it today. Whatever method they used, the final arrangement was the result of teamwork, the "composition" gradually taking shape by a process of mutual suggestion and rejection until everyone was satisfied with the result. This is not so unusual in our own day, either. Many of our jazz and popular combos follow a similar procedure, and are not unlikely to announce a new number as one that "we composed."

The original soloists of the Davidic musical service, Asaph, Heman, and Jeduthun, appear to have been at the same time leaders of the several singing groups. Over them Chenaniah had initially been placed, suggesting that he must have conducted the actual performance, leaving the preparatory work to them. But Chenaniah, "master of the singers in the song" of David's early musical organization, seems no longer to have been alive at the formal installation of the sacred service. In his stead Heman, Asaph, and Jeduthun appear to have become conductors of the entire musical service.

For the seventeen musicians of the early Davidic ensemble a single conductor should have made out very well with three assistants for rehearsals. But for the 288 musicians of the Temple organization even three conductors might have been overworked preparing and presenting some twenty-one weekly performances, exclusive of rehearsals.

This may explain why in the final organization of the Temple service each of the twenty-four singing groups had its own leader, all of these in turn being subordinated to the three chief conductors, as repeatedly stated by the chronicler: "under the hand of Asaph," "under the hand of their father Jeduthun with the harp," and "all these were under the hand of their father for song in the house of the Lord, with cymbals, harps, and lyres, according to the king's order to Asaph, Jeduthun, and Heman."

Inasmuch as the character of Hebrew Temple music was similar to Egyptian, it was probably conducted in much the same way. As early as the twenty-eighth century B.C. we find records of hand signs and finger motions that were used by Egyptian musicians. On a mural in the tomb of Amenemhet I at Thebes (c. 1550 B.C.) we see a conductor snapping his fingers and pounding time with his right foot, although this, in the ancient world, did not indicate "time beating" as we know it. Rhythm in antiquity was a rather different matter, as we shall see further on.

To indicate the vocal line the conductor traced with his hand the melody's rise or fall. Various finger positions urged the choir to louder or softer singing, and even movements of the head had meaning. By today's standards it does not seem very precise, but as a method it survived far into the Middle Ages of Europe. In time, written signs were made from the visual signals and these, after several centuries, developed into our modern system of notation.

Before any performance, of course, the correct pitch for the voices had to be given. For this the Hebrews used a sort of pitch pipe, but since the notes it struck did not belong to the music itself, they were not considered part of the service. This task, therefore, fell to the Nethinim, literally the "given ones," who performed certain lowly Temple functions. They had originally been war captives or conquered peoples, whose descendants formed a servant class.

For the Levites, education of the young was an integral part of their service, but since their economic needs were assured they received no remuneration for this. Their method of teaching must have been efficient and thorough. The fact that no singer might become a full-fledged member of the Levitical musical guild until thirty years of age indicates that the years of preparation were long

and arduous, his basic training probably starting in early childhood. Before being admitted into a Temple choir he underwent
a grueling five years' apprenticeship, during which he was not
only drilled in choral singing and accompaniment but was required to fix in oral memory all the voluminous and complex details of the ritual. Once accepted, he would serve for twenty
years, or until the age of fifty, when the vocal qualities of a singer
normally start to decline.

Although we know little about their role, there is good reason to
believe that women also took part in the musical service, a case in
point being the three daughters of Heman who are mentioned in
the Chronicles along with his fourteen sons. As we have seen, each
of the sons was made choirmaster of a choral unit. It may be that
the daughters served in the vocal ranks, since the passage states
that "they were all under the hand of their father for song."

Singing in the Temple was reverent and serene, but there is no
reason to suppose that it was in any sense monotonous or drab.
Rather, it was probably marked by dramatic changes of tone color,
by skillful alternation of soloists and chorus, or of several choral
groups. Such enlivening effects, however, would have been principally vocal, since the voice was paramount in the musical service.
Other Oriental peoples might use musical instruments to generate
hysterical adoration of their gods, and even the Sons of the Prophets, as we have seen, found that this hastened a state of prophetic transport. But as David had conceived the Temple musical
service, instruments were meant to support but never to intrude
upon the vocal utterance.

Song was the winged vehicle by which praises and petitions were
wafted to the Almighty. The words, therefore, were all important. It was essential that Yahweh should hear them clearly and with
no hindering instrumental clutter. As a rule, each singer accompanied himself, the strings of his harp or lyre helping to keep him
on pitch and also providing a controllable balance between voices
and instruments. Strings predominated, as best suited to the sedate
character of Temple music. Technically, also, they were better
able to follow the intricate patterns of Oriental melodies than
woodwinds, which in those days were still rudimentary.

After the fashion of the Orient, instruments, in the main, merely
duplicated the vocal melody in unison or at the octave. Stone and

wall carvings left by neighbor nations suggest that the Hebrews, at least from the time of David, possessed in addition a knowledge of the fifth interval and possibly the fourth, in which case one of the choirmaster's tasks must have been to determine the tones and intervals that should accompany a given melody.

From all such conjectures we arrive at a general idea, at least, of how rehearsals may have proceeded. To begin with, the music was "composed," i.e., the most important part, the vocal melody, was jointly worked out in practical sessions. Then the instruments that would duplicate this in unison were chosen and coached. After this the functions of the accompanying, or accenting, instruments were fixed note for note.

All this was practiced until everyone had mastered all details assigned to him. Finally, everything was rehearsed together, again and again, until a satisfactory result was obtained. This methodical, conscientious rehearsal technique was one of the reasons the artistry of Levitical performances became famous in antiquity.

Through more than ten centuries, sometimes in the face of acute danger, the systematic rehearsal work of the Levites would continue with fanatical zeal. Despite the lack of musical notation, Hebrew music was preserved through the vicissitudes of later ages by the skill and fervor of these Levitical music masters. It was their unshakable belief in their mission as apostles of their art that managed to keep such music alive in the face of national catastrophes, wars, idolatry, captivity, and wide dispersion.

8

THE SACRED PSALMS

THE HEAVY YEAR-ROUND schedule as well as the diversity of offerings demanding each its appropriate vocal accompaniment brought the need for a large and varied musical liturgy. The Temple, with its colorful appeal to all the senses, quickly became the fountainhead of an inspired outpouring. Disciplined by ritual needs and fired with spiritual purpose, devotional music now was joined to poetry with an expressive force never to be surpassed.

The pent-up creative urge of the Hebrew spirit, denied expression in pigment and stone, eagerly embraced this new art form, which had the full sanction of the nation's religious laws. Poets and musicians vied with one another to enrich the sacred service. The song of praise, a feature of worship since the days of Moses, and refined and fostered by David, now became a consciously wrought tone-symbol of faith in God and humility before his works. This endeavor to serve God in word and music led to the creation of one of the world's immortal treasuries of poetry, the Book of Psalms.

The authorship of most of the psalms probably will be shrouded forever in mystery. Still, we can perhaps determine the class, at least, to which the poets of the psalms belonged by examining the beliefs of those times.

Music in antiquity was looked upon as a divine gift, closely allied to the gift of prophecy. So intimately related were they that Hebrew prophecy was virtually born out of the spirit of music. The poet and the prophet also were blended into a single notion, for the Hebrew prophets were at the same time poets. Even though their utterances may not always have achieved the level of poetry, they were distinguished by a literary style and a delivery that was either sung or chanted. The poet, too, felt that he could convey his message most effectively to the sound of music, as in Psalm 49:

> Hear this, all ye peoples . . .
> My mouth shall speak wisdom, and the meditation of my
>   heart shall be of understanding.
> I will incline mine ear to a parable; I will open my dark
>   sayings upon the harp.

In antiquity whatever was solemnly sung or chanted carried greater authority than if it were merely spoken. Like other ancient peoples, the Israelites confidently believed the singer to be in the grip of some prophetic inspiration. This may be why the Levitical singers also came to be called prophets and seers, since they obviously seemed inspired by Yahweh to pour out their feelings in song.

Such seers as Asaph, Heman, and the few others whose names have come down to us must have been not only gifted singers but distinguished poets as well. Their accomplishments, in any case, were so outstanding, even among the artistically prominent Levitical singers, that the chroniclers saw fit to preserve their names for posterity. Inasmuch as literature and poetry had long been cultivated systematically by specially trained priestly and Levitical families, there seems every reason to look to the ranks of Temple functionaries for the authors of a great majority of the psalms.

Composing music for the sacred service or adapting it for ritual use was a prime duty of the singers. They knew the needs of the liturgy and the style in which its poetry should be cast. Since the purpose of music was to clothe the devotional utterance, who was better qualified for such a task than those who had been born into a tradition of serving the Lord through song?

We can safely suppose that they not only created and sang the psalms, preserving the tradition of their performance through many centuries, but that they also inscribed their exalted poetry with laborious care on scrolls of narrow parchment and papyrus, bequeathing to ages and to faiths not yet born the legacy of Jewish devotional genius in the Book of Psalms.

Today this forms a collection of 150 lyric poems, in five sections, or books. Its Hebrew title, *Sefer Tehillim*, means a book of songs in praise of God. Later, the Romans gave it the title *Psalterium*, meaning hymns sung to the psaltery. It is from this that we get our present name for it, the Psalter.

We can be sure that the Psalter originally contained more psalms than it does today. Many were doubtless lost over the ages, many others, for one reason or another, removed from the collection by various editors. What remains, however, is a unique anthology of lyrico-religious poetry, which early became and is today the basic liturgical songbook of the Jews.

Every human emotion is expressed in the psalms, each of which deals with some aspect of man's relationship to God. Some are a plea for God's protection, as Psalm 16:

> Preserve me, O God, for in thee I take refuge.

Others reflect the anguish of the guilty soul, as in Psalm 38:

> O Lord, rebuke me not in thy anger,
> nor chasten me in thy wrath!

Some express humility before the beauty of the natural world, as in Psalm 19:

> The heavens declare the glory of God;
> and the firmament showeth his handiwork.

Or a calm confidence in God's omnipotence, as in Psalm 24:

> The earth is the Lord's and the fullness thereof,
> the world and those who dwell therein.

Although virtually all are addressed to the deity and have a strong devotional cast, songs from many different categories make up the Psalter, indicating that its compilers drew from all sources of popular poetry. Among the earlier Hebrews, songs for their religious rites may have constituted a primitive hymnal. The Israelites' devout alliance with their God must have inspired more than one folk bard to compose poems extolling Yahweh's majesty and his protection of his chosen people. Such songs of praise and thanksgiving, of prayer and repentance, provided the foundation for the later Book of Psalms.

But we can also find in certain psalms fragments from the many songs of harvest and vintage, work songs, love songs, and wedding songs that must have carroled across the early period of folk poetry. All, to be sure, have been given a suitably religious coloring, but traces remain that clearly point to the popular origin of such verses as those of vernal thanksgiving in Psalm 65:

> The pastures are clothed with flocks; the valleys also
> are covered over with corn; they shout for joy, they
> also sing.

The historic ode, preserving in song the memory of some great national event, was another species of song incorporated into the Psalter. Examples of these are Psalm 30, which tradition says was sung at the dedication of the Temple, and Psalm 137, which reflects the grief of the captive Hebrews by the rivers of Babylon:

> . . . We wept,
> when we remembered Zion.

Finally, we find certain prayerful meditations, the phrasing of which indicates that they may have been models for later psalm writing. Such is the hymn of praise that the young David offered after the Lord had prospered him over his enemies (deservedly so, as David pointed out) and that we find later incorporated almost without change in Psalm 18:

> I love thee, O Lord, my strength.
> The Lord is my rock, and my fortress.

Historical evidence favors the belief that a considerable part of the Psalter originated well before the Babylonian captivity (587 B.C.). As we noted earlier, the Babylonians and Assyrians took over ancient Sumerian hymns and used them in their own liturgy. In view of the Israelites' close cultural ties with both nations it seems probable that they also adopted this liturgical custom very early.

Certainly the Babylonian, no less than the Egyptian, examples must have been intriguing to the Levitical poets, particularly after the Sanctuary was erected in Jerusalem and the sacred service flowered into its solemn and impressive ceremonies. Indeed, although the Hebrew psalms reflect a higher religious concept, we find striking parallels in form, language, and idea between them and certain Babylonian poems.

More than a few Egyptian attitudes likewise penetrated them, a well-known instance being the resemblance between Psalm 104:

> O Lord, my God, thou art very great!
> Thou are clothed with honor and majesty,
> Who coverest thyself with light as with
> > a garment,
> Who hast stretched out the heavens like
> > a tent . . .

and the "Hymn to the Sun," attributed to the young pharaoh Ikhnaton (Amenhotep IV):

> Thou risest beautifully, O living Aton,
> > Lord of Eternity;
> Thou art glittering, beautiful, strong;
> Thy love is great and mighty,
> Thy rays furnish vision to every one
> > of thy creatures . . .

Canaanite influence is also found in many passages of the text. Psalm 29, among others, is believed to be of Canaanite origin. But despite such occasional infiltrations, the most searching modern scrutiny of the psalms confirms that the Psalter, on the whole, is a genuine creation of the Jews.

For all this, scholarly opinions are sharply divided as to when the various psalms were written, as well as to their possible authors. A majority date many of them from the period of the early kingdom (during the reigns of Saul, David, and Solomon, in the eleventh and tenth centuries B.C.), when the schools of prophets and the Levitical caste alike reached a crescendo of psalmodic outpouring. Portions may have been added a couple of centuries later during the reign of King Hezekiah, which was also a fertile period for sacred music.

The Psalter's fourth book is generally believed to have been written at the time of the Babylonian exile or shortly thereafter (sixth century B.C.), and the remaining portions during the two or three centuries immediately following.

The modern dating of a majority of the psalms after 400 B.C. is seriously questioned by many scholars of note, some of whom think it possible that certain ones may have been written in the time of Moses, or even of Jacob. Others contend that all the psalms were written only after the return from Babylon.

Most scholars agree that the Psalter received its final form around 200 B.C. Such estimates are in agreement with the historical development of musical culture in ancient Israel. There appears, indeed, to be a striking parallel between the gradual growth of the Psalter and the evolution of Jewish sacred music.

Most psalms carry in their heading the name of their presumed author. Of the 150 psalms contained in the Psalter, seventy-three are credited to David, twelve to Asaph, eleven to the sons (descendants) of Korah, two to Solomon, and one each to Moses, Heman, and Ethan. Thirty-four carry no author's name. In talmudic literature these are called "orphan psalms."

Since David is traditionally supposed to have authored the majority, his name has been affixed to the entire collection, which has commonly been known as The Book of Psalms of David. Modern biblical criticism, however, has largely abandoned the belief that the proper names in the headings necessarily represent the author of any given psalm. The opinion today is that each designates some earlier collection from which the particular psalm was taken.

It may be, too, that the names refer to certain groups of Temple singers, and that a psalm so headed originally belonged to the special repertoire of a given group or family. Or it may have been taken from a hymnal compiled (although not necessarily composed) by them. It is reasonable to suppose that each choral group might have its own favorite hymns, or be especially qualified to perform certain ones, which thus might become traditionally identified with it.

Such group names, attached to a small collection of psalms, were retained in the individual headings in the final order of the Psalter. Biblical researchers have found traces of at least ten such previous smaller collections, ranging from the days of the early kings until after the return from Babylonian captivity.

We shall probably never know for certain how many of the psalms actually were composed by David. Some scholars maintain that he authored none of them. Others think it likely that his name in the headings of nearly half the psalms indicates not their author but, with a few exceptions, the first of several smaller psalters gathered under his name after the return from Babylon, from which these psalms were taken by later compilers of the final Psalter. This earliest compilation of Davidic psalms may have been a prayer book, since they are for the most part prayers.

To be sure, there is no proof that David may not have written all of those attributed to him, as well as any number of the so-called "orphan psalms." At least one modern scholar would divide the credit for a majority of them between David and Hezekiah, or their court poets.

Patently, it is next to impossible to determine either the authorship or the time of origin of a collection such as the Psalter, into which items from a period covering almost nine centuries have been incorporated. An additional handicap is the fact that, in all probability, many of the hymns and psalms were not written down immediately but were preserved orally for generations. This must have resulted in any number of deletions or additions, and of changes, either unintentional or arbitrary. Moreover, the introduction into public worship of certain psalms not originally intended for this purpose may have caused some readjustment in the original text.

Sometime before the third century B.C. the Psalter became canonized. Thereafter, as a sacred book, it might not be altered. But during the preceding 200 years there had been nothing to restrain any number of editors from seeking to modernize it by replacing certain archaic or obsolete expressions with terms common to their own time. Since the Psalter was not compiled as a work of literature but as a practical tool of religion, no qualms were felt about radically altering the text to adapt it to the immediate needs of the religious service.

The literary production of antiquity was largely anonymous. Like the great poems of Egypt, Persia, India, Babylonia, and Assyria, the Bible was the work of many unknown authors over long periods. With the exception of the Prophets and the books of Ezra and Nehemiah, the authors of the biblical books are not known to us by name.

According to tradition, Moses is the author of the Pentateuch. In reality these first five books of the Old Testament were handed down to posterity as anonymously as the rest of ancient Hebrew writings. Throughout the Pentateuch, Moses is referred to only in the third person and as one clearly distinct from the narrator.

Even the prophetical books, although they carry the name of an author, were apparently not written by the prophets themselves but by disciples intent on perpetuating their master's ideas and counsel. They were not intended as "literature" in the later sense of the word; rather, they were propaganda pamphlets whose sole purpose was to preserve the religion of Yahweh and its priestly institutions. Since it was essential for their acceptance that the books proclaim whose teaching they contained, the prophet's name was attached to them.

There is no reason to suppose that the Psalter is an exception to the general rule governing the literature of antiquity. In later times a Davidic tradition arose, built around the idealized figure of the king and representing him, apart from his other virtues, as the author of nearly half the psalms. The Greek version of the Psalter attributes even more to him, and the Syriac version almost all. The most generous estimate of many modern scholars is that David perhaps authored half of those that bear his name.

Moses' authorship of Psalm 90 is extremely unlikely, inasmuch as this appears in the fourth book of the Psalter, which was not compiled until long after the first three. No compiler would have overlooked the chance to include so distinguished a name in the very earliest psalmodic collection.

Solomon's meager representation is puzzling. Insofar as the time factor is concerned, the first of the two psalms ascribed to him (Psalm 72) and incorporated into the second book could well have been written by him. In view of his fame and his publicized talents as a poet and sage, it is surprising that no more than these two psalms are credited to him.

It may be that a number of these actually were incorporated into the Psalter at one time and subsequently divorced from their identifying titles. We can safely assume that in the turbulent centuries following his reign the majority of Solomon's proverbs and psalms were lost.

The sons of Korah were members of a group of Levitical scribes who from the time of King Hezekiah until well after the return from Babylon (roughly from 724 to 444 B.C.) carried on a prolific literary activity. The eleven psalms attributed to them contain a number of historical records and references, which hints that they may have helped to write the historical books of the Bible.

The Asaphites were another Levitical family whose literary activities extended over several centuries. The twelve psalms ascribed to Asaph may also originally have been part of a small separate collection, as may the two respectively attributed to Heman and Ethan (or Jeduthun).

(According to a modern view, Ethan and Jeduthun meant the same person, "jeduthun" being not a proper name but a corrupt version of the Hebrew phrase, (al) jede ethan, "(upon) the hands of Ethan," i.e., in charge of the choir group led by Ethan. Apparently the authors of the Chronicles, or their later copyists, misread the word in the psalm headings and took it over into their own text as Jeduthun.)

But however adulterated the songs of the Psalter, or however varied in form and content, they have one thing in common: they are lyrico-religious songs designed for liturgical use. The Psalter went through several stages before attaining its present form, absorbing sundry smaller collections, adding or eliminating single songs, markedly changing others. Yet the ultimate purpose of the final book was the same as that of the primary collection: to serve as a hymnal for public worship at the Temple.

9

THE CHARACTER OF
HEBREW MUSIC

How WERE THE psalms sung? What did they sound like as they poured from the throats of the Temple singers beside the brazen altar in the huge court of the sacrifices?

For centuries these questions were to keep biblical scholars and, later, musicologists embroiled in a welter of conjecture and speculation. Numerous theories were advanced, and during the nineteenth century sundry attempts to reconstruct the ancient Hebrew melodies in modern musical notation served only to becloud the issue further. After the fashion of the time the psalm texts were treated to stiffly conventional harmonies, in an effort to make them resemble Protestant chorales in a four-part setting. Or they were endowed with extravagant vocal leaps to an accompaniment of broken chords in the manner of piano exercises for beginners.

Whatever the approach, all such earlier attempts made the basic error of trying to apply the principles of Western music to the ancient Hebrew prosody. When such efforts failed it seemed to confirm the belief of many that the verses in the Psalter had never formed a hymnal at all, but merely a collection of poetry serving as prayers that had been uttered, at most, in a free recitative style.

Today we understand their nature better. Ancient Hebrew music, we now realize, was a product of Oriental music culture and followed its aesthetic laws. These differ appreciably from those of Occidental music, and neither can be fully interpreted in terms of the other.

It was obvious that a fresh approach had to be made, but from what direction? Surprisingly, the Bible itself furnished a leading clue. For centuries this had been hiding in plain sight in the psalm headings themselves, which for the better part of 2,000 years had been invested by scholars and churchmen alike with any number of conflicting and esoteric meanings.

Many psalms in the Psalter, as a casual glance will show, contain in their headings terms which seem to have no bearing upon the text itself. Such terms as *gittith, shoshannim, al taschith*, and others, for none of which any modern translation has yet been found, are scattered among the headings of some fifty psalms in the first three books of the Psalter. Scholarly arguments, ranging widely, found some agreement on the theory that the terms indicated musical instruments, ignoring the fact that whereas references to musical instruments abound within the psalm verses, none of the disputed terms are to be found therein.

It seemed certain, at any rate, that the baffling terms originally had good reason for being in the psalm headings. Continuing to probe, more recent scholars were able to operate in the clearer light provided by the new science of archeology. Among the more helpful discoveries turned up by archeologists' spades during the past century was a fragment of stone slab found in Assyria. Dating from 2000 B.C., this bore inscribed on it the titles of some 300 Sumerian and Assyrian songs, sacred and secular, which apparently were well-known melodies of the time. The entire slab, only the upper half of which was recovered, had doubtless contained many more.

What particularly excited biblical scholars was the fact that the songs listed in the stone "catalogue" had evidently been meant to furnish musical settings for a variety of psalmodic and liturgical texts. Other relics recovered by archeology disclosed the fact that ancient Syrian hymn writers had customarily provided their poems with musical instructions, for example: "To be sung to (the melody) 'I will open my mouth with knowledge.'" This practice, it seemed clear, had been universal in the music of antiquity.

Reasoning from this, biblical scholars concluded that many of the hitherto enigmatic terms in the Hebrew psalm headings had served a like purpose: they were the titles or the catchwords of songs that had been popular in ancient Israel, and it was to their melodies that the psalms had been sung.

The enigma of the psalm headings, however, was still a long way from being solved. For one thing, how did the ancient Temple singers manage to adapt a given melody to the text of a particular psalm? Many psalms are much longer than any popular song. Most of them are very uneven as to rhythmic beat, and all of their verses vary greatly in number of syllables and in the way these are naturally stressed.

To understand how they surmounted such problems we need to know a little about the character of Oriental music, which is much the same today as it was for the people of early Israel. In the first place, what we in the Occident think of as song or melody cannot be applied to the ancient singing of the psalms. Oriental music does not possess our kind of melodic structure, which is divided into musical motives and phrases that recur in a predictable pattern. Today, as in antiquity, Oriental music is based on small, nuggetlike groups of tones, each belonging to some particular Oriental musical "scale."

These little nuggets, or melodic kernels, are stereotyped musical patterns, usually comprising only a few notes. To us they may not sound much like tunes, but to the Oriental ear, trained for centuries to recognize dozens of them, they are miniature, self-contained melodies. This principle of ready-made melodic kernels is the foundation of the entire musical structure of the Orient and the Near East. In India such a melodic formula is called a *raga* (literally, "color," "mood"), but in Israel's neighboring countries of Arabia and Persia it is called a *makam*.

The way in which these makams are put together to form an organized melodic system constitutes the basis of Oriental music theory. Each makam is composed of two, three, rarely four, motives, which are flexible enough to accommodate a varying number of syllables. Each makam also is bound to a particular tempo, mood, pitch, accentual pattern, and scale sequence from which the singer may not depart. The artistry of the Oriental musician consists in his ability to arrange and combine his limited number of motives—composing, in the truest sense of the word, a fresh vocal expression that is further embellished with a variety of coloratura effects.

This is the direct opposite to our Western conception of music, in which the work itself is paramount. For us, the notes as the composer wrote them are fixed and inviolable. When we attend a symphony concert, for example, we can rest assured that the conductor is striving for the utmost fidelity to the composer's wish, as preserved in the printed score. Any conductor who arbitrarily altered the development section of a Brahms symphony or presumed to weave spontaneous variations on the rondo finale of a Beethoven concerto would speedily be looking for a job in another field. The widest latitude allowed the Occidental performer relates only to matters of relative tempo and expressive shading—and even in these he is more often than not taken to task by one or another dissenting critic.

In Oriental music, on the other hand, interpretation is virtually more important than the original musical idea. The latter is merely the raw stuff out of which the skilled performer himself creates the art work by improvising variations upon it; and his Oriental audience, experienced in listening, is able mentally to separate these from the basic melody. Of the ragas of his native India the late poet Rabindranath Tagore observed:

> In our country the understanding portion of the audience think no harm in keeping the performance up to standard by dint of their own imagination. For the same reason they do not mind any harshness of voice or uncouthness of gesture in the exponent of a perfectly formed melody; on the contrary, they seem sometimes to be of the opinion that such minor external defects serve better to set off the internal perfection of the composition.

Their effect upon the European listener was expressed by the German philosopher, Hermann Keyserling, after hearing certain Hindu ragas:

> Nothing calculated, no definite shape, no beginning, no end; a surge and undulation of the eternally flowing stream of

life. Therefore, always the same effect upon the listener; it is not wearisome, could last forever, since nobody ever gets tired of life.

Yet a raga—the Hindu parallel to a makam—consists of only a few tones, compared to our Western melodies. It is on the bare framework of these few basic notes that the skilled Oriental performer builds an intricate melodic structure, often so ornamented today that the original idea is festooned beyond easy recognition. Runs, trills, appoggiaturas, portamentos, melisms—all kinds of vocal decoration are mosaically worked into ever fresh patterns. There is no preestablished point of return, no *da capo*, as in Western music, to a beginning from which the process may repeat. Unlike Occidental melodies, which are usually square-shaped and subordinate to the overall structure, Oriental melodies are like mountain streams that bubble from a seemingly inexhaustible source, taking on in their meandering an infinite variety of shapes and colors.

To see how this might work, let us take as a makam a tune that everyone knows, such as "My country, 'tis of thee." These first five notes we will call one motive; "sweet land of liberty" will give us a second motive, and "of thee I sing" provides us with a third. (Of course, this would never do as an ancient makam for many reasons, but it is as familiar to us as were their own makam melodies to the early Hebrews.)

Now let us pretend that you are a Levitical singer in the Jerusalem Temple and that the psalm you are to sing for a particular occasion—perhaps a special act of the ritual or a High Holiday—must be based throughout on these three motives, which make up its makam or melody pattern. During the years you studied to be a Temple singer you learned rote-perfect the many rigid rules that must govern your use of the various motives that make up all the different makams. You know, for instance, that some motives may follow each other, while others may not, and that certain motives must begin and end your song.

Bearing these and other restrictions in mind, you can then proceed to alternate and combine your motives as you will. You can embroider them with vocal trills and grace notes, and between the basic notes you can even add whatever short passing notes are needed to fit a motive to various passages of the text. The more inventive you are in doing all this, the finer artist you will be considered.

But you must never change suddenly to another makam of a different mood and tempo, as, for example, "Frankie and Johnny," and try to combine its melody motives with the first. Your audience would know at once that you had committed an unpardonable musical error as well as violated the sacred ritual, for every makam used in the Temple service was associated with a particular devotional activity, and was believed to exert its own spiritual and moral force upon the listener.

So now we see how the principle worked. Through their skill in variation, common to any trained singer of the Orient, the ancient Levitical singers were able to adjust such melodic kernels to any number of verses, long or short. It was necessary only that they choose makams that were universally familiar, so that these might be used as musical patterns for the psalms not only in their own time but by future generations. The popular songs referred to in the various psalm headings—gittith, shoshannim, and the rest—were evidently such well-known makam types of the time, which long remained familiar through oral tradition, but which were ultimately forgotten during the social and political upheavals of the centuries.

Such common coinage of makams not only helped to preserve the psalms, but was an essential factor in their creation. Authors of the earlier psalms doubtless drew upon a much wider sampling of popular melodies and of folk tunes than were finally accepted into the permanent Temple liturgy. Too, after the Oriental fashion, the psalms may have been written with a particular melody pattern or makam in mind. The fifty psalms that survive with such indications in their headings may each have once been part of a group of psalms designed to be sung to a particular makam.

The fact that such melody patterns are found only in the first three books of the Psalter suggests that those initially used had already fallen into oblivion by the time the later books were compiled, several centuries later. Subsequent makam types may have cropped up and become popular, but the fate of the older ones may well have deterred the Temple musicians from designating any new ones for the later psalms. Instead, the choice of these appears to have been left to the musicians of the time.

There are no written records to tell us how the melodies of ancient Israel were shaped and sung. But of one thing we can be sure. The meticulous organization of the Temple ritual was not confined to externals. If Asaph, Heman, Jeduthun, and their colleagues were governed by a rigid pattern of daily ceremonies, the music they performed was no less scrupulously organized. A sense of order, as such, was the distinguishing characteristic of Hebrew life in antiquity, and of all cultural domains liturgical music was perhaps most efficiently organized.

Whatever its debt to other cultures—and this was large—the music of the Jerusalem Temple was formed on the principles of law and logic that govern every expression of art in any age. It had not only an artistic standard by which a piece or its execution was judged; it had a system, a rational discipline, by which a national style could be expressed within the general musical context of the antique Orient.

Changes in its art take place inevitably in any culture that endures for several millennia. Even in the tradition-bound Orient major political or economic changes brought corresponding changes in other spheres; sober Egypt itself, as we have seen, was forced to modify its musical expression to meet the changing times.

Any sweeping statements, therefore, as to precisely how Hebrew music sounded at the time of the First Temple (c. 1000 B.C.) would be both presumptuous and unwise. The music of ancient Israel, which may be said to have endured from before the Exodus to the first century of the Common Era, or roughly from 1300 B.C. to A.D. 70, would itself have undergone certain changes as the climate of Hebrew life varied over the course of fourteen centuries.

In archaic times and down to the first years of the kingdom, Hebrew music would appear to have been based largely on a pentatonic, or five-tone, scale (without semitones), like the black keys on the piano. In those early years of artless, spontaneous singing, women customarily took the lead, dancing to their small frame hand drums. This practice, common to the ancient Near East, is still found today in certain primitive areas, from which scholars have been able to deduce the form that such ancient folksongs may have taken.

In the light of modern evidence turned up by the late Robert Lachmann's studies on the North African island of Djerba, we may suppose that early Hebrew folksongs, as sung by women, depended on a small store of well-worn melodic turns, which were made to serve time and again for various songs. No systematic rhythmic pattern divided the melody into bars; the drumbeats, following at regular intervals, merely fell on each period of the melody, and no hard-and-fast tonal relationships had yet been developed.

Women's singing, like their dancing, tends in primitive cultures toward small, contained steps. Their melodies, simple and symmetrical, stay within a narrow tonal compass, scarcely exceeding intervals of a second or a third, and reflect the seemly domestic pattern of their daily tasks—soothing babies, spinning, weaving, grinding grain. In view of women's prominence in the musical life of early Israel the form of their songs may well have played a significant part in shaping the structure of Hebrew folk melodies.

The Sons of the Prophets, who flourished before and for some time after the establishment of the sacred musical service, also accompanied their songs with hand drums, but we must suppose that —again reasoning from modern examples of primitive music—the form of their melodies was bolder, with wider masculine strides between the notes. The ecstatic character of their singing suggests, too, that once a hypnotically repeated group chanting had reached a certain emotional pitch, one or another more inspired member would soar into free improvisation.

Work songs, on the other hand, whether of men or women, reflected the rhythmically repeated pattern of the task, often performed in group unison, and tended toward greater regularity of rhythm, hence of melodic structure, than songs sung by a solo performer accompanied by instruments, as among the emerging group of professional singers at David's royal court. Egyptian murals of a thousand years earlier show trained singers signaling to their accompanist, indicating that such court songs had always possessed definite improvisatory features.

The Levites, as a hereditary caste, also had their own musical tradition, dedicated like themselves to devotional matters. They may even have regarded certain songs, even certain kinds of music, as peculiarly their own, which no other class was allowed to perform. Representing, with the priesthood, the educated minds of their time, they knew something of the orderly processes of mathematics and astronomy. The splendid logic of the heavenly bodies wheeling across the dark-vaulted sky over Jerusalem could scarcely have failed to leave its mark on the Temple scholars seeking to establish a sound theoretical basis for their sacred music.

All such elements were part of Hebrew musical culture when the Psalms were first being shaped to the needs of the Temple service. Traditional folk melodies fused with the freer forms of cultivated music to give them on the one hand a musical structure that admitted of a formal discipline, and on the other a melodic flexibility to meet the diverse requirements of the official cult liturgy. This duality would enable them to meet and assimilate changes that might otherwise have proved their undoing throughout succeeding ages.

To gain an idea of how the melodies may have sounded we must always bear in mind that they were Oriental in character. Instead of our major and minor scales, Oriental music is based on intervals (tone steps) quite different from ours. Oriental gradations between tones are much subtler and are virtually impossible to reproduce in our Western musical notation.

When we listen to Oriental singing, for example, we hear any number of intermediate tones, which sound as though the performer were singing now flat, now sharp, while any accompanying instruments sound curiously out of tune. Such delicate, "microtonic" intervals seem indefinite and unmusical to our ears, although to one familiar with them they are often more aesthetically satisfying than our square-cut Western melodies.

Both the Near and Far East regard as attractive certain vocal affectations that inspire the Western listener with something less than admiration. One of these is a markedly nasal quality of tone. Another is a vocal tremolo so pronounced as to sound almost like sobbing. This, achieved by pressure on the throat, is still used by Oriental singers, who regard it as a legitimately artful device. That it was already a common practice in high antiquity we know from the famous Assyrian bas-relief in the British Museum, which depicts the victory reception of Sennacherib's grandson, Ashurbanipal (668–626 B.C.), and shows among a band of musicians a singing woman who is pressing her fingers against her throat. Certain Egyptian murals also show singers using the same device, by which particularly sharp and shrill tones were produced. In other pictures of antiquity the artist has painted wrinkles between the eyebrows of the singers, presumably to portray the strain of forcing high-pitched nasal tones through a tightly constricted throat.

Still, for the ancient Hebrews the words remained the important thing, bearing as they did a message to their God. The music of the psalms was not meant to entertain the worshiper but to furnish an exalted form of address to the Almighty. Although the Levitical singers drew upon the tradition of Oriental music for the form of their sacred expression and employed the basic features common to all Oriental singing, they appear to have kept the Temple performances relatively free from vocal abuses until quite late in their history. Excessive ornamentation or exaggerated vocal effects were contrary to the dignified spirit of early Temple music and would have been frowned upon by the stern guardians of their craft.

For sacred singing the importance of the verbal message formed a point of departure from the rhythmically stricter form of popular singing. Whereas the common people continued to sing their strophiclike folksongs—less for their lyrics than as an accompaniment to the bodily patterns of their work or dance—Temple singing took on a rhythmically freer character to accommodate the natural flow of the sacred text.

If, as we must suppose, this followed the pattern of most Oriental melodies, those of the psalms may have been constructed within the frame of four descending intervals, comprising two whole tones and one semitone, and coming to rest on the lower, or fourth, note. We call this a tetrachord, from the Greek *tetra*, meaning "four." Any melody exceeding this narrow frame established a new tetrachord, which, added to the first, formed a set of eight notes or, in Western thinking, an "octave" composed of two disjunct tetrachords:

If the two tetrachords shared a common pivotal note, a seven-step, or heptatonic (*hepta* = seven), series was created, containing five whole tones and two semitones, as in our diatonic scale:

No hard-and-fast conclusions may ever be possible as to what extent the early pentatonic folk melodies prevailed in ancient Hebrew Temple music. It would appear, however, that the archaic, five-note gamut of popular song was expanded in ritual music to a six- or seven-note sequence. Curt Sachs, whose work helped lay the foundation for all subsequent research in ancient music, declares that in the ancient Western Orient, "Singing, at least in the last one thousand years B.C., was heptatonic without any trace of pentatonism." Other authorities, notably Joseph Yasser, maintain, on the other hand, that biblical chant had basic and very strong pentatonic traits.

Whatever their scalar structure, the melodies were modal—a term that implies much more in its Eastern context than in ours. A mode is usually defined as a sequence of tonal intervals organized in a particular way, but in the Orient this is further characterized by the way in which certain beginning, middle, and concluding motives are employed within the melody.

Modes used for the Hebrew psalms were chosen to suit the character of the text. The Pentateuch and, later, the Prophets, Psalms, Lamentations, and other books of the Old Testament, had each its prescribed mode, with a particular melodic pattern (makam) composed of some two to four motives. Special melodic patterns, perhaps keeping their pentatonic, folksong character, were retained for lyric portions of the Pentateuch, such as the song of Lamech and the Red Sea song.

Western music has three basic elements: melody, harmony, and rhythm. Oriental music, being largely vocal, makes melody its prime element. Singing of any sort is invariably accompanied, but such instrumental accompaniment merely supports the melodic vocal line, never subordinating or conflicting with it. Because of this unchallenged supremacy, Oriental melodies over the centuries have developed great refinement and subtlety.

The psalms sung in the Temple therefore had no chordal structure as do our modern hymns. Like all music of antiquity, choral singing was monophonic, having only a single, unharmonized line. Monophony, however, did not mean monotony, for out of this endlessly spun thread of melody the Oriental gift for variation wove an ever-changing design.

This monophonic character of ancient Hebrew music has been persistently linked with a misunderstood biblical passage that relates that at the dedication of Solomon's Temple "the trumpeters and singers were as one," making "one sound to be heard." The unison of voices and instruments lifted on this occasion in solemn, unharmonized accord ("one sound") has been pointed to by some as reflecting a Jewish philosophical conception of the world, aiming in every part at uniformity. Such an interpretation is based on a patently erroneous premise. Monophony is neither a product of Jewish cultivation, nor does it reflect any "Jewish world view." It is simply a common feature of Oriental music, and the "one sound" mentioned refers to the uniform intonation achieved by the immense musical forces—a phenomenon so rare in the imprecise tonal habits of the Orient as to warrant scriptural mention.

Harmony, as we know it, has played no part in Oriental music. To the Western ear harmony conveys a sense of tension and relaxation, as certain chords resolve into others more reposeful, and vice versa. It is a major organizing principle of Western music. The role that harmony plays in the West is played in the East by rhythm, which accounts for the preponderance in its music of drums, cymbals, and other instruments of indefinite pitch. Most of its tunes, whether sung or played, are accompanied by one or several of these, and if none is available, by clapping of hands or stamping of feet.

But again, the Oriental idea of rhythm differs from ours. For us, rhythm is governed by the time units made up of longer or shorter pulsations (beats), which determine the pace, or tempo, of a piece. (In waltz tempo, for example, the musical stress falls on every third beat: ONE, two, three, ONE, two, three; in polka tempo, on every other beat: ONE, two, ONE, two, and so on.) Oriental rhythm has no such mechanical beats with regular stresses, strong or weak, falling at preestablished points in a melody. We must keep this in mind when we consider the role of rhythm in those portions of the Bible that were written, like all poetic literature of antiquity, to be sung.

The Old Testament comprises both prose and poetry, but the decision as to what constituted either was long disputed. The psalms, for instance, were uniformly conceded to be poetry, whereas the remainder, aside from certain lyric episodes, was regarded as prose.

Loftiness of idea and expression, however, may lift even simple prose to the level of poetry, particularly since notions of either are highly flexible when the consideration is purely literary. The problem of where to draw the line was long debated.

It was not until poetry, during the past century, was freed from its attachment to a strict meter, with lines of a set length and an often inflexible rhyme scheme, that many of the biblical books began to be seen for what they are—poetry of an extremely high order and surprisingly modern in form.

In its expanded concept, meter alone, regular or irregular, could now be taken as the real test of poetic form. Accordingly, nearly all portions of the Old Testament, aside from sheer narrative or pronouncements of law, are today classed as poetry. To these belong —in addition to the Psalms—the Proverbs, the Song of Songs, Lamentations, Job, much of Ecclesiastes, important sections of the Prophets, and among the Apocrypha, parts of Ecclesiasticus (Ben Sirach), Judith, Tobit, and certain others.

In none of these do we find the lines chopped into equal lengths, but this does not mean that they are without meter. (Meter means the number of feet in a line of poetry, with each foot containing one accented syllable and a variable number of unaccented ones.) Thus:

A time / to weep / and a time / to laugh,
a time / to mourn / and a time / to dance.

These lines from Ecclesiastes each contain four feet, although such symmetry in Hebrew poetry is uncommon. Here, however, the unstressed syllables vary, the third foot showing two before the heavy accent, whereas the rest show only one. We are dealing here, of course, with the lines in their English translation; stresses in the Hebrew text would normally fall on different syllables.

Three or even four unstressed syllables may precede the accented syllable in Hebrew poetry, since it was not concerned with the number or kind of feet but with the rhythmic flow of speech, which naturally stresses the important syllable in a text. For example:

> I will lift up mine eyes unto the hills
> From whence cometh my strength.

Here the natural accent is so irregular and subtle that to force a mechanical meter upon it would quite distort the beauty of the lines.

In the main, then, Hebrew rhythm was determined, not by the number of syllables in a line, but by the natural fall of the accent. This conscious irregularity kept it from freezing into the formal mold of classical verse, and left the poetic thought unconstricted by the mechanics of meter. Such rhythmic latitude is not uncommon, either, in English poetry, long portions of which must be read by accent rather than by meter. Shakespeare abounds in these, as in the lines from *Cymbeline*:

> Fear no more the heat o' the sun,
> Nor the furious winter's rages.

John Donne, also:

> Death be not proud, though some have called thee
> Mighty and dreadful, for thou art not so.

On the other hand, examples of a vigorous folk poetry sometimes gleam from the earlier biblical books, showing much greater rhythmic regularity and an unmistakably songlike character, such as the Red Sea song, the Well-digging song, and the paean of Deborah and Barak. The reason for their stricter meter may be that in nomadic times such songs were customarily sung by groups of women, who were dancing to the rhythm of hand drums. Like all ancient folksongs, these probably had a rather square melodic shape easier for the untrained singer.

Other examples included within the narrative portions of the Scriptures, such as the song of Lamech, Moses' song of praise, and David's lament for Saul and Jonathan, show a stanzalike structure that suggests that they, and others like them, are remnants of ancient bardic songs.

Hebrew poetry and its musical rendering evidently underwent a change with the institution of the sacred musical service. Influenced perhaps by the freer accentual rhythms of the religious liturgy, later poetic writings, most of which stemmed from the Temple academy, took on a less strict form than in nomadic times.

As a rule, the lines of a verse started on an upbeat, that is, with one or two unstressed syllables, since most Hebrew words, in their classical diction, are accented on the final syllable. In singing, such unstressed syllables were given perhaps an eighth-note value while those stressed were held for at least a quarter-note, or a group of shorter notes tied together. Syllables ending a phrase or a period were later extended with elaborate vocal embroidery during the special services held at festival seasons.

Two lines of a verse customarily formed a period, i.e., a rhythmically rounded idea, as in Psalm 93:

> The Lord reigns; he is robed in majesty;
> The Lord is robed, he is girded with strength.

That is one period, followed immediately by another:

> Yea, the world is established; it shall never
>   be moved;
> Thy throne is established from of old;
> Thou art from everlasting.

In both examples, as we can see, the second line parallels the thought of the preceding one. This "parallelism" was a frequent feature of ancient poetry, as far back as the Sumerians. Hebrew verses are studded with similar parallelisms, in which a line paraphrases the thought of a preceding line, but in a different meter. We see this in the song of Lamech as well as in the poetic visions of the prophets, and throughout the psalms—for example, Psalm 99:

> The Lord reigns; let the people tremble!
> He sits enthroned upon the cherubim; let
>   the earth quake!
> The Lord is great in Zion;
>   he is exalted over all the peoples.

Here we have two verses, the second halves of which amplify and confirm the sentiment expressed in the first half.

The musical counterpart of this poetic parallelism is known as antiphonal singing, in which one group sings the first half of a verse while another group answers with the second half. In the Temple service the first half was sometimes sung by the chief soloist, and the second half by the Levitical chorus, in which case it became responsorial singing, a form that is still used today in the Roman Catholic Church.

In the Jerusalem Temple the role of the chief singer was quite as important as that of the choir, and often more arresting. The choir's role had to be fixed in rehearsal, since spontaneous improvisation by any singing group would be musical anarchy. The chief soloist, however, was given freer rein to turn his utmost skill toward a varied treatment and a spontaneous ornamentation of the vocal melody. To what extent he availed himself of the common Eastern devices of a vocal tremolo and a nasal tone we do not know. In the modern Near East the Jewish chanter is supposed to have a sweet, expressive voice, preferably tenor. "Sweet" may have meant something quite different to the listener of 3,000 years ago.

The fact that many psalms are addressed "to the chief singer" indicates that there must have been other Temple soloists as well. Various singers in the choir may occasionally have been singled out for solo passages, at which time their own skill in variation came on trial.

Psalm singing in the Temple evidently started out as the exclusive prerogative of the Levitical singers. The Psalter, containing psalms especially written for certain services and others adapted to ritual use from songs of the common people, was designed by and for professional Temple singers. But as the congregation grew familiar with certain psalms, it seemed only natural for them to indicate their agreement with the sentiments vocally. (As when they replied "Amen!" to David's psalm at the installation of the Ark in the tabernacle.) Since a feeling of closeness to Yahweh was an essential part of their faith they wanted to join in the songs of praise. Tentatively at first, they began to interject single words (acclamations), and then to repeat certain half verses as refrains, as they had long done in their songs of daily life.

This custom went at least as far back as the Red Sea song, in which, we recall, Miriam answered the women as they sang. The women who greeted Saul and David were another instance of such antiphonal singing among the common folk. For adapting this to sacred usage there was precedent in the customs of older civilizations. We know from archeological discoveries that in the sacred liturgy of Babylonia and Assyria short acclamations served to introduce certain ceremonies. Assyrian hymns show recurrent refrains that were apparently sung by a priest-soloist and answered by a chorus. In the Rig-Veda songs of ancient India entire verses were repeated virtually word for word as a refrain. Even today antiphonal singing is commonly heard in Abyssinia, Upper Egypt, and other Near Eastern communities.

A few psalms, written in the first person singular (e.g., Psalms 3 and 5) seem best suited to solo psalmody, while others, such as Psalm 46, call for simple choral chanting throughout. The great majority, however, appear designed for antiphonal singing; certain ones, in fact, seem to require the participation of the congregation. The format of Psalms 44, 47, 80, 99, and sundry others shows the need for a response after each verse. Psalm 136 is obviously designed for responsorial singing, the leader singing the verse, perhaps with a variety of vocal effects, and the chorus or congregation the melodically unvarying refrain throughout:

> O give thanks to the Lord, for he is good,
> (For his steadfast love endures forever).
> O give thanks to the God of gods,
> (For his steadfast love endures forever).
> O give thanks to the Lord of lords,
> (For his steadfast love endures forever).

Often, refrains for the congregation are indicated at the beginning, as in Psalms 106 and 107; sometimes at both beginning and end, as in Psalms 103, 104, and 118. In addition to responses that are clearly indicated by the text, the practice of interjecting single words or short phrases, begun spontaneously, became a tradition in rabbinic times, when a cue was given the congregation to ensure their responding uniformly.

The jubilant *Hallelujah* (praise the Lord) was frequently uttered by the worshipers at the beginning or end of a psalm, sometimes both. The opening lines of Psalm 133 contain three such exclamations: *Hallelujah* (praise the Lord), *Hallel* (praise), O ye servants of the Lord; *Hallelu* (praise) the name of the Lord.

The most substantial responses, however, were the doxologies, the formulas of glorification sung by the congregation that end each psalm concluding a book of the Psalter. Since this is divided into five books, there are five such terminal psalms: 41, 72, 89, 106, and 150. The last psalm is in itself an appropriate concluding doxology for the entire collection:

> Praise (the Lord) with trumpet sound;
> Praise him with lute and harp!
> Praise him with timbrel and dance;
> Praise him with strings and pipe!
> Praise him with sounding cymbals;
> Praise him with loud clashing cymbals!

In all the doxologies the active role of the congregation was not only a musical but a ritual necessity, and it is likely that such glorifications were customarily added in actual performance to many psalms that do not show any in the Psalter.

10

THE ENIGMA OF THE PSALM
HEADINGS

FOR ALL OUR progress in biblical research, many psalm headings continue to baffle and challenge scholars as they have for centuries. Such headings almost certainly contain marginal notes relating to the musical performance, jotted down for the use of the choir leader who, then as now, would have needed some sort of lead sheet.

The beginning or end of a psalm was the logical place to add any such notations as to the melody, or makam, to be used, the instruments required, and any peculiarities of interpretation that were to be observed. These were set down in a form readily understood by any Temple singer, although it would have meant nothing to the average layman.

This did not matter so long as there was a corps of trained Temple musicians to interpret and carry out such instructions. But over the course of ages the meaning of the terms became obscure, and not surprisingly, in view of natural language changes, the many political disruptions, and other hazards, as well as the esoteric nature of the terms themselves.

By the third century B.C., even the scholars who made the first

(Greek) translation of the Old Testament no longer understood the terms, and were obliged to take them over phonetically from the original Hebrew. So, also, did the first Latin translators. The early Church fathers characteristically attributed to them all sorts of moral, allegorical, and mystical implications.

Not all the terms, to be sure, are obscure. In fifteen psalm headings we find the word, "song." In its original Hebrew form, *shir*, this meant a lyric poem sung at joyous occasions. For the Israelites the act of praising their God was an occasion of joy and so this name was given to liturgical songs of praise, especially to those performed by the Levitical choir. As the earliest term for the psalms it was probably used in the headings of various pre-Psalter collections, or hymn books.

Fifty-seven headings carry the designation, "psalm." The Hebrew word for this is *mizmor*, the root of which indicates a song performed to instrumental accompaniment as against the popular dance-song, or roundelay, which was commonly accompanied by tabrets or hand-clapping. In the Psalter it perhaps indicated a psalm to be sung by the chief soloist or one in which soloist and chorus alternated.

Occasionally we find the two terms, mizmor and shir, together. A psalm may have been designated as a "song" in one early collection and as a "psalm" in another. When such collections were absorbed into the final Psalter, both terms evidently were retained.

Psalms 17, 90, 102, and 142 have the designation *tefillah*, "prayer," indicating a threnodic form of supplication. The word is also found at the beginning of Habakkuk 3, and in the postscript to Psalm 72, where it seems to have been used as a generic term for personal prayers.

Of all the psalms, none have been more intriguing than the fifteen, numbered consecutively 120 through 134, which are called "Songs of Degrees" or "Songs of Ascent." One tradition holds that the Temple Levites sang these at the Feast of Tabernacles while gradually mounting the fifteen steps leading up to the Court of the Israelites—a psalm for each step.

Another theory is that they were sung by repatriates returning from Babylonian exile as they toiled up, or ascended, the high hills to Jerusalem. If they actually were songs of pilgrimage it is more probable that they were sung by the pilgrims "going up" to the three great harvest festivals. The short verses, written in an unaf-fectedly popular vein not found in other psalms, make it easy to believe that these songs of ascent gradually took shape among the yearly caravans of pilgrims that marched from all corners of Israel to the holy site of Jerusalem. In time they were probably made into a small songbook, whose collective title, "Songs of Ascent," may have been affixed to each of the songs when the collection was taken into the Psalter.

The words le hazkir, "to bring to remembrance," are found in the headings of Psalms 38 and 70. This is sometimes interpreted as a plea of the psalmist to be remembered of God, but more prob-ably it refers to an ancient memorial service at which, along with a handful of flour and oil, incense was thrown into the sacrificial fire.

Psalm 7 has in its heading the term shiggaion, as does also, in a different spelling, Habakkuk 3. This seems to be related to an As-syrian term meaning a plaintive song of several stanzas, which in Babylonia accompanied special rites. The Assyrian meaning is "to lament vehemently," from which we may deduce a kind of dithy-ramb, a wild, passionate song with rapid changes of rhythm. Such a song perhaps infiltrated the early Canaanite tribes, from whom the Israelites adopted it as a penitential or lamenting song.

The headings of six psalms (Pss. 16 and 56 through 60) contain the word miktam, a term whose meaning has been so completely lost over the ages that most English Bibles do not even try to trans-late it. The root of the word is ketem, meaning "gold"; one theory, therefore, holds that these psalms were inscribed in gilded letters and placed in the sanctuary, like certain Egyptian and Babylonian prayers that were carved on stone slabs and erected before the gods in gratitude, or to petition, for some favor.

More probably miktam means that one or another well-known song was to be used as a melodic pattern. The title or first line of such a song usually accompanies miktam in the headings. Thus Psalm 22 was to be sung to the tune of "The Hind of the Dawn"; Psalm 56 to "The Dove in the Distant Fir Trees"; and Psalm 60 to "The Lilies of the Testimony."

Divorced from their ancient context, such titles make little sense today. But we must remember that they were written nearly 3,000 years ago. It is not likely that our own descendants, 3,000 years from now, would be able to "dig" such currently tuneful sentiments as "Rock Around the Clock" or "Strike Up the Band."

Several psalm headings, to be sure, contain song titles without the word miktam. Yet this need not negate our theory. Although the psalms were sung to familiar makams from the first, the headings were later additions. Some translations of the Bible include none, others only a few. The Syriac version even has entirely different titles.

One reason may be that early biblical scribes, aware that such additions were not part of the psalms themselves, did not transfer them to later copies as scrupulously as they handled the actual text. This would explain the variations in such ancient manuscripts as have been preserved, the frequent inversions of letters, and the fact that some manuscripts contain words that are left out in others. Moreover, so long as the tradition of early Temple music was still alive and the musical terms were still current, many indications, however important, could be omitted from the headings without endangering their clarity.

Later scribes copied the headings with all their simplifications and abbreviations. Eventually these came to represent the authentic version, and after the psalms were canonized around the third century B.C., they became part of a sacred and inviolable text.

In the heading of Psalm 60 there is, in addition to "Miktam of David," the word le-lammed, meaning "to teach," apparently to the youth of Israel. It is unlikely that this was the only psalm so designated; probably most, if not all, of the psalms bearing miktam in their headings were similarly intended.

The various psalms containing miktam originally may have formed a small independent collection, with Psalm 60 as the initial poem, expressing in its heading the purpose of the entire group, i.e., "to be taught to youth." When the Psalter took final shape this initial psalm may have become detached, and le-lammed thus have lost its meaning as a generic term.

The preceding terms appear to relate to the character of the psalms themselves. But there are many equally disputed terms that presumably have to do with the musical performance. Not all of these, to be sure, have remained incomprehensible. Some, indeed, are so obvious that their interpretation should never have been in doubt.

Such is the term *la-menazzeah*, which derives from the Hebrew verb *nazzah*, "to shine" or "to lead," thus indicating that the psalm was entrusted to "the leader" or "the chief musician." And here we uncover a remarkable similarity between the psalms and one of our Occidental vocal forms, the cantata.

La-menazzeah seems to have been attached only to psalms whose texts suggest that they were performed either by a soloist throughout, or by soloist and chorus alternately, thus corresponding respectively to our solo cantata and our mixed cantata. On the other hand, psalms with no such instruction may have been sung by the chorus alone, thus representing a parallel to our choral cantata.

If we apply the principle of our solo cantata to the text of psalms headed by la-menazzeah, we find their contents dividing into cantatalike sections. Psalm 5, for example, divides into passages for alternate solo and choral singing. In verses 2 to 4 the psalmist speaks in the first person (soloist), in verses 5 to 7 in the third person (choir), in verses 8 and 9 again in the first person (soloist), and in verses 10 and 11 in the third person (choir). Verse 12 affords a suitable ending by soloist and choir together.

Psalm 12 is a typical example of responsorial singing. In the even-numbered verses—2, 4, 6 and 8—the psalmist, as soloist, speaks directly to God, while the chorus responds in the odd-numbered verses, amplifying and extending the thought. Such examples of cantatalike structure are not hard to find. On the other hand, Psalms 13 and 54, owing to their introspective nature, are suited for performance by soloist alone.

In addition, the natural vanity of the performing artist may have caused more than one psalm to be earmarked for him. The chief soloist was the singing virtuoso of the time and fully aware of his artistic status. For all the solemnity of the Temple rites and the devotion of the congregants, the effect of his artistry upon his audience must have been considerable. The fact that fifty-five psalms are headed "to the chief singer" testifies to the power such soloists must have enjoyed.

Outside of the psalms, la-menazzeah is found only in Habakkuk (3:19), which according to the author's own statement was designed, like the psalms, for performance with musical accompaniment: "for the leader, with my string music." Habakkuk's song of praise is really a psalm that seems originally to have belonged to the precanonical Psalter, from which it was subsequently removed for reasons unknown. In it the musical instruction appears not in the heading but at the end.

And here we come to a revolutionary new theory regarding the musical instructions for the psalms. First, however, we must realize that all ancient manuscripts, whether Hebrew, Greek, or Latin, were written with no breaks or separations between words and with no indication of chapters or paragraphs.

The biblical verses were divided, not by the scribes who first wrote them down, but by subsequent editors, and mainly by the Masoretes, the third-to-sixth-century Hebrew scholars who were chiefly responsible for their final form.

This is especially significant for the Book of Psalms. We may safely assume that the Hebrew text that served as the basis for all later translations was substantially identical with that which we possess today. However, like other ancient manuscripts, the psalms followed upon one another without any separation, thus leaving the door open to all kinds of personal interpretation as to where a psalm might begin or end. This incertitude resulted in different arrangements of the psalms in the various Bible versions, such as the Hebrew, Greek, Latin, Syriac, Arabic, and others.

Not until our present century was a fresh light thrown upon the matter, when James W. Thirtle, the noted English scholar, after comparing the psalm texts with their headings, concluded that the terms in most of the headings applied more logically to the preceding psalm. Thus, instead of being attached to the beginning, the musical instructions for the early Temple singers had been jotted down as a postscript at the end of the psalm.

This appears to be borne out by Habakkuk's song, which, as we have seen, carries his musical instructions at the bottom, and by a hymn of thanksgiving sung by King Hezekiah (c. 750 B.C.) upon his recovery from a sickness, and ending:

Therefore we will sing songs to the stringed instruments all the days of our life in the house of the Lord.

It is surprising that this possibility had not occurred earlier to the innumerable scholars who had pored for centuries over the psalms. Thirtle's theory was to be supported by archeology, which has furnished striking analogies from antiquity. Sumerian and Babylonian psalms, it was found, customarily carried as a postscript what Hebrew psalms appeared to carry in their headings: the nature of the psalm, the melody or makam to which it should be sung, the accompanying instrument, the author, the purpose of the psalm, and sometimes even the collection to which it belonged.

Although in a few instances (e.g., Pss. 49, 140, etc.) the Hebrew instructions seem more appropriate as headings, there seems every reason to accept Thirtle's arrangement. To avoid confusion, however, we shall continue to deal here with the psalm headings as they are traditionally arranged.

A term that always appears with la-menazzeah is *neginoth*. This was a collective term for stringed instruments, so together the instruction would read: "to the chief musician, with stringed instruments." As a rule psalm-singing was accompanied by the usual Temple instruments. When for any reason a different instrumental or vocal arrangement was desired, the change was specified.

This appears to have been the case with Psalm 46, which contains the instruction, "on alamoth," or "according to alamoth." So baffling is this term that most English Bibles do not even try to translate it. Some scholars construe it as the title of some well-known song of the time, others as a musical instrument.

Since *almah* in Hebrew means "maiden," alamoth may refer to the range of the female singing voice, i.e., soprano. Thus the heading perhaps called for the psalm to be sung either by a women's chorus, or a boys' chorus, or to the accompaniment of a small, hence higher-toned, harp. There is also the possibility that certain male Temple singers sang in falsetto, since this was a popular practice throughout the ancient Near East.

If, following Thirtle, we apply the instructions to the preceding psalm (45), the first possibility is strengthened. This psalm, surnamed "A love song," is a nuptial ode and uniquely suited for female voices, particularly a maidens' choir.

At the other extreme we find the term *al ha-sheminit* in Psalms 6 and 12. Again, most modern English Bibles leave it untranslated. Its literal Hebrew meaning is "on the eighth," or "over the eighth." Thus it may have meant that the melody sung by one group (female) was to be sung by a second group (male) an octave lower, as is usual when men and women sing together in unharmonized fashion. Another theory is that it indicated an eight-stringed instrument, perhaps a lyre with unusually long and lower-sounding strings.

It may also be that there were eight modes in Temple use, each assigned to a particular section of singers. Or, since ancient ritual was closely associated with the calendar, the term may have referred to one of eight melodic formulas designed to be sung serially as part of some seasonal observance.

The headings of Psalms 53 and 88 contain the term *al mahalath.* This was already obscure by the time of the early translators, and nearly all English Bibles since have taken it over phonetically. If it can be related to music, it may signify that these two psalms were to be accompanied by pipes. Inasmuch as vowels were a later addition to the Hebrew text, it is possible to interpret many words in more than one way. If we read it as *meholoth,* it could refer to a victory celebration "with dancing."

The situation is similar with *el ha-nehilot* in Psalm 5. Tracing the word back to the Hebrew for "pierce," it suggests the pipe, hence indicating woodwinds as the accompanying instruments. If we read it as *nehalot* ("inheritance"), it could signify a commemoration of coming into the Hebrew "inheritance," the Promised Land.

Psalm 30, titled "A Song at the Dedication of the House," intimates that this was sung either at the dedication of Solomon's Temple or of the Second Temple; possibly also at the rededication of the desecrated sanctuary during Hezekiah's reign. It may also have received its title in later centuries, when the sanctuary was "dedicated afresh with songs and harps and lutes and with cymbals" by Judas Maccabaeus in 165 B.C.

The meaning and purpose of certain terms have become almost hopelessly lost over the centuries. Such a term is *al shoshannim,* usually translated "lilies," in the headings of Psalms 45, 69, and 80. If this is not a song title it may indicate a seasonal psalm, sung perhaps at the Passover services.

The words "Destroy not," found in the headings of Psalms 57, 58, 59, and 75, appear to signify the beginning of an ancient penitential song. Legend has it that Moses, in behalf of his erring people, prayed forty days and forty nights on Mount Sinai: "Destroy not thy people and thy inheritance." His prayer would seem to have constituted the leitmotiv of these later songs, designed to be sung in times of national peril.

Scholars are divided with regard to the meaning of *al mut lab-ben*, found in the heading of Psalm 9. Some agree that al mut may be a corrupt spelling of alamoth, "maidens," thus indicating a maidens' choir, but they have taken the matter no further. The second word, however, gives us *ben*, meaning "son" or "boy," which might equally indicate a boys' choir.

Heman, we recall, had fourteen sons and three daughters, all of whom were "under" him for song, so the possibility of a choir (or choirs) of boys and girls is clearly there. That this has not been explored may be partly owing to the fact that the text of Psalm 9 is unsuited to such a youthful group.

Things become different, however, if we apply Thirtle's principle and regard the instruction al mut labben, not as a heading to Psalm 9, but as a postscript to Psalm 8—a short, joyous paean whose very text invokes the innocence of youth:

> O Lord, our Lord,
>   How majestic is thy name in all the earth!
> Thou whose glory above the heavens is chanted
>   By the mouth of babes and infants . . .

No term throughout all of the psalms is more baffling than *selah*. More than any other technical term in the Psalter, this mysterious little word, inserted seemingly at random within the text of 39 psalms, has excited the imagination of scholars of all times and has given rise to an entire literature based solely on attempts to interpret it.

Selah appears sixty-seven times within the psalmodic text, and four times at the end of a psalm. Of the psalms containing it, all but eight have in their heading the indication la-menazzeah. Since this is patently a musical reference, scholars agree that selah must also be one. This is confirmed by its only biblical appearance outside the Psalter, in Habakkuk 3, which, as we have seen, is itself a psalm.

From early times, selah has been thought to signify some sort of break in the singing. St. Augustine, writing in the fifth century A.D., declared:

"It is (as some think) either a Hebrew word meaning 'So be it!' (Amen!), or a Greek word indicating a break in the psalmody (whenever the psalm is performed with singing). In fact (it) signifies a pause in singing."

John Chrysostom, another early Church father, held that King David customarily assigned each psalm to a particular choral group. When the text contained varying moods, he had the contrasting parts sung by alternating groups. Selah, according to this theory, was then used to indicate where such changes should occur.

Rabbinic tradition adds that in later times, although the psalms were not alternated between choral groups, they actually were sung in several sections, the breaks between these being indicated by trumpet blasts. The Talmud relates that during one of the daily services in the later Temple, upon the precentor's clashing the cymbals the Levites began their song. When they arrived at an arranged break in the psalmody, the priests then blew the trumpets and the congregation prostrated itself in worship. This procedure, occurring at every such break in the singing, may have been indicated by selah.

That selah signifies some kind of pause or break was never doubted. The only question was: what kind of break? Some scholars have interpreted it as indicating an interlude of strings, played either softly to induce meditation or forcefully to contrast with their usual soft accompaniment. Others have held that it meant a change of melody or of tempo, an instruction to repeat the last verse or return to the beginning, a marginal note indicating the end of a choral stanza, or a place in the service where benedictions or prostrations of worship interrupted or closed the singing.

The fact that selah appears at the end of Psalms 3, 9, 24, and 26 suggests that, as they stand today, these psalms are incomplete; either that verses that originally followed selah have been deleted or lost, or that certain psalms, now separated, really belong together. In the Septuagint, for example, Psalms 9 and 10 constitute a single psalm, so that there selah appears within the text. It is possible, too, that whatever ritual act was connected with selah may sometimes have taken place at the end of a psalm, where the term may have indicated some sort of instrumental postlude.

Selah probably is not found in every place where an interlude would be called for. Our preserved manuscripts are quite inconsistent, perhaps because a word not belonging to the text and having no bearing on the contents was not copied as carefully as the text itself, at least prior to the fixed Hebrew canon. Too, there are obvious errors of the copyists. Human errors are unavoidable even in a holy book. Occasionally selah may be hidden in a wrong spelling. Many other selahs have been lost. In certain early Greek and Latin manuscripts more selahs are found than appear in the Hebrew and English texts.

Too, since selah was a notation for the singers, it may have been inscribed only in copies used for rehearsal. It could also be left out in these, since the Temple singers, under normal conditions, would know what to do even without it.

That selah may have indicated some sort of ritornello in which the instruments took over forcefully seems rather logical in view of the sheer physical limitations of the human voice. The main burden of the musical ritual in the Temple rested upon the Levitical singers. In lengthy performances—and psalm-singing was precisely that—soloists as well as choristers could have used an occasional breather.

Too, there may well have been outstanding instrumentalists among the singers. Performers in all times, and virtuosos in particular, have seldom been reluctant to take over the spotlight.

11

MUSIC AND THE HARVEST
FESTIVALS

IN THE TEMPLE each sacrificial action had its own meaning and required its own musical setting. Gradually a tradition developed in which each devotional act was attended by its particular psalm.

Thus the daily burnt offerings, the expiatory gifts, and the libations had each a different musical format, as strictly enforced as all other parts of the ritual. A different psalm was assigned for each day. On the first day of the week, Psalm 24 was sung in remembrance of the first day of creation. No reason is known for the choice of the other daily psalms. On the second day the Levites sang Psalm 48; thereafter through the week, Psalms 82, 94, 81, 93, and on the Sabbath, Psalm 92, which bears this indication in its heading.

The psalm of the day was intoned, rabbinic writings say, as soon as the high priest stooped to pour the libation of wine on the altar. Opening with a clash of cymbals by the chief soloist, the psalm came traditionally to be sung in three sections, between each of which the music fell silent while the priests sounded the silver trumpets. Upon this signal the worshipers prostrated themselves before the altar in adoration.

Sacrificial offerings at the Sabbath morning and evening services were double those of weekdays, consequently the musical setting was much more elaborate and colorful. At the pouring of the Sabbath wine libation the Levites sang:

> It is a good thing to give thanks unto the Lord . . .
> Upon an instrument of ten strings, and upon
> > the psaltery;
> Upon the harp with a solemn sound.

Like the psalm for weekday libations, this was performed in three sections, similarly ritualized. The Sabbath also had an additional libation ceremony, during which the Levites intoned the Song of Moses:

> Who is like unto thee, O Lord, among the Gods?

This rather long musical service was divided into six portions, each of these being further broken into three parts, at which the worshipers' act of adoration was signaled by trumpet blasts. At the Sabbath eve service they sang, in addition, the Red Sea song.

At the conclusion of the daily offerings in the morning, the first fifteen verses of Psalm 105 were intoned, and after the evening service Psalm 95 was sung.

Calling on the name of God was always performed by the high priest to the accompaniment of Levitical singing.

Even more important than the Sabbath in some respects was the new moon, in whose observance Moses had commanded that the trumpet be blown over the sacrifices of the peace offering.

Ceremonies connected with the new moon appear to be as ancient as the human race itself. When Abraham had been a boy beside the Euphrates, the people were never sure when the old moon disappeared that a new moon would take its place. Their rites at these times were prompted by fear, and during the full moon they kept to their houses to avoid the evil spirits they believed roamed abroad at that season.

The ancient Hebrews continued to welcome the new moon as eagerly as their pagan forebears. For all their trust in Yahweh they felt a certain uneasiness at such times, since they depended on the new moon for their calendar, to know when to plant or harvest their crops, or to expect the life-giving rains. Its appearance, therefore, called for certain festive ceremonies, and these, after the time of David, centered in the Temple.

None but the high priest, or the king as actual head of the cult, had the power in those days to proclaim the new month's arrival. On the last evening in the old month the priests and Levites gathered in the Temple courtyard to scan the sky for the thin new rind of silver crescent. The first to see it rushed the reassuring news to the Temple, whereupon trumpets were sounded and the start of the new month officially proclaimed.

That night, bonfires on the higher hills around Jerusalem announced the fact to outlying towns and villages, which celebrated with communal and family feasts. In later ages further bonfires spread the news in a network of blazing beacons as far as the Euphrates to the east and Egypt to the west, where many Jews now lived.

Within the Temple at Jerusalem the new moon was celebrated with a feast and with special offerings on the evening of the first day, during which the stirring verses of Psalm 29 were sung, providing that the event happened on a weekday. If it occurred on a Sabbath, the regular Sabbath psalm was sung. In the seventh month the celebration of the new moon was considered a higher holiday, and on this occasion Psalm 81 was sung as the wine libation was poured:

> Raise a song, sound the timbrel,
> The sweet lyre with the harp.
> Blow the trumpet at the new moon,
> At the full moon, on our feast day . . .

All these were public offerings and their volume alone was considerable. Yet it was dwarfed by the abundance of private offerings. With the approach of the High Holidays these grew so numerous that even the increased priestly forces were hard put to perform all the ritual requirements.

Since the most minute observance of these was thought to be essential for securing God's goodwill, the singers often had to assist the overburdened priests. And inasmuch as the offerings were always accompanied by singing, the normal daily task of the singers in itself must have been heavy. On High Holidays they probably provided an almost continuous musical service.

Among the psalms sung at these, the Hallel psalms were most prominent. To these belonged the Egyptian Hallel, as Psalms 113 through 118 are called in rabbinic literature; the Great Hallel, Psalm 136; and Psalms 146, 147, and 148, which are known simply as the Hallel psalms. All of these became traditionally attached to the great harvest festivals that were celebrated nationally as a religious ordinance.

As desert shepherds the Israelites' chief source of subsistence had been their flocks and herds. Like other nomads they had celebrated nature's renewal in the spring with a festival, at which the firstlings of the lambing season were sacrificed as fertility offerings to ensure the year's food supply. Having no cultivated crops, they originally had no festivals connected with the harvest.

Once in Canaan, however, they quickly settled into the agrarian life already established there and adopted the harvest festivals of the Canaanites. From then on their festival cycle was governed by the seasonal changes of the crops, token offerings of which were ritually consecrated to Yahweh.

The Israelite farmer's calendar was marked by three important events, beginning with the barley harvest. Like the earlier shepherd feast, this occurred in the spring, for in Canaan's subtropical climate grain ripened early. Eventually the two festivals—the nomadic offering of a firstborn lamb and the agrarian offering of the first grain—combined into a single festival lasting seven days. In time this came to commemorate only the Exodus from Egypt and was known as the Feast of the Passover, or the Feast of Unleavened Bread, in memory of the hurried meal the people ate when fleeing from the soldiers of pharaoh.

Seven weeks after the Passover feast the spring wheat was ripe for cutting. The end of this harvest was celebrated as the Feast of Weeks, so named because the Israelites, having as yet no written calendar, figured its date by counting seven weeks from the second day of Passover. The word "Pentecost" is the Greek term for the fiftieth day, namely, the day on which the harvest usually started.

In early fall the ingathering of the entire yield of orchard, field, and vineyard was celebrated as the Feast of Ingathering, or Feast of Tabernacles. This was the great thanksgiving week in ancient Israel, ending the year's agricultural cycle and inaugurating the New Year, for like most of their neighbors, the Hebrews observed their New Year in early autumn.

Initially the three festivals had equal religious importance, but as time passed the Feast of Tabernacles gained precedence, becoming known as the Feast of the Lord, or simply as The Feast. According to Mosaic Law, every adult male was required to visit a sanctuary on each of the three religious holidays. For generations the sanctuary at Shiloh, where Hannah had gone to pray for a son, had been a popular site of harvest celebrations, and others were established in cities central to the surrounding farming communities. But after the Temple was built sacrifices were not permitted elsewhere, and a pilgrimage to Jerusalem thrice a year became a religious ordinance that everyone was expected to observe.

Far from considering this a hardship, the people carried it out with eagerness and joy. Their entire year was oriented toward the thrice-yearly pilgrimage to the Holy City, crowned by its high-tiered sanctuary of white limestone and the even more sumptuous royal palace adjacent.

For the entire family the custom provided the most festive events in their lives. It broke the tedium of the farmer's indenture to plow and livestock. In hundreds of villages scattered throughout Israel the thrice-yearly exposure to urban customs guarded the people against the disuniting provincialism that had undermined the Canaanite tribes. Town, city, and mud-hut village—all regarded themselves as suburbs of Jerusalem, linked to the Golden City by ribbons of pilgrims stretching like colorful streamers across hills green with young spring wheat or tawny with the stubble of grain full garnered.

For the Feast of the Passover each family carried with it a sheaf of barley carefully cut from the first ears to show golden in the field, along with a young lamb for a sacrifice and a family feast. Pilgrims from farther off might buy one in Jerusalem's thriving sheep market. Within the Temple courtyard, awaiting their turn with thou-

sands of other pilgrims, the men sang psalms or chanted ritual formulas while the women eagerly exchanged gossip with friends not
seen for many months.

The men were admitted to the sacrificial court in groups of
thirty. As each slaughtered his lamb to a ritual accompaniment, the
Levitical singers, with their harps and lyres, intoned passages from
the Great Hallel while the people joined in. Psalm 136 was considered especially appropriate for this occasion because of its references to Israel's liberation from Egypt.

At dusk, those who had arrived early enough joined friends and
relatives to feast within the courtyard. Pilgrims from more distant
communities held their own feasts within their goathair tents
pitched thickly for miles around the Holy City.

Seven weeks later, with the wheat and barley stored away, the
people made ready to celebrate the Feast of Weeks. Now the summer fruit was beginning to ripen, and in the orchards bright bits of
colored string tied around the first fig or pomegranate or cluster of
grapes to show a blush of purple or crimson marked these apart as
offerings for the ceremony. Cakes and bread for the family feast,
along with two special loaves for the Temple altar, were baked of
flour freshly ground from the new wheat crop.

Once more up the long slope to the Temple the processions
wound, bright this time with the first fruits from orchard and vineyard. On their heads the women carried baskets heaped with figs
and scarlet pomegranates, red and purple grapes, golden honey-
combs on beds of cool green leaves. Fat jars held fresh-pressed olive
oil, and bulging wineskins bumped against the sides of laden donkeys.

Behind, as far as the eye could see, the processions stretched over
hills still covered like a careless patchwork with tufts of green. The
fragrance of early summer warmed the air. Wild lilies dotted the
fields and oleanders splashed their pink and orange blossoms
against the gaunt brown rocks. The cheerful sound of many pipes
joined with the voices of the pilgrims as they sang one or another
of the Songs of Ascent:

> I was glad when they said to me,
>   'Let us go to the house of the Lord!' . . .

Jerusalem . . . a city . . . bound firmly together,
　To which the tribes go up . . .
　As was decreed for Israel,
To give thanks to the name of the Lord . . .

Behold, how good and pleasant it is
　When brothers dwell in unity!

Except on the first day of the festival and on the Sabbath, Temple music during the Feast of Weeks was brightened by the sound of reed pipes. At regular services throughout the year the instrumental accompaniment was held to the more sedate timbres of harp and lyre, but the festive nature of the great harvest celebrations called for a livelier sound. For this also, at least in later days, the sweet, high voices of choirboys, sons of the Levitical singers, augmented the vocal choirs during the Hallel psalms that accompanied the dedication of the paschal lamb. As in the Passover service, the congregation also took an active part musically, responding after each verse with a jubilant "Hallelujah!"

The great yearly event, however, was the Feast of Tabernacles. Now all the harvest was gathered and the people, free from orchard and field, could make a leisurely pilgrimage and spend a carefree week in the exciting atmosphere of the Crown City.

At every morning service throughout the week the worshipers, swaying palm branches, encompassed the altar in a dancelike procession, singing the last five verses of Psalm 118: "O Lord, we beseech thee, send us prosperity." When the priests sounded the trumpets they retreated from the altar, intoning, "Homage to thee, O Lord, and to thee, O Altar." On the seventh day the altar was thus encompassed seven times.

During this feast three symbolic ceremonies, all richly provided with music, became popular features, although none was directly connected with Temple worship. These were the rite of water libation, the ceremony of carrying wood for the burnt offerings, and the popular festivity known as Beth-ha-Sheuba, which took place in the Temple court with a rousing display of song and dance.

The rite of water libation had its roots in a primitive belief in sympathetic magic, which will be discussed in a later chapter. To an agricultural people dependent on the soil for grain and for grazing pastures, rain was a matter of life or death. Droughts in Canaan had been known to last for seven years, so it was in deadly earnest that the ritual of insuring a good rainfall was performed, appropriately at the start of the fall rainy season.

To assure this, each morning during the Feast of Tabernacles, a golden pitcher was filled with water drawn from the pond of Siloam just outside the city, and carried by the high priest in a solemn procession to the Temple. When the cortege reached the entrance known as the Water Gate, it was greeted by a blast of trumpets.

The water, together with a little wine, was then poured upon the altar as a libation to the Lord. During the ceremony the priests again sounded the trumpets, whereupon the music started and the Levites sang the Hallel as on the Passover. On this occasion also, except on the first day and the Sabbath, pipes were added to the usual strings.

At the ceremony of carrying wood, which was held in the vineyards around Jerusalem, maidens, dressed in white, and young men sang songs antiphonally and performed round dances. Even so, enough wood got gathered, we are told, to take care of the whole year's needs of firewood for the altar.

The first day of the festival concluded with a popular entertainment in the Temple court, which was aglow with the lights from torches and chandeliers. A full complement of Levitical singers played upon harps, lyres, pipes, and cymbals. The ceremony was especially festive in the short-lived Third Temple. There, in the brilliantly illuminated Court of the Women, its gallery alive with the rustle and color of gay dresses, girls and young women watched distinguished elders of the congregation, dancing with burning torches, wind nimbly among the pillars and sing antiphonally hymns and songs of praise and joy.

On the fifteen steps leading up to the Court of the Israelites stood the Levites, accompanying the singing and dancing with their instruments. According to one tradition, they sang on this occasion the fifteen Songs of Ascent.

Music and dance, combined with the harvest moon, seem to have generated a kind of religious ecstasy not uncommon at nocturnal ritual feasts in the ancient Orient, as well as among primitive religions in general.

The rejoicing lasted until cockcrow. Then, at a trumpet signal by two priests, the throng formed a huge procession and marched to the sound of the Levitical orchestra through the Court of the Women to the eastern Gate. Here the ceremony ended, but with a curious reference to a time in their prehistory when their forebears had evidently been sun worshipers. For as the sun rose the priests recited, "Our fathers . . . worshiped the sun toward the east, but as for us, we are the Lord's and our eyes are turned to the Lord."

The Feast of Tabernacles would continue to be celebrated down the centuries. During the social oppression of rabbinic times its gay nocturnal festivities were so treasured that the saying arose: "He that has never seen the joy of Beth-ha-Sheuba has never in his life seen joy."

12

MUSIC IN SECULAR LIFE

THE MUSICAL LIFE of the ancient Hebrews was by no means centered wholly in the Temple. Music in one form or another entered into nearly every activity of daily life. Alone or in groups, with instrumental accompaniment or without, they sang upon every pretext. Song was the common language, uniting them in the shared round of daily chores that animated their vigorous folk life.

No people of antiquity has left a more eloquent account of the role music played throughout their history than the Hebrews have left us in the pages of the Old Testament. Here we find references to songs of triumph, of derision, of mourning; to drinking songs and marching songs; to the song of the builders and the layers of cornerstones; to songs of the courtesan and of the watchman; to love songs, dance songs, and songs of the palace.

Although for our purposes the references are much too casual, this very fact confirms the permeation by music of every area of ancient Hebrew life. The biblical chroniclers, writing for their own age, felt it unnecessary to elaborate in regard to customs that were so universally known.

Like other ancient peoples, the Israelites had harvest and vintage songs, as well as songs for the various professions and crafts. In general, any work involving some rhythmic activity had its own songs: nurses rocking babies, wagoners driving teams of oxen, vintners treading grapes, sailors pulling at the oars, weavers tossing shuttles—all knew the secret of lightening the drudgery of labor and expediting the task with rhythm.

How completely song colored their everyday life may be judged from a rabbinic passage:

> The song of thanksgiving was sung to the accompaniment of lutes, lyres, and cymbals at every corner and upon every great stone in Jerusalem.

Singing was an important part of every social occasion. No banquet ended without a final round of merry songs, as we infer from Ecclesiasticus:

> A concert of music in a banquet of wine
> Is as a signet of carbuncle set in gold.

And,

> As a signet of an emerald set in work of gold,
> So is the melody of music with pleasant wine.

But at no occasion were the songs more abundant or merry than at the most joyful event in the life of the Israelites—the wedding. Here music and songs were indispensable. Surprisingly, the Bible mentions this only cursorily. Yet it contains a rich assortment of wedding songs if we rightly interpret a document that has been almost universally misunderstood. This is the Song of Solomon, or translating the Hebrew title literally, the Song of Songs.

Today there is little doubt that these verses were accepted into the sacred canon only by being given an allegorical interpretation. For they quite evidently are nothing more or less than a collection of love and wedding songs, reflecting the sensuous, roguish, rather naughty character of those still sung at rustic weddings, especially in the Near East.

The verses deal throughout with love between the sexes, and this in an unabashedly earthy fashion. Early churchmen must have had a formidably difficult task to attribute an allegorical meaning to this kind of erotic folksong.

The book, however, carries the name of Solomon, which made it a venerable relic from the ages of divine inspiration. Any scrap of writing preserved from such times was considered sacred. Thus the early canonizers, faced with such an embarrassing holy text, undertook to disguise its erotic contents. With a resourcefulness peculiar to their calling, they construed its verses as dealing with Yahweh's love for Israel and his matrimony with his chosen people —a favorite theme of the prophets since Hosea.

Solomon, of course, is only nominally the author. Actually the author is the people itself. Like popular poetry in general, the Song of Songs developed gradually out of the life and feelings of unsophisticated poets and minstrels. It may first have been crystallized into single little songs, which were subsequently collected by scribes and embodied in a book.

It follows the general rule of antiquity in that the name of its compiler or editor was not preserved. Instead, the name of some distinguished patron of the arts—in this case Solomon—was attached, either to ennoble it or, less innocently, to pass it off as a literary fragment from Israel's golden age.

But neither Solomon's name nor the book's adoption into the canon can alter the fact that we are here confronted with wedding songs, loaded now with facetious, now with erotic, content. They are genuine folksongs, composed by unknown, naïve popular poets, and as such they constitute a pure type of "utility music."

In rabbinic times the Song of Songs was regarded as a purely secular book. Young men sang its verses in public taverns, an act of impiety that incensed the more zealous rabbis. In modern times it has frequently been elaborated into one or another dramatic play involving music and dancing. But such ventures fail to appreciate its essentially lyric quality. Just as the Book of Psalms is the most exquisite collection of religious poetry, so the Song of Songs represents the finest compilation of secular poetry in the Old Testament.

Dramatic representations of nature myths were common among all nations of the ancient Near East. For the Hebrews, however, the religious edicts that forbade their making any graven images were apparently extended to all kinds of representation, either of objects or persons. Their literary efforts, therefore, bypassed the drama in any form and manifested themselves chiefly in lyric poetry.

The Song of Songs is an anthology of poems, variously chaffing and suggestive, but wholly lyrical throughout. That they were designed neither for theatrical nor sacred purposes becomes evident when we read them in the light of certain popular Syrian wedding customs that have continued into our own times.

In these, the bridegroom and bride are called king and queen during the seven days of the wedding festivities, beginning with the morning on which they rise as a young couple. They take their seat on the only available "royal dais," the threshing floor, from which they preside over a mischievous and merry "court."

During the "royal week," dances, jokes, and pranks are performed before their "throne." A major role is assigned to songs describing the marital bliss of the newlyweds. These songs deal mostly with the beauty of the young couple and their wedding ornaments, and refer to the bride as "the most beautiful of women." Numerous dances are performed in her honor.

In the Song of Songs, too, the lovers are referred to as the "young royal couple," and the erotic allusions represent merely the rude jokes that are customary at all rustic weddings.

The "daughters of Jerusalem" in the verses are the bride's girl companions, with whom she perhaps performed group dances. Finally, the "Shulammite" stands for none other than Abishag, the Shunammite virgin, who became King David's last wife. She was proverbial as the most beautiful of the daughters of Israel, hence her name was bestowed in song upon the rustic bride.

With this the whole cream-puff structure of a dramatic play falls to pieces. From king and queen, from Solomon and the lovely Shunammite, nothing remains but jesting wedding songs and a lively entertainment. However, we can be grateful that, because of its canonization, a marvelous example of secular lyric poetry from ancient Israel has been preserved that indubitably would otherwise have been destroyed along with other secular offshoots of Hebrew poetry.

What is evidently another example of popular wedding songs has been equally canonized in Psalm 45, the verses of which deal throughout with the nuptials of a young couple who are addressed by their merry friends as king and princess.

First, the bridegroom is hailed in song, perhaps by the best man or some gifted singer among the company:

> My heart overflows with a goodly theme;
>   I address my verses to the king;
> My tongue is like the pen of a ready scribe.

The singer goes on to extol the bridegroom as a prince and warrior:

> You are the fairest of the sons of men . . .
>   Gird your sword upon your thigh, O mighty one . . .
> In your majesty ride forth victoriously.

Here we find reflected a custom still general among the Islamic world, in which the Arab bridegroom rides forth to greet his bride in full battle array.

Now the "king" waits for the bride to emerge from the bridal bower for the wedding ceremony:

> Your divine throne endures forever and ever,
>   Your royal scepter is a scepter of equity . . .
> From ivory palaces stringed instruments make you glad;
> Daughters of kings are among your ladies of honor;
> At your right hand stands the queen in gold of Ophir.

Next, the bridesmaids take up the song, counseling the "princess":

> Hear, O daughter, consider and incline your ear:
>   Forget your people and your father's house;
> And the king will desire your beauty.
> Since he is your lord, bow to him.

The bride is then escorted to the bridal bower, where her new spouse now awaits her:

The princess is decked in her chamber with gold-woven
robes;
In many-colored robes she is led to the king,
With her virgin companions, her escort, in her train.
With joy and gladness they are led along
As they enter the palace of the king.

Poetic invention and a rich fund of humor lifted the acts of
daily living far above the humdrum for the people of ancient Israel. The Bible has left us generous examples of the first. For instances of the second we must search with an intuition born of
affection, but they are there to be found.

Throughout the Scriptures the close affinity between music and
general thinking is a leading motif. Thus, a man's pleasant manners are characterized by a musical simile:

And lo, you are to them like one who sings love songs with
a beautiful voice and plays well on an instrument.

Sorrow also expressed itself in song:

In the days of my trouble I seek the Lord . . .
In the night I will call to remembrance my song.

Music consoled man in his affliction:

Where is God my Maker, who giveth songs in the night?

Psalms too were sung in secular life, and although these had only
a slight religious motivation, their popularity reflected the extent
to which religious ideas and precepts colored the folk habits of the
people. Certain psalms, in fact, apparently belonged to both aspects of the nation's life. These were the Songs of Ascent, mentioned earlier, all of which had a strong folk character. It seems
probable that before these were taken into the Psalter they were
sung at secular occasions, and only later became a musical concomitant of religious ceremonies.

Musical instruments belonged to the most cherished goods of daily life. Tabrets and pipes were among the treasures of the prince of Tyre. A popular enlivener of fashionable banquets was the lyre, and playing it was among the more discriminating pleasures of the ancient elite. In the tenth century B.C., playing the lyre was still considered something of a novelty for the wealthy amateur, and there must have been more than a few in the higher social brackets who entertained themselves and one another by singing idle songs to its accompaniment. Young men with time on their hands amused themselves by inventing new instruments, in flattering emulation of their sovereign, David, and mastering these became a social accomplishment.

Another favorite, the lute, was well suited to intimate gatherings. In Solomon's time it quickly became popular with the avant-garde, partly owing to its exotic character, but principally because its fewer, more versatile strings made it easy to accompany the ballads and love songs that entertained small fashionable gatherings.

Singers at court or at wealthy houses were always accompanied. Soloists often accompanied themselves. If not, they instructed their accompanist by gesturing with the right hand, palm up or down, thumb up or down, sometimes thumb and forefinger forming a circle, the other fingers stiffly outstretched.

For all its profuse flowering, the music of ancient Israel was basically utilitarian. Although it ultimately developed great spiritual and ethical significance it was from the first, and to a large extent remained, a practical and many-purposed art. It served religion, deepened the solemnity of state occasions, and enriched the life of the common people, individually and collectively.

Utility music of all epochs follows its own internal laws. Thus it is not surprising that aside from certain natural differences the practical requirements of ancient music-making had much in common with our own. Then as now instruments had to be manufactured and kept in good repair. Performers had to learn how to play them, as solo instruments, for ensemble playing, or to accompany singing. Before any performance there first had to be something to perform; this involved the composing and arranging of music, and its rehearsal. All this required much preparatory work as well as the coordination of many musical factors, all of which presupposes some kind of musical organization.

It seems highly probable that the secular musicians, like those of the Temple, were similarly organized into a guild, whose purpose, naturally, was to safeguard the professional interests of its members. Precedent for this appears to reach far back into Hebrew history. There is good reason to believe that even the folk bards of heroic times had some kind of singers' guild. These poet-singer-musicians of ancient times amassed a treasury of songs on which they could draw at will, just as did the singers of Homer or the medieval wandering minstrels.

Ballad singers, they were far more than mere entertainers. Traveling from place to place with their fund of ancient lore, they commanded great respect and exerted a powerful influence on public opinion, especially in times of national decision. Their words were eagerly attended; "Therefore the ballad singers say" was a common phrase in the early days of Israel.

Their ancient organization survived in a changed form. After the establishment of the early kingdom they lost their political significance but gained in popularity, becoming a national institution of professional entertainers without which private and public festivities would have been infinitely poorer.

The increased social life of the time caused a demand for their services that united them into a permanent professional guild. This never became as tightly knit or as powerful as the entrenched hereditary guild of the Temple musicians; neither did it enjoy the privileges or the royal patronage of that exclusive body, which admitted only the closest of kin to membership and utterly rejected any non-Levite.

For the broad dissemination of music among the masses, however, the secular musicians accomplished infinitely more than the Levites. Their art had its roots in the people and served the people. Anyone with the desire and the aptitude could hope, by study, to become one of their order.

Through their liberal attitude, perhaps unprecedented in antiquity, a breach was made in the long tradition of a single musical caste. The musical profession was no longer the privilege of a tribe or a class. Not birth but talent now determined who might become a musician. History furnishes no more dramatic evidence of this than David's spectacular rise from shepherd to court minstrel and ultimately to king. Music's emergence into a free-lance profession, freely competing and untrammeled by ritual or religious fetters, was one of the most significant developments in its early history.

Unlike the Levitical musicians, whose economic needs were taken care of by the people, the secular musicians were dependent on the income earned through their professional engagements. Few could have lived on an income derived solely from teaching. The great majority were performing musicians, playing at public or private events, such as weddings, banquets, funerals, and other occasions at which music was customary.

One source of income may have been the manufacture and repair of musical instruments. Among the many trades and professions mentioned in the Bible, that of instrument-makers is lacking. Nevertheless it must have existed, for with a few possible exceptions the multitude and variety of instruments used in the ritual service, as well as in secular life, could hardly have been imported.

Perhaps the biblical chroniclers considered it self-evident for a musician to make and repair his own instruments. Rabbinic literature refers repeatedly to the repairing of these, but without mentioning instrument-making. We may assume that many secular musicians manufactured them for their own and general use as a substantial addition to their income. The Levitical musicians, on the other hand, had to make and maintain their own instruments in good shape as part of their duties, without extra pay. In urban life there developed a class of skilled craftsmen whose trade was regulated by the law of supply and demand. In view of the demand there must have been for musical instruments we must conclude that a craft of instrument-making also flourished, which through the years slowly wrought improvements in the tone and technical qualities of pipes and stringed instruments.

The extensive cultivation of music opened a large field for music teachers as well. During the prosperous reign of Solomon a rising class of wealthy merchants built their own palaces in Jerusalem and undertook to learn the arts of cultivation. Music and singing were taught their sons and daughters, and the lyre and the lute were as much a part of every well-appointed home as our parlor grand of yesteryear.

A special field of music instruction may have been the art of mournful wailing, performed exclusively by women. That this had to be learned is confirmed by the biblical passage: "Teach your daughter wailing, and every one her neighbor lamentation." Such teachers were evidently wailing women themselves, experienced in the art.

The funeral wailing of the Hebrews was antiphonal and had analogies among other ancient peoples. A report about the funeral of an Assyrian king mentions mourning songs performed by the music master and his "daughters," or assisting female singers, in which the mourners participated antiphonally: "The wives of the deceased wailed; the friends responded."

In Babylonia, sacrifices in memory of the deceased always took place with funeral music and mourning ceremonies performed by professional lamenters. Wailing women and men intoned the funeral songs, while the mourners expressed their grief in loud moans, tore their garments, pulled their beards, clipped their hair, and cut themselves with knives. Psalms of lamentation for wailing women as early as 2350 B.C. have been uncovered at Lagash.

Such mourning rites belonged to all Semitic peoples of antiquity. In Israel's early times the mourning ritual likewise included lacerating the body (later replaced by the tearing of garments), cutting the hair, removing footwear, and other symbolic gestures.

The ceremony of mourning was minutely regulated in ancient Israel. At funerals of public figures the people manifested their feelings by such exclamations as that in David's lament: "How are the mighty fallen!" In the second book of Chronicles we find a reference to a Book of Lamentations, now lost.

At private funerals the women of the house were assisted by professional wailing women, who performed the songs of mourning antiphonally, as evidenced by the Scriptures:

And the land shall mourn, every family apart; the family of the house of David apart, and their wives apart; the family of the house of Nathan apart, and their wives apart . . . all the families that remain, apart, and their wives apart.

Besides wailing songs, the musical background of the funeral ceremonies included the playing of pipes, which were the mourn-

ing instruments par excellence of ancient Israel. Even the poorest
man had to hire for the funeral of his wife at least two pipers and a
wailing woman. Wealthier citizens might, of course, hire as many
as they could afford, indicating that the volume of music at funerals was in ratio to the wealth and social standing of the deceased.

The other instrument generally used was the *rebiit*, a rather
large drum whose dull sound must have blended appropriately
with the gloomy mood of the occasion. Both pipes and drum accompanied another fixed feature of mourning in early times. This
was the funeral dance, which will be discussed in the chapter on
the dance.

We do not know whether the "wages" the secular musician received for playing at public or private events, as well as any "fee"
for lessons, were in money or in kind. Probably the latter, since
this was customary in all societies based on a primitive economy.

The Bible contains no data about such payment, but to a free-
lance performer such wages already represented the dignified hon-
orarium of the artist. In Europe this notion did not mature until
the rise of public concerts in the mid-eighteenth century, but its
artistic and social implications were already present in ancient Israel.

There the secular musician was in no sense a poor and despised
itinerant. He never represented the outcast fraternity that in
medieval Europe brought popular music into discredit. In ancient
Israel he belonged to a respected and well-liked class. He had a
remunerative profession and his livelihood was assured by the people's innate craving for music. He was the recognized representa-
tive of popular art, conscious of his mission and sure of his influence upon his audience.

Thus the social condition of the Hebrew secular musician was far
ahead of many other features of his time, and was, in fact, to find
its parallel only in our own day. More than by the institution of
Temple musicians, the artistic status of the ancient Hebrews is evidenced by the sociologically advanced estate of their secular musicians.

13

THE MUSICAL INSTRUMENTS
OF ANCIENT ISRAEL

THE VERY FACT that music played so large a part in the life of ancient Israel makes it impossible for us to know as much as we would like about its musical instruments and customs. The biblical chroniclers wrote for a contemporary audience. It never occurred to them that 3,000 years later people would be trying to puzzle out the meaning of musical terms that to them were household words.

Take the case of the most popular stringed instrument of antiquity, the lyre, whose Syrian name, we recall, was kinnor. This was virtually universal in ancient Israel; it was "David's harp," and it is mentioned in the Bible forty-two times. Nowhere is it described. (Ill. 7)

Even the origin of its name is in doubt. It may be connected with the Syrian word, *kenara*, or the Arabic-Persian *kunar*, both meaning "lotus." The durable wood of the lotus plant was much used in the Near East, and very possibly for musical instruments as well. In antiquity it was not uncommon for an instrument to take its name from the material of which it was made. (In Greece, *lotos* was both the name of the plant and the flute made of lotus wood. Among the Romans the pipe, *tibia*, took its name from the animal shinbone that provided the early whistle pipes.)

An ancient lake in Israel and the town beside it were both called Kinneret. Traditional explanations were that the lake was shaped like a lyre, or that the townspeople excelled in playing or manufacturing the instrument. Rabbinical lore further suggests that it was called Kinneret because the fruits of its orchards were "sweet as the sound of the kinnor."

Modern research has concluded that the Hebrew lyre was similar to the early Greek *kithara*, which was popularly called the "Asiatic lyre." Pictures of this in Assyrian and Egyptian antiquities show an instrument with curving side arms joined at the top by a crossbar, from which strings stretch down to fasten to a sounding board. The player holds it either horizontally before him, the base pressed against his chest, or in an upright position under the arm. No doubt the Hebrew lyre was similarly played.

That the lyre was probably taken to Egypt by Semites migrating from the east is borne out by a mural (c. 1900 B.C.) that shows an Egyptian prince being approached by a procession of Semitic—possibly Hebrew—nomads, asking royal permission to settle in Egypt. The immigrants appear to be traveling metal-workers, for their two donkeys carry what look like two pairs of goatskin bellows. Like the tinkers of the Middle Ages, they may have eked out their slender living by entertaining with music, for one of the immigrants is a musician who holds under his right arm what appears to be a lyre with eight strings, which he manipulates with his left hand while his right holds a plectrum. The instrument's body resembles an almost square board with a large section cut away to form a frame for the strings. This is thought by some to be a possible prototype of the Hebrew lyre, which thus would have entered Egypt about the time of Abraham. (Ill. 10)

Another possible forerunner of the Hebrew lyre is an instrument depicted on an ivory carving from Megiddo, near Syria. Dating from around 1200 B.C, or about the time Moses led the Israelites to Canaan, this shows a Canaanite king sitting on a throne flanked by winged lions with human heads. He drinks from a bowl as one of his musicians entertains him on a lyre with ten strings, strung horizontally and plucked with the fingers. The instrument was evidently common to Canaan before the Israelites arrived there from Egypt, and may greatly have influenced the later form of the Hebrew lyre.

The strings of the lyre were of various thicknesses, to produce either a clear, singing tone or a deeper humming sound. As a rule they were frailer and higher in tone than those of the harp, since they were made from thinner catgut.

The lyre was the musical companion of joyous occasions, and the melodies played on it were mostly of a sweet, bright character. It was a versatile instrument, more intimate than the harp and much used to accompany singers, in which case the single string plucked with a plectrum would merely double the vocal melody, after the Oriental manner.

Although the lyre was more often used to accompany the voice, it could be very eloquent when played alone, with the fingers of both hands sweeping the strings freely. Such solo playing must have been rather uncommon in David's time, for the Bible four times especially remarks the fact that he "played with his hand" before King Saul. David, it would appear, had not only fashioned a creditable instrument for himself, but he had spent the lonely hours on his shepherd's hillside learning to play it with rare skill.

Over the centuries, improvements were conceivably wrought in the primitive lyre. The sounding board may have been enlarged, the tuning mechanism refined, the frame ornamented after the Greek fashion. But such superficial changes would have left the fundamental structure intact. Probably several types of lyres, differing in size and number of strings, were used by the ancient Hebrews. This might explain certain disagreements in descriptions of them by contemporary and later writers. (Ill.6)

St. Jerome, writing in the fourth century A.D., stated that the lyre had six strings. But Josephus, the prolific Jewish historian of the first century, who was closer to Hebrew tradition, asserted that it had ten strings and was struck with a plectrum, whereas the harp had twelve strings and was plucked with the fingers.

The early rabbinic sages were far from unanimous with regard to the number of strings for either lyre or harp, since, like the early translators of the Bible, they were not familiar with either instrument. They frequently confused them, sometimes declaring them to be identical, "except that the harp has more strings."

A second instrument played by both men and women in secular life, as well as a favorite accompaniment for voice, was the nebel (harp), mentioned in the Scriptures twenty-seven times. Its Semitic meaning is "to inflate" or "to bulge," hence it was also the Hebrew term for the inflated skin bottles or clay jugs used to hold water or wine.

As nabla, the Greeks attributed its invention to the Phoenicians, more precisely to the Sidonians, who were famed for music. In later centuries the Latin poet Ovid would urge young Roman patricians to "Learn to sweep with both hands the genial Phoenician harp (nabla); suitable is it to merrymaking."

Since the Bible does not mention the nebel until relatively late, in the time of Samuel, it is probable that the Hebrews did not take with them from Egypt the vertical, bow-shaped court harps of that land. Rather, they may have adopted the vertical, angular harp from the neighboring Phoenicians during their early years in Canaan.

The harp was one of a family of more or less similar instruments grouped under the Greek term *psalterion*. These may have shown differences with regard to size, number of strings, volume, sonority, and tuning, but their construction and technique of playing must have followed a like pattern. One classical writer called the harp an "upright psaltery," indicating that psalteries in general were horizontal.

In the strict sense psalterion signified a particular stringed instrument that was played by the fingers of both hands; it was easily accessible from both sides, had several strings and a harplike shape. In a wider sense instruments were also called psalteries whose strings were stretched over a horizontal sounding body and which therefore could be played from one side only, with a plectrum or with little sticks.

Although the harp was larger and lower pitched than the lyre, there may also have existed a small harp and a large lyre. This would clear up the puzzling reference to two of the early Davidic choral groups, one of which, we recall, was appointed to perform "with harps set to alamoth" (i.e., in the range of maidens' voices), the other "with lyres on the sheminith." The first might then refer to small, high-pitched harps, the second to large, low-sounding lyres, both with their usual roles reversed—the harps now doubling the vocal melody while the lyres assumed an occasional accompanying function.

Through the centuries attempts have been made to identify the term nebel with the bagpipe, because of the word's meaning "to bulge." Today, however, there is virtual agreement that the nebel was the upright, portable angular harp, with a rounded, skin-covered body rising vertically from the string holder. It may have existed in various sizes and with different tunings, but over the ages its basic form was modified only in minor details. (Ill. 8)

As in nearly all antique harps, the strings faced away from the player, without the forepillar of the modern harp. The skin encasing the body for greater strength and sonority, as well as the ornamental inlay that often reinforced this, doubtless contributed to the bulging appearance.

The *asor*, referred to only three times in the Old Testament (Psalms 33, 92, and 144), is thought to come from a root meaning "ten." Hence the asor is generally believed to be an instrument of ten strings.

The question is: what kind of instrument? One opinion holds that it was the ten-stringed lyre mentioned by Josephus. Another, that it was a Phoenician zither, a small, rectangular instrument with ten strings strung parallel to the shorter sides and played upright, perhaps as a favorite of women.

Still another theory is that the Hebrews adapted it from an Assyrian harp, which in its turn may have descended from a ten-stringed horizontal angular harp of the Sumerians. The catalogue of Sumerian songs carved on the stone slab mentioned earlier contained a list of liturgies meant to be performed with instrumental accompaniment. Among "recitations with pipe," "songs with the reed pipe," "songs with the long flute," and "songs with the hand drum," one inscription reads: "Twenty-three songs of the breast (i.e., love songs) for the (Semitic) instrument of ten (strings)."

Halil, abub, and *ugab* are the three terms found in biblical and rabbinic writings that indicate woodwind instruments, individually or collectively.

The Hebrew word halil, which occurs six times in the Old Testament, indicates a pierced hollow tube, and is more accurately

translated "pipe" than "flute." The familiar transverse flute of today evolved several centuries later; it had no mouthpiece, the player
blowing against the sharp edge of an opening near one end.

No such horizontal woodwind was apparently known to the
Near East in the days when David was organizing the Temple music. Pipers of the time everywhere used a vertical instrument akin to
the *aulos* of the Greeks or to the shawm, a medieval ancestor of
the modern oboe. This primitive shawmlike pipe was fitted with a
double reed, but instead of holding this against his lips as in today's
oboes, the player took the entire mouthpiece into his mouth, which
in Oriental fashion he then used as a kind of windbag, inhaling
through his nose while maintaining a steady force of air through
the instrument.

Many pictures from antiquity show a double oboe with a single
mouthpiece from which two divergent pipes descend. The melody
was played through one pipe while the second probably sustained
a high drone, or bourdon note, as is still common to Oriental playing.

The Old Testament contains no direct references to the double
oboe, and later rabbinic references to its use in the Second Temple
are inconclusive. It seems more probable that a single pipe of
oboe type was used in the sacred musical service. Since there was
no lip pressure against the mouthpiece to control the tone color,
the early vertical pipe emitted only the naturally shrill, strident
tones of the double reed. The Mishnah, the first rabbinical commentary on Hebrew writings, reports that when pipes were played
in the sanctuary at Jerusalem their sound was heard as far away as
Jericho. This need not be taken literally, but it suggests that their
penetrating timbre carried a considerable distance.

Some believe that no pipes of any sort were used in the First
Temple, since they are not among the instruments mentioned at
David's establishment of the sacred musical service. However, both
biblical and rabbinic references appear to confirm their use in the
early ritual. As we have seen, they were among the instruments
used by the Sons of the Prophets, whose ceremonies profoundly influenced David's conception of the sacred service.

Talmudic tradition states that pipes were played at the sacrificial
altar twelve times during the year, and mentions the ceremonies
involved. To be sure, it does not indicate whether the First or Sec-

ond Temple is referred to, but inasmuch as the Second Temple patterned its ritual minutely on that of the First, it seems certain that if pipes were used in one they were used in both.

In antiquity, pipes were made of reed or wood, as a rule. Sometimes the wood was covered with metal, usually gold or silver. Only occasionally were they made entirely of metal. One such metal instrument, discovered in the royal tombs of Ur (c. 2800 B.C.), consists of two slender silver tubes, each with four fingerholes. Except for the mouthpiece, which doubtless disintegrated over the centuries, it is very similar to the double oboe seen in numerous Egyptian tombs.

Among the Israelites metal pipes may have been preferred by professional pipers, and those of wood or thighbone were common secular instruments. But the Temple musicians were more conservative, preferring, for the few occasions when they were permitted, pipes made from reed, "because the sound was sweeter."

Like the Greek aulos, the Hebrew halil was of Asiatic origin. The Phoenicians had a small, span-long pipe from Syria, of shrill, lamenting tone, which was used in ritual mourning for Kinnyras, whom they identified with the Greek Adonis. As used by the Hebrews, this short Syrian pipe had a bright, gay sound and was a general favorite, since it was easy to learn to play.

Despite its shrill sound the Israelites were extremely fond of the instrument in whatever form, and made it a part of all occasions for rejoicing, as at the coronation of Solomon:

> And the people piped with pipes and rejoiced with great joy, so that the earth rent with the sound of them.

At the harvest festival as well as the offering of the first fruits, the playing of pipes in the procession of pilgrims was traditional:

> Ye shall have a song as in the night when a feast is hallowed; and gladness of heart, as when one goeth with the pipe to come into the mountain of the Lord, to the Rock of Israel.

Its shrill, exciting timbre also was able to engender a state of ecstasy, which was probably its function as used by the Sons of the Prophets. A later use of this sort is related in the apocryphal Acts of Thomas, which declares that on his visit to India a Jewish flute girl, standing behind the apostle, played the pipe until he achieved a state of transport. The words he uttered in his rapture were understood only by the girl.

One of antiquity's most versatile instruments, the pipe could assume any character, gay, exciting, pensive, or mournful. It made an appropriate funerary instrument, and was used for this by all peoples of the time. The Babylonians used pipes mainly for lamentation. In a Sumerian hymn of atonement the penitent weeps: "Like the reed NAA, I am in sadness"; and in the lament of Ishtar for Tammuz, the Babylonian goddess moans: "A reed of lamentation is my heart." Two thousand years later Aristotle would remark: "Why do those who are sad and those who are enjoying themselves both make use of the flute?"

The term abub was used by rabbinical writers as a synonym for both halil and ugab, all three designating a similar instrument. Rabbinic lore states:

> There was a flute (abub) in the sanctuary which was smooth (i.e., of pleasing quality), made of reed, and dating from the time of Moses. At the king's command it was overlaid with gold, but its sound was no longer sweet. The overlay was removed and its sound became sweet as before.

Widespread notoriety was given the instrument in antiquity by the abub-playing flute girls of Syria. In later days many of these lived in the basement of the Roman Circus, which became jocularly known as "the meeting place of the flute girls." Probably some of these found their way to Israel, where the anathema of the sages against immoral life in general was directed equally toward the musical instrument of their calling. (Ill. 3)

The hostility against the orgiastic aulos and the similarly sounding halil was continued by the early Church fathers. Clement of Alexandria, in the second century, warned his congregation against the chromatic (to him, dissolute) melodies of the heathen Greeks and ordered them to return to the traditional diatonic psalmody of David.

Ugab, one of the two instruments that legend ascribes to Jubal, the world's "first" musician, was probably a generic term for all wind instruments. It may originally have meant a particular instrument, and later been extended to cover all kinds of pipes, including certain softer-toned flutes. The role of these in antiquity is hard to define because of the interchanging of terms for oboe-like pipes with those for the flute proper, i.e., having no mouthpiece.

The development of these is traced on various Egyptian and Assyrian monuments, which show end-blown flutes of various lengths, double flutes with tubes set parallel or at an angle and blown simultaneously, and a nose flute played through one nostril, a variety of which is still used by Egyptian natives today. Finally, on an Etrurian relief of the second century B.C., we find an example of the modern transverse flute.

The hatsotserot, from a word meaning "convoker," were long straight trumpets built by the Israelites after models in Egypt, where they were familiar instruments in both religious and military life long before the biblical exodus. We find pictures of them in preserved monuments as early as 1415 B.C.

In Tutankhamen's tomb two trumpets were found, one of silver, the other of bronze. The Louvre Museum has another ancient Egyptian trumpet of gilded bronze, which is dated some 1,000 years later. Tutankhamen reigned about the year 1360 B.C., a little more than a century before the exodus of the Israelites, which is believed to have occurred around 1240 B.C. Thus the Israelites were living in Egypt before, during, and after the age of Tutankhamen, which makes it logical to assume that they took over their own trumpets from the Egyptians.

Wood or bamboo tubes with a bell of gourd or animal horn and capable of sounding one or two notes were common throughout the primitive world. According to Greek and Roman sources, metal trumpets, modeled after these, were invented by the Etruscans, the first bronze casters of the Mediterranean basin. This pre-Roman people evidently introduced them to the Egyptians as well as to the Greeks and Romans.

Josephus gives a detailed description of the Hebrew trumpets that agrees essentially with their prototypes pictured on Egyptian antiquities. According to him they were "a little short of a cubit in length" (about 16 inches), their straight tube being somewhat larger than the halil and further widened at the lower end into a bell-like shape to strengthen the tone. The mouthpiece was rather broad. Thus their form was similar to what today we call heralds' trumpets.

The trumpet is the only Hebrew instrument of which we possess at least one contemporary picture. The Arch of Triumph that the Emperor Titus erected in Rome after the destruction of Jerusalem shows among the captured Temple vessels borne in triumphal procession the two sacred silver trumpets, which the sculptor must have copied from the originals. (Frontispiece)

Several coins issued during the second Maccabean revolt (A.D. 132–134) show on their face two trumpets. These are clumsily designed and foreshortened to fit the space, but the bell-like widening of the tube is clearly visible. (Ill. 2)

Like the Egyptian trumpets, the Hebrew instruments were made of metal, either of bronze or, for the sacred trumpets, of hammered silver. When God, according to Scripture, commanded Moses to make two trumpets, he specified only the material and the occasions of their use; the shape was already known to Moses. Although none but Aaron and his descendants, the priests, might sound the sacred trumpets, secular trumpets were blown by others than the priesthood, as for instance by royal heralds upon the coronation of kings. Those used in secular life were probably made of bronze, like their Egyptian counterparts.

The construction and sound of the Hebrew trumpet was basically that of today's natural trumpet, except that the biblical instrument was not curved. It was jointed in several sections, which sometimes fell apart.

The two sacred trumpets were identical in dimensions, an acoustical necessity since they were blown in pairs to produce powerful unison blasts. At first they may not have exceeded two or three easily produced tones, such as the octave and the upper fifth, and possibly the second octave.

In their early stage they were used principally for signal purposes, both within and without the sanctuary. As with the primitive trumpets of other ancient peoples, their tone must have been coarse and uneven. In the fifth century B.C. Aeschylus refers to the Greek trumpet as "yelling," and Roman authors characterized the tone of the straight Roman trumpet (tuba), which was similar to the Hebrew, as horribilis, raucus, rudis, and terribilis. They were even harder on the trumpets of other countries. Plutarch, in the first Christian century, compared the tone of the Egyptian trumpet to "an ass's bray."

As with the loud instruments of other ancient Oriental peoples, the trumpets' original purpose was to arrest God's attention. With the maturing of Hebrew religious concepts such loud invocation was largely abandoned, although as late as the second century b.c., during the Maccabean revolt, the sacred trumpets were blown while the people called upon God "with a loud voice."

A spiritually loftier purpose of the instruments is inherent in the biblical command that they be sounded "for a memorial before your God," that is, as a symbolic reminder of God's presence—a reversal of the primitive intent to arouse God's attention by noise, shouting, and loud instruments.

The Egyptian trumpet was used primarily as a signal instrument before and during battle. Thus the signals that Moses adopted for his own people may represent the code of signals used by the Egyptian army, since Moses was apparently familiar with all aspects of Egypt's government, both priestly and military. The two silver trumpets that signaled the Hebrew armies, however, differed from the Egyptian models in being a matched pair. The two trumpets found in Tutankhamen's tomb were not matched, one being silver, the other bronze, and differing in length.

The Hebrew sacred trumpets were blown at all religious feasts, the new moon, the daily burnt offerings, the peace offerings, as well as at all important ritual ceremonies. They were used at the transfer of the Ark to Jerusalem, at the dedication of Solomon's Temple, the dedication of the rebuilt walls around Jerusalem, and at all general feasts.

The ritual announcement of the Sabbath was sounded by the trumpets from the Temple roof, so that the people working in the fields could hear the call. Between the first and the last blast of the Sabbath call some time elapsed, in which any immediate task had to be finished. Upon the second trumpet call the Sabbath started and every activity had to cease.

With the collapse of the Hebrew nation and the ensuing chaos, certain musical notions disappeared or became confused, among them the distinction between the uses of the hatsotserot and the shofar; even the terms for the two instruments were used inter-

changeably. English versions of the Bible fail to discriminate between them, translating both arbitrarily as trumpet, bugle, cornet,
or shawm. Only the Jewish version consistently renders hatsotserot
correctly as trumpets.

The shofar is the only instrument of ancient Israel that survived
the centuries in its original form and that is still used in the Jewish
liturgy, although with greatly curtailed functions. The Hebrews
took over the shofar from the Assyrians, the word itself, as we saw
earlier, being derived from the Assyrian *shapparu*, "wild goat" (of
the ibex family). More often, however, the Jewish shofar is made
of a ram's horn.

The original form of the shofar was curved like the natural horn.
Later, treatment involving steaming would change the natural
shape, producing straight shofroth with a distinct bend close to the
bell-like end. In the Second Temple both curved and straight
forms were used. In rabbinic times the shofar blown at the New
Year was of wild goat's horn and straight, with the mouthpiece
overlaid with gold. Flanking the player that blew it were two
priests with silver trumpets. The shofar blew a long note, the
trumpets a short one, since the duty of the day fell upon the shofar. On fast days the roles were reversed. The shofar for this was a
ram's horn in its naturally rounded state, with its mouthpiece overlaid with silver. The player was flanked by two priests with silver
trumpets, which blew a long sustained note, the shofar a short one.

After the destruction of the Temple the embellishment of shofroth with gold, silver, or other showy ornamentation was prohibited, and in this unadorned form the instrument still functions
today.

The primitive shofar was made by cutting off the tip of the
natural horn or boring a hole in it. The instrument had no mouthpiece and could produce only crude sustained tones. The shofar
with a mouthpiece represents a more developed form, but even so
it remains limited to two, sometimes three, tones, the octave, the
upper fifth, and the second octave. It goes without saying that the
shofar could not carry out any musical assignment but was restricted to the simple functions of a signal instrument.

Many transformations could be wrought upon the natural horn.
It could be scraped to make it smooth. Its curved form could be

straightened. The bony portion of the skull, in which the horn was embedded, could be chiseled out and left attached to the horn for greater resonance and volume. Even a damaged shofar, if expertly repaired, might be ritually used again, provided it was mended with self-material. It might be carved with inscriptions, but it could not be painted. Neither could it be cut to improve it. (Ill. 5)

During the Temple's existence the shofar might be blown at New Year in any city near enough to Jerusalem to hear the shofar blasts from the Holy City. After the Temple's destruction it was decreed that it might be blown wherever there was a congregation.

At the New Year the shofar was originally blown in the early part of the morning service, but subsequently this was changed to a later hour. The reason for this was a tragic occurrence, related in the Talmud. It seems that the Jewish shofar blasts resembled the military signals of the Roman army stationed in Palestine. As a result the Roman authorities once suspected that the Jews were preparing an attack on them and that the shofar blasts served to call the men together.

To prevent what they took to be an armed revolt, Roman troops were suddenly dispatched in the early morning to the synagogues, where a frightful carnage was committed among the worshiping Jews before any explanation could be made. For a while after this the Romans forbade the shofar to be blown at all, and to enforce this they sent spies around every six hours. Eventually, it appears, the Jewish religious leaders were able to convince the occupation authorities that the shofar blasts had only a ritual significance, for in subsequent years the shofar was again sounded, even in the morning service. It was also retained in the evening service to which it had been transferred.

As with the trumpets, the daily number of shofar blasts was strictly regulated: "Never less than twenty-one and never more than forty-eight." This ordinance became the basis for much rabbinic argument after the destruction of the Temple, when the function of the sacred trumpets had to be assumed by the lowlier shofar. Some rabbis, poorly versed in musical matters, interpreted the three shofar blasts as one, while others held that they represented three separate sounds.

Today's synagogue service uses four different shofar blasts:

tekiah	("blast"), a relatively short pick-up note on the tonic (or first tone sounded), leading to a sustained note on the fifth above and ending in some shofroth with the higher octave;
shebarim	("breaks"), a rapid alternation of tonic and fifth; ending with a sustained note on the fifth;
teruah	("din"), a rapid staccatolike repetition of short notes on the tonic, ending with a long note on the fifth;
tekiah gedolah	("great blast"), basically identical to the *tekiah* but using longer note values and ending with a long sustained note on the fifth or, in some shofroth, on the octave.

The shofar used in today's Jewish ritual is normally a straight tube fourteen to fifteen inches long, with the widened bell bent slightly sidewise. Since its interior is rather rough and the instrument usually is blown through a mouthpiece of irregular shape, its pitch is highly variable and not always distinct. Shofroth vary also as to the number of their available harmonics. Some can produce only two, possibly three, and rarely four sounds of their respective natural series.

Of all the Israelite instruments the shofar is mentioned most often in the Bible—seventy-two times, which indicates its importance in the religious as well as secular life of the people.

In times of war it was the regular signal instrument for assembling the warriors, attacking the enemy, pursuing the vanquished, or announcing victory. Its role in war is evident from any number of biblical events: Ehud's fight against the Moabites; Gideon's war against the Midianites when, we are told, 300 warriors blew the shofar to intimidate the enemy; Saul's combat with the Philistines; Joab's fight against Abner, and many others.

In postbiblical times its use was even more diverse. Shofar blasts now announced the Sabbath. It was used along with pipes as a funerary bugle whose sound had the magic power to frighten off

evil spirits. At ceremonies of excommunication its blast could signal the banishment of a member from the congregation or the
rescinding of the ban. It proclaimed droughts, blights, and other
natural catastrophes. If rain was scanty, the people fasted or blew
the shofar, and if no rain at all fell, they did both.

If pestilence attacked a city or it suffered an earthquake (which
appears to have been not uncommon in those days), the inhabi-
tants both fasted and sounded the shofar. Nearby towns might also
blow it, but were not required to fast.

> For these things they sound the shofar in every place:
> blight or mildew, locust or caterpillar, wild beasts or the
> sword.
> For these things they sound the shofar even on the Sab-
> bath: for a city that is encompassed by gentiles or by flood;
> for a ship that is storm-tossed out at sea. They sound the
> shofar because of any public distress.

It was also usual to hold public prayers accompanied by shofar
blasts in times of impending economic calamity, such as the decline
in trade or the purchasing power of money.

> Linen garments in Babylon and wine and oil in Palestine
> have become so cheap that ten are sold at the price of six.

This amounted to a drop of forty percent, which even in a relatively primitive economy affected both producer and purchaser.
Public prayers were, therefore, in order and the shofar's part in
these was again to draw Yahweh's attention to the people's plight.

Toward the end of Israel's national existence a latent struggle
developed between priestly and secular forces with regard to eliminating the trumpets in the sacred service in favor of the shofar.
This struggle was decided with the destruction of the Temple by
the Romans in A.D. 70. Since the trumpets were associated with the
sacrifice, permissible only in the Jerusalem sanctuary, the cessation
of this ritual ended their use as well.

The shofar, on the other hand, continued to perform its normal
functions—to announce the New Year, introduce the Sabbath,
usher in the new moon, and carry out certain rites on the Day of

Atonement. In addition it now took over those of the trumpets. Thus the shofar became what it remains to this day, the only ancient musical instrument in the Jewish sacred ritual.

Two other words for horn also appear in the Bible. One of these is *keren*, which means "firm" or "solid" and refers to the hard horn of the neat, a kind of cattle. Like the shofar, the keren served as a signal instrument. It was made exclusively of neat horn and apparently had no metal parts. Since the biblical text never connects the word keren with the sacred service, it was evidently a purely secular instrument.

The word "yobel" we met with earlier, in its meaning of ram's horn and its legendary association with Jubal, the father of all musicians. It is first found in Leviticus of the Old Testament when God ordains that every fiftieth year shall be for the Israelites a *shanat ha-yobel*, "year of the horn" or "year of sounding."

This year, ushered in on the tenth day of the seventh Hebrew month (the Day of Atonement) by loud blasts of the yobel horn, was dedicated as one of general moral reassessment among the Hebrews. Property values and years of servitude were reckoned from it. An Israelite who had fallen on lean times and hired himself out as a bondsman, either to another Israelite or to a stranger, would be freed in the year of the horn; and if he was redeemed before this time, the worth of his unserved years would be figured to the nearest such year. During its twelve months the Israelites might neither sow nor reap, and all property had to be restored to its rightful owner.

When the Bible was translated into the (Latin) Vulgate, the phrase shanat ha-yobel became the Latin *annus jubilus*, the Latin J having the sound of Y. It is from this that the idea of a year of jubilee arose, implying a festive period, which was not indicated by the Hebrew term. Even the earlier (Greek) Septuagint confused the matter, holding that in such a year all slaves were automatically freed and that their liberation was accompanied by blowing the horn. Any bondsmen released on the year of jubilee were Israelites. Slaves, either bought or captured from alien tribes, were an inheritable possession.

The horn announcing such a year was not the ordinary shofar but an exceptionally powerful instrument with a peculiarly loud blast. It was probably put together of several parts, the most important being a bell-like endpiece, which was removable and functioned like a megaphone, not only increasing the sound but giving it a hollow, ominous quality, well-suited to supernatural happenings.

The yobel horn's apocalyptic tones joined with lightning and thunder to create a mystic setting for God's revelation to Moses on Mount Sinai. With remarkable dramatic sense, the biblical chronicler suggests the gradually increasing sound of the big horn—"when the horn soundeth long . . . and the voice of the horn exceedingly loud . . . and when the voice of the horn waxed louder and louder"—conveying the idea of a continuous crescendo to match the uproar of the elements.

The yobel horn also played a salient part in the famous siege of Jericho, but since other supernatural factors were also involved this incident belongs more properly to the chapter "Music and Superstition."

Hand drums, of which the Hebrews had as many as other ancient peoples, were grouped under the collective term *tof*, a word that in itself suggests the sound of the instrument. The term came to the Hebrews from the Sumerians by way of Assyria, but for an idea of what such hand drums looked like we again must rely on pictures from other countries of antiquity.

Such percussion instruments were extremely important in Oriental music, since, as we have seen, they served the purpose that rhythm does in our Western music. Both the Egyptians and Assyrians had many varieties, such as a square-shaped species with lightly arched bays on its four sides, a small circular hand drum, and a long cylindrical type, which hung on ribbons from the neck and was played with both palms or with a pair of slightly curved sticks.

We may suppose that the Hebrew hand drum consisted in general of a wooden or metal hoop covered with the skin of a ram or wild goat and that it was played either with the fingers or the clenched fist. Nowhere in the Bible do we find any hints as to the playing of hand drums with sticks. Nor do we know whether metal rings or small metal plates were fastened to the hoop to produce a jingling sound as on the later tambourine. There is no evidence either whether the hand drum had a skin on only one side or both. The hand drum was the most primitive, consequently the most common instrument of ancient Israel, and easily played by anyone. As in Egypt, it was played mostly by girls and women, although occasionally also by men, as we saw in the case of the Sons of the Prophets. Music often gave rise to spontaneous dancing, led traditionally by women, whose hand drums furnished the rhythmical background.

The only percussion instruments admitted unreservedly into the sacred service were metal cymbals. These, played in pairs, are named only in the plural, as *meziltayim* or *zelzelim*, taking their names from their shimmering sound.

Virtually all antique peoples possessed some kind of metal cymbals. The Assyrians had two kinds: a flat, saucerlike type, held upright and struck together sideways, and a rather bulging, bell-like sort with long handles, played by striking the inverted cymbal against the lower one.

Egyptian cymbals had a broad flat brim and a large bulge in the center that increased their resonance. They were held upright and struck sideways. The Hebrew cymbals may have been similar; according to Josephus these were large bronze plates played with both hands.

Greek cymbals were made of a bronze alloy and were small enough to be used by dancing women. In the New Testament the apostle Paul distinguishes between "sounding brass" and "tinkling cymbals." The first is usually construed as a trumpet, the second as the Greek cymbals of that day. However, it is more probable that the Hebrew Paul referred to the Jewish cymbals, paralleling the two kinds mentioned in Psalm 150, the "loud cymbals" and the "high-sounding cymbals."

These presumably differed in size and possibly in material. The "loud cymbals" may have been larger, made of bronze, and held upright, with a sound that was harsh and penetrating. The "high-sounding cymbals" were smaller brass instruments, lighter in weight and brighter of sound, played vertically.

The Israelites apparently did not know how to prepare the proper alloy for cymbals, as well as other metal articles. When once the Temple cymbals became damaged, in later times at least, artisans had to be called in from Alexandria. The Talmud relates this in a passage that curiously echoes one quoted earlier:

> There was a cymbal in the sanctuary from the days of Moses, made of bronze, and its sound was pleasant; then it became damaged. The sages sent for craftsmen from Alexandria in Egypt, and they mended it, but its sound was not pleasant anymore. Thereupon they removed the repair and its sound became as pleasant as before.

Like the first quotation, this is manifestly one of those tall tales so often found in rabbinic lore.

Shalishim and *menaanim* both signify shaking instruments, like the Egyptian sistrum, though perhaps less ornamented. The sistrum consisted of a metal frame in which rods were inserted, carrying loose rings that jingled when the instrument was shaken by its handle. They appear to have been extremely ancient; Sumerian tombs contained them, and they were known to the Babylonians and Assyrians as well.

Two other sound devices remain to be mentioned, although neither is precisely a musical instrument. The *paamonim* were the little bells attached to the lower seam of the high priest's garment. These tiny golden bells had an unobtrusive tinkle, just loud enough to indicate the whereabouts of the high priest but not to interfere with the ceremony.

Mezillot were larger bells, or perhaps tiny plates or even buckles, that were hung around the necks of horses to keep away evil spirits by their jingling.

Quite a number of additional instruments were also known and used in later Talmudic times, but these, although interesting in themselves, do not properly belong to the music of ancient Israel.

14

THE STRUGGLE
AGAINST APOSTASY

SOLOMON'S WISDOM AS a ruler, his building of the Temple, and the splendor of his court have tended to overshadow his more personal gifts as a poet and musician. That he was the true son of his father is indicated by the Bible's assertion that "he spoke three thousand proverbs, and his songs were a thousand and five."

Perhaps he actually did write that many. More likely it is the kind of flattering exaggeration that Oriental despots expected— and received—from their court chroniclers. In any case, only fragments of any such output are preserved: in the Proverbs, Ecclesiastes, and possibly in the Book of Psalms.

Music is occasionally referred to in the Proverbs: "An evil man is ensnared by his transgressions, but a righteous man sings and rejoices." "And I was daily his delight, playing before him always." "When it goes well with the righteous, the city rejoices." "He who sings songs to a heavy heart is like one who takes off a garment on a cold day." Certain proverbs appear to be complete songs; such is Proverb 31, sometimes called the Song of the Virtuous Woman:

1.
Gold and mosaic *kithara,*
found in the Great Death-pit at
Ur. (*After Woolley*)

2.
The sacred temple instruments (*Kinnor* and
Hazozarot) shown on Bar-Kokba's coins
(132-135 C.E.).

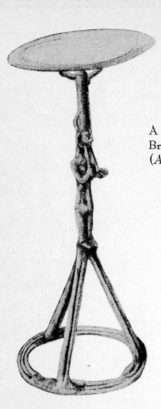

3.
A Jewish flute girl holding a bowl.
Bronze figure found at Megiddo.
(*After Benzinger*)

4.
Semitic captives (probably
Israelites) playing lyres under the
eye of an Assyrian guard.
(*After Wellhausen*)

5.
Yemenite *shofar*, richly carved
with biblical quotations (40 inches
long, 3 inches in diameter). (*Courtesy
of Mt. Sinai Memorial Center,
Los Angeles, Calif.*)

6.
Seven-stringed Abyssinian *kissar* with
Jewish Shield of David. In the
Palestinian Archaeological Museum,
Jerusalem. (*After Gradenwitz*)

7. & 8.
Kinnor.   *Nabla.*
(*After M. R. Brondi*)

9.
Semitic lyre player. Ivory carving
found at Megiddo (13th century B.C.E.).

10.
Semitic lyre player entering Egypt, as
pictured on the Beni-Hassan monument
(circa 1900 B.C.E.). This instrument is
the prototype of the Jewish Kinnor.

> A good wife who can find?
> She is far more precious than jewels.

In certain passages of the Proverbs we hear the echo of similar sentiments expressed a thousand years earlier by the Egyptian king Amenemhet I, as one of many instances in which the poetical output of Israel was colored by the style and thought of her two senior neighbors, Egypt and Babylonia.

It may also be that the Proverbs are a compilation of the rich folk wisdom of many generations. In Israel's heroic age, scribes sometimes wrote down the songs of the folk bards as well as other popular songs. From these were later compiled several collections of battle songs, ballads, and songs of the ancient glory.

Several such collections are alluded to in the Bible, so we know that there existed at one time a Book of the Wars of the Lord, containing songs celebrating Israel's victory over the Moabites and the defeat at Heshbon of Sihon, king of the Amorites. Another collection of minstrelsy was the Book of the Righteous (sometimes called the Book of Songs), to which belonged David's lament for Saul and Jonathan. A biblical reference to still another lost historical document may have been the Lord's command to Moses to "write down" the story of the victory over the Amalekites. Assuming that Moses did so, this may have formed part of the lost Book of the Wars.

Some modern scholars believe that it was none other than King Solomon himself who ordered and supervised the compilation of such ancient songs. Considering his own literary gifts and strong sense of tradition, we can believe that he would have been eager to preserve the spiritual heritage of his people, to leave as a legacy more lasting than stone for the generations that would come after. Unfortunately, it did not turn out that way. Such collections either were lost during the turbulent era following his reign or were deliberately destroyed by later biblical editors in order to establish the Bible as the only "inspired" document.

If Solomon possessed the prophetic insight that Israel traditionally ascribed to its sages, some premonition of the evils that would befall his land after his death may have colored his recorded utterances. Ecclesiastes, which contains some of the most transcendent literature in the Old Testament, is filled with melancholy reflections upon the vanity of life by one who had tasted it to the full and had found that folly and wisdom can equally betray the heart of man.

"I made me great works," mourned Solomon in song. "I builded me houses; I planted me vineyards. I gat me men-singers and women-singers, and . . . instruments of music, and those of all kinds." But nothing had power any longer to cheer the disenchanted king. The phrase, "men-singers and women-singers," perhaps referred to those of the royal court, but it might have alluded equally to the singers of the sacred service. Not only were these "under the hand" of the king, but the Temple's nearness to Solomon's overawing residence made it, in effect, a chapel of the palace, to which the king had his own private entrance.

Solomon was a man less simple-hearted than David. He had most of the faults of an Oriental monarch: he taxed his people cruelly, he liked to live high, and he had a king-size lust for women. But he also had the faculty, curiously noninsular for his time, of seeing things in the round. This may make for wisdom, but it does not easily make for happiness.

Solomon did not depart this life as contentedly as his father had done. David knew that his kingdom would rest in able hands. Much of Solomon's bitterness may have come from knowing that he must leave his kingdom to a son, Rehoboam, who possessed none of his father's gift for dealing with people.

When the elders of Israel came south to ask for a reduction of their heavy taxes, the new king met them with arrogance. "If my father made your yoke heavy," he said, "be assured that I shall make it twice as heavy."

His words sealed the fate of the Hebrew realm. The men of Israel returned home, permanently estranged from the house of David. They stoned the royal tax collector and declared Israel a separate kingdom under Jeroboam. The best that Rehoboam could do was try to strengthen the kingdom of Judah, which was smaller than Israel but contained the gem of the ancient Near East, the Golden City of Jerusalem.

To it fled the priests and Levites, abandoning their lands in the northern kingdom, where there was now no place for the religion of Yahweh. Israel had never been as strongly committed to the

Davidic line and its hereditary priesthood as had Judah. It was not too hard for Jeroboam to turn the people to pagan practices modeled on those of Egypt. He gave them golden calves to worship and created his own priesthood to function in the groves and high places that he peopled with a host of idols.

Judah welcomed the faithful who continued their pilgrimage to the Holy City, and the sacred musical service itself remained unchanged. But in the fifth year of Rehoboam's reign, the king of Egypt invaded the land. The Judeans, splintered from their stout brethren to the north, were no match for his twelve hundred chariots and sixty thousand horsemen. For the remainder of his reign Rehoboam was a vassal of the pharaoh, and under Egyptian influence idolatry also came to Judah.

The country was in distress; the people abandoned the God of Abraham; "the priests with the trumpets of alarm" called for repentance and summoned the faithful to fight against unbelief. Not before Asa, King of Judah (957–918 B.C.), succeeded to the throne was idolatry proscribed. The people renewed their covenant with Yahweh and "swore unto the Lord with a loud voice, and with shouting, and with trumpets, and with horns."

Asa's son, Jehoshaphat (918–894 B.C.), continued his father's good works and restored the sacred service to its former splendor. Once more the Levitical singers "stood up to praise the Lord . . . with an exceeding loud voice." Jehoshaphat also ordered that the Law of Moses be taught the people, as the patriarch had commanded. For several generations this had not been done, so the king sent nine Levitical singers and two priests to go about all the cities of Judah, teaching the Ten Commandments and the other Mosaic Laws. In the local sanctuaries they intoned the passages in the half-sung chant used for all sacred readings.

Such public teaching of religion and morals was a prime duty of the Levitical singers and one of the great innovations of the Hebrews. For them religion was a matter for all the people, not merely for a special caste or to be observed ritually at certain times. Their religion colored all their daily actions, and since it was concerned not with an ideal, other-worldly estate but with a system of ethics by which man could live in amity with his fellows here and now, it was essential that the people should know the sacred rules by which this might be practiced.

Jehoshaphat was a strong king, and under him Judah again grew powerful. As they had to Solomon, the Philistines brought tribute of silver and the Arabians brought flocks of long-haired goats. But such prosperity aroused the envy of neighboring tribal chiefs. The armies of Moab and Ammon joined with those of Mount Seir to attack the land, and Jehoshaphat realized that he was hopelessly outnumbered. Desperate, he proclaimed a general fast, and all the people gathered at the Temple and stood before the Lord with their wives and their little ones.

As the king prayed for guidance, the spirit of the Lord came upon a Levitical singer named Jahaziel. And in the curiously woven melodies of the Orient, he told them in song what it was that they must do.

"Be not dismayed by this great multitude," he sang, "for the battle is not yours but God's. Tomorrow go down against them; you will not need to fight. Take your position, stand still, and see the victory of the Lord on your behalf."

Then Jehoshaphat bowed his head to the ground and all the people did likewise. And the singers stood up to praise the Lord, the God of Israel, "with a very loud voice."

Early next morning the troops went forth. "Have faith in the Lord," the king adjured them. Before the soldiers he ranked the Temple singers with their harps and lyres. And as they all marched off to battle, the singers, dressed in their long Levitical robes and hallowed for a holy mission, went ahead of the troops singing:

> Give thanks to the Lord,
> For his steadfast love endures forever.

At the end of a valley stood the armies of Moab and Ammon and Mount Seir, a formidable host of archers and spearmen and of chariot drivers reining tight their plumed battle horses. Opposite them the army of Judah ranked itself and stood, as the king had ordered, while the singers continued to pour forth their songs of praise and faith.

Then an amazing thing happened. Suddenly the armies of Moab and Ammon turned upon the forces of Mount Seir, slashing through the ranks of their ally with sword and spear and the sharp knives that studded their chariot wheels. This done, they turned upon each other in a furious snarl of hand-to-hand combat until every man among them had dropped lifeless to the ground. It took the astonished soldiers of Judah fully three days to gather up the spoil. A fourth day they devoted to thanking the Lord in what would afterward be known as the Valley of Berakah, or Valley of Blessing, from the wealth of blessings and praises that rose to Yahweh in song and chant. Then, Jehoshaphat at their head, they returned to Jerusalem, rejoicing with harps and lyres and trumpets.

Things were not going so well in Israel, however. On its throne sat a king named Ahab with a Canaanite wife whose name was Jezebel. Jezebel persuaded Ahab to worship the rain god Baal, and the king commanded that everyone else must also take part in the worship and its pagan debaucheries. This aroused the prophet Elijah to righteous wrath.

"As God lives," he swore to the king, "there shall no rain fall in these years unless I give the word." Sure enough, no rain fell, and in a few seasons there was sore famine. Ahab sent for the prophet.

"Gather all Israel at Mount Carmel," Elijah demanded. "And the four hundred and fifty prophets of Baal who eat at Jezebel's table."

When this was done, Elijah ordered the prophets of Baal: "Take one bullock and lay it in pieces on the wood, but light no fire under it. I shall do the same with another bullock. Now you call on the name of your gods, and I will call on mine, and the one that answers by fire, let him be God."

And all the people said, "It is well spoken."

From morning until noon the prophets of Baal leaped up and down at his altar, in the contorted, limping dance of their cult, crying the rain god's name in high-pitched panting yelps or hoarsely muttered incantations. But no fire lit their sacrifice.

"Cry louder," mocked Elijah, "for he is a god, you say. He must be away on a journey. Or maybe he is asleep and must be awakened!"

Then all the prophets of Baal cried even louder and cut themselves after their custom with knives and lances until the blood gushed out upon them. Leaping and dancing, they sang their pagan songs and chanted magic incantations until nightfall, but with no result.

When they had given up, exhausted, Elijah gathered stones and built an altar to Yahweh and laid his offering upon it, drenching it with twelve jars of water. This done, he called upon the name of the God of Israel, and at once the fire of the Lord consumed the burnt offering—altar, stones, and all. Then the people believed, and slew the prophets of Baal, and held festival. And scarcely were they done feasting when it came on to rain.

Ahab's daughter, Athaliah, carried on the family talent for wickedness. She married Jehoshaphat's son and went to live as queen in Jerusalem, where she quickly got a taste for ruling. When her son, Ahaziah, came to the throne she made his decisions for him, and all of her counsel was evil.

Ahaziah almost immediately met a violent end, but Athaliah had no intention of relinquishing her power. To make certain of this she slew all of his royal relatives and hired men to murder his little sons who were still in the royal nursery.

But it happened that their aunt was married to the high priest, Jehoiada, a man faithful to the ways of Yahweh. Secretly she crept into the nursery and stole the tiniest baby, Joash, so the queen's hired assassins did not find him. For the next six years little Joash lived in the Temple with his aunt and uncle, while his evil grandmother ruled the country with a high hand and brought back all the idolatrous customs of her Canaanite forebears.

But Jehoiada, the high priest, was determined that the sacred psalms should once more resound in the Temple of the Lord. When little Joash was seven years old, Jehoiada met secretly with certain Levites and military leaders. Swearing them to secrecy, he showed them the king's little son and told them of his plan.

The following Sabbath the companies of Levites reporting for their turn at Temple duty went straight to Jehoiada, who gave them spears and shields out of the Temple armory. And thus they stood, each with his weapon ready, in a solid phalanx before the great altar of the sacrifices.

Then before the astonished congregation the high priest led forth the little king, big-eyed with wonder at the gleaming array of shields and spears and the tall ranks of Levites guarding the house of the Lord. Jehoiada lifted him up on the high bronze dais in the middle of the great court so all the people could see their rightful king. Upon his head Jehoiada set the golden crown and in his hands he placed the sacred scroll of the Testimony. Then they anointed Joash king and everybody clapped their hands and cried, "Long live the king!"

When Athaliah in the palace heard the singing and the shouting she rushed to the Temple. And behold—there stood the tiny king upon the royal dais with the crown upon his head and with the chieftains of the land and the priestly trumpeters at his side. And all the people were rejoicing, and the trumpets were sounding; and the Temple singers, rank on rank with harps and lyres, were almost bursting their throats with joyful psalms of praise and glory to the Lord God of Hosts.

The wicked queen rent her clothes and shrieked, "Treason! Treason!" But no one paid her any heed. The captains seized her, carried her out of range of holy ground, and slew her. Then the high priest, followed by all the people singing and rejoicing in a grand procession, escorted the little king from the Temple, on through the high gate, into the royal palace. And there, to the sound of the Levites' harps and lyres, they sat him upon the throne of the kingdom.

Joash was a good ruler so long as Jehoiada was alive, but in his later years he forsook the faith of his fathers. During the turbulent centuries following his reign a succession of kings occupied the thrones of Judah and Israel. Some were faithful to the Lord, and under these the Temple singers and the ceremonies enjoyed royal support. More, however, strayed from the religion of Yahweh to follow the idolatrous customs of their neighbors or sought to combine the two.

In many places Yahweh was worshiped with pagan ceremonies and pagan songs on the high places against which the prophets inveighed. In others, temples to various idols were housed in sacred groves, where sacrifices were made to the sound of orgiastic music. Worship of the gods of Syria, Phoenicia, Egypt, and Philistia, as well as the ancient Canaanite gods of Baal and Ashteroth, was hard to eradicate from the folk customs of the people, and under the reign of apostate kings it flourished by royal sanction.

During such periods, sometimes lasting several decades, the

power of the king was never strong enough to overthrow permanently the deeply entrenched observance of the Yahweh cult. As
the traditional faith this was carried out, openly or in secret and
despite all hazards, by a dedicated priesthood and equally dedicated Temple singers. Since their musical art was based entirely on
oral tradition, even a few months of suspended activity might
easily have jeopardized it. That it was always able to resume as if
no interruption had occurred testifies to the perseverance and
artistic conscience of the early Hebrew musicians.

Outside the Temple too segments of the faithful continued
to follow the ancient faith. The Sons of the Prophets, although no
longer identified with academic life, continued to serve the Lord,
attaching themselves to such prophetic figures as Elijah and Elisha
and supporting their struggles to return the people to the ways of
Yahweh.

But the majority of the people followed the king's lead, observing the rites established for pagan worship, calling on the
names of the various deities, and praising them in heathen songs,
such as those sung by the prophets of Baal at Elijah's test of
divine power on Mount Carmel. The ravings, the invocations
(i.e., singing), accompanied by savage dances and noisy music,
were traditional features of all such ceremonies.

Music suffered not only in the religious sphere. The entire
social fabric of the country was affected, and with it music reflected the moral laxity encouraged by the official flouting of the
true faith. Formerly music had served as an embellishment to life;
the rustic merriment of youthful wine treaders and the pleasures of
princely banquets were alike enhanced by song and music. But
as certain classes became wealthy, luxury and debauchery spread.
Music changed its role, becoming the noisy accompaniment of
carousals.

The prophets and other thoughtful men stormed against such
revelry, and since music was now made a part of this, they included
it in their diatribes, admonishing the people to repent.

Job poured out his wrath against the ungodly "who sing to the
timbrel and harp, and rejoice at the sound of the pipe." Amos, too,
was inflamed by the self-indulgence of the nobles: "Woe to those

who lie upon beds of ivory and stretch themselves upon their couches . . . who sing idle songs to the sound of the harp, and like David invent for themselves instruments of music."

With equal vehemence, Isaiah scourged the sins of gluttony and debauchery: "Woe unto them that rise up early in the morning, that they may follow strong drink, that tarry late into night till wine inflame them! And the harp and the psaltery, the tabret and the pipe, and wine are in their feasts." And describing the divine judgment: "The mirth of tabrets ceaseth, the noise of them that rejoice endeth, the joy of the harp ceaseth; they drink not wine with a song."

Even Yahweh himself rejected the Temple offerings: "Take away from me the noise of your songs; to the melody of your harps I will not listen."

For Jeremiah, writing 200 years later, the most dread punishment that could befall the sinful was an existence without song: "Then will I cause to cease from the cities of Judah and from the streets of Jerusalem the voice of mirth and the voice of gladness, the voice of the bridegroom and the voice of the bride." In Lamentations he mourned: "The elders have ceased from the gate, the young men from their music. The joy of our hearts is ceased; our dance is turned into mourning."

But when the people should return to God there would again be the joys of music. After repentance and atonement, chanted Jeremiah, "shall proceed thanksgiving and the voice of them that make merry . . . and they shall come and sing in the height of Zion." Israel "shall go forth in the dances of them that make merry . . . then shall the virgin rejoice in the dance, and the young men and the old together." Zephaniah was confident that "the daughter of Zion shall sing again," for the Lord would show mercy to his repentant people. "He will rejoice over thee with song . . . he will joy over thee with singing."

Such prophecies reflected music's authority over the Hebrew spirit. They are the more significant in that they largely represented for the people the words of God himself as revealed through his prophets. Such utterances of the Lord, so rich in musical metaphors, are among our most dramatic proofs of the ethical loftiness of music in the concept of ancient Israel.

But many factors, political and military as well as social, operated against the firm establishment of the Yahweh cult. Sometimes, if a battle went against the Hebrews, the temptation to espouse the god of the winning side brought new deities into the local pantheon, as in the case of Ahaz, King of Judah. Ahaz already followed several pagan cults, but when the Syrians carried off a portion of his people captive he sacrificed to their gods as well, reasoning: "Because the gods of the kings of Syria help them, therefore will I sacrifice unto them, that they may help me."

For nearly a thousand years the great struggle of the nation's leaders—its prophets, its priesthood, and its consecrated kings—continued to be twofold: an external struggle with surrounding nations for military supremacy and an internal struggle to preserve its ancient faith against the recurrent inroads of alien cults.

The extent to which the Levitical musicians assisted in this may never be fully assessed, but it cannot stand too far below that of the prophets. Like the prophets, they were concerned with persuading a young, impressionable people of the power and majesty of a single, all-encompassing deity, the creator and mover of everything that is. To accept him was to accept the Law of Moses, with its religious strictures, its demand for self-scrutiny, and its inflexible moral standard of right and wrong.

The neighboring peoples had a much easier time of it in this respect. They had many gods—a chief one, usually, but any number of lesser gods as well—who might be wooed with gifts and sacrifices and leapings about the altar. If one god grew angry or unresponsive, there were plenty of others to whom they could turn. Thus they could keep going from god to god without ever having to come to terms with their own conscience.

This posed serious competition for a deity who would not share his authority with any other and who demanded the utmost loyalty and rectitude from his followers. To make the people understand his requirements and the paternal affection behind them throughout a thousand years of headstrong generations was not the smallest task of the Levitical singers. Like the prophets, they dealt in ideas, clothed in poetic form to spark the imagination and buoyed by song to wing directly to the heart.

Faithfully, in good times or bad, under benign kings or kings indifferent to their message, the Levitical singers persevered in their task of extolling the glories of God. Fortunately for their efforts, they had behind them the weight of a sternly practical musical organization. Ties of blood, especially strong among early peoples, cemented the singers into a loyal fraternity. The hereditary nature of their office and an inbred reverence for tradition combined to make their guild a powerful agency, alert to foster and protect the interests of its members.

During periods when the Temple music was under official ban, the guild saw to the material welfare of the singers and encouraged the systematic rehearsals by which they kept alive their songs and the tradition of their performance. When, from time to time, their perseverance was rewarded by a king loyal to the ancient faith, this organizational discipline guaranteed their resumption of their public duties with complete fidelity to the Davidic tradition.

Thus they were never wholly in eclipse. But more than three hundred years were to elapse after the time of David before another king as devoted to their cause would sit upon the gilded ivory throne in Jerusalem.

15

TWO MUSIC-LOVING
MONARCHS

HEZEKIAH (724–695 B.C.), SON OF Ahaz, set out from the first to
undo the damage that his father had wrought upon the Temple
and the sacred service. Ahaz had been about as wicked as a king
could be. He had sacrificed to strange gods. He had ordered a
pagan altar for the Temple and had taken the original one for his
own use. When the Lord failed to help him against the Syrians
he shut up the Temple, plundered the holy vessels, and extinguished the perpetual flame before the Ark. But worst of all, he
sacrificed his own children by fire, after the custom of the Canaanites.

Against these terrible things the prophet Isaiah thundered
denunciation. Ahaz, like his father and grandfather before him,
turned a deaf ear to the noble old prophet, but Hezekiah, growing
up, was gripped by the urgency of his words. By the time he came
to the throne Hezekiah was unswervingly committed to the side of
the Lord.

As his first royal act he flung open the doors of the Temple.
Then he brought in the priests and Levites and said, "Now sanctify
yourselves, and sanctify the house of the Lord God of your fathers,

and carry out the filth from the holy place. Do not be negligent, for the Lord has chosen you to stand in his presence and to minister to him and burn incense."

Then the Levites arose, all the sons of the great tradition, the sons of the Kohathites and of Merari, the sons of the Gershonites and of Elizaphan, and the sons of Asaph, and of Heman, and of Jeduthun. For eight days they ritually cleansed and sanctified the house of the Lord. Then they reported back to the king.

Early next morning Hezekiah and the city officials went up to the Temple bearing a host of sacrificial offerings, for the sins of Israel under his father had been very great. Hezekiah was determined that during his reign things would be quite different. During his boyhood, while the Temple had been shut up, he had sworn that his very first act as king would be to restore the sacred service.

Now he was about to witness the ceremony for the first time, as was more than one member of the large congregation that stood gazing in awe at the beauty of the newly restored sanctuary. At the east end of the huge bronze altar, once more in its rightful place, the singers in their finespun Temple robes stood ranked by their several choirs as Hezekiah had ordered, so that everything might proceed according to the tradition established by King David.

In their hands were many of the instruments that had also been King David's: the harps and lyres and cymbals—perhaps for this special occasion a number of pipes as well. With what loving care and reverence these had been preserved was known only to the Levitical families who had cherished them as a legacy of trust through successive generations. They were too precious to be used for any but the most special of occasions, and since the days of Solomon there had been no occasion so worthy as this rededication of the sanctuary that he had built.

When the priests were ready, the king signaled for the ceremonies to start. And as the burnt offering began, the singers began their song to the Lord, while the trumpeters sounded and the whole assembly worshiped. Perhaps Psalm 30, said to have been sung at the dedication of the Temple, may have been sung at this rededicatory service as well.

Following this the king, and the princes too, requested the

singers to perform certain favorite psalms of David and of Asaph. The fact that the singers sang whatever was asked "with gladness" proves that despite the scant time they had to prepare for the event they were able to perform any psalm requested with complete skill and confidence. Once more the unrelenting discipline of their order had paid off handsomely. Everyone from the king on down was happy that matters went off so well, "for the thing came about suddenly."

The rededication of the Temple had taken place at the time when the yearly Passover would have been celebrated, a custom that had not been observed for many years. Unwilling to wait any longer, the people unanimously voted to hold this the following month.

Hezekiah invited all Israel and Judah to come to Jerusalem. Messengers went with the king's letters from city to city, urging the people to turn again to the God of Abraham, who stood ready to forgive and to welcome them back to his sanctuary. In the northern kingdom of Israel the messengers were laughed at and mocked by some, but others gladly made their first journey in many years to the hill-girt citadel of the Lord, joining the pilgrims from Judah who thronged to their reclaimed sanctuary bearing lambs or young goats for a family feast.

All told, "a very great congregation" assembled at Jerusalem to keep the feast of the Passover that year. At the ceremonies, which were carried out with all the reverence and fervor of earlier days, the Levitical singers again took part beyond their usual duties. Ritual dictated that the head of each family had to dedicate his festal lamb to the Lord, but only if he had first confessed and atoned for any transgressions.

Such hymns of confession may also have involved the Levitical singers, for they were perhaps presented with a special musical setting. Because the Passover had been called suddenly, many pilgrims had not had time to observe this rule. In order that all might join in the general feast the Levites prepared the Passover lambs for them, while the king himself asked the good Lord to "pardon everyone that prepares his heart to seek God, even though not according to the sanctuary rules."

For seven days they held festival. In regular shifts throughout each day the singers kept their places, "singing with instruments of strength unto the Lord," which suggests that these may have been increased along with the vocal choirs by the addition of further strings and, since it was the Passover, of pipes.

If women were part of the vocal chorus, their voices may have been accompanied by a small, higher-sounding harp that was tuned to alamoth (i.e., "in the range of maidens' voices"). Psalm 46, the only one preserved that bears this in its heading, would have been especially appropriate for an occasion meant to reaffirm the people's trust in Yahweh. This seems to have belonged to the repertoire of the sons of Korah, so it may be that its performance was the privilege of that Levitical clan, or that they had provided an arrangement for it that became traditional:

> God is our refuge and strength,
> A very present help in trouble.

The ten-stringed harp (asor) may have been called for by a new psalm composed especially for the occasion. Psalm 33 may have been such a one:

> Praise the Lord with the lyre,
> make melody to him with the harp
> of ten strings!
> Sing to him a new song,
> play skilfully on the strings,
> with loud voice.

Whatever songs were sung in addition to the traditional Hallel psalms, the Levitical singers again proved their vocal and instrumental skill. So impressively did they perform, in fact, that the king himself was moved to praise them. It was perhaps owing in no small measure to their artistry that the congregation unanimously voted to extend the celebration another seven days. This time the king himself feasted the people and there was great joy among them, for not since the time of David and Solomon had there been the like in Jerusalem.

Hezekiah was a gentle person and perhaps the most wholly lovable king who ever sat upon the throne of Israel or Judah. His only wish was to serve his Maker and his people, and he did this faithfully throughout his entire reign. In return, God prospered him. He wound up with "very great possessions" and a stable kingdom that gave him time to cultivate the arts.

His scribes copied the Proverbs of Solomon, and under his patronage the art of psalm-writing once more flourished. It is thought that a substantial portion of our present Psalter stems from his reign. He reestablished the traditional cycle of the Levitical singers, appointing them to utter psalms of praise to the Lord in a regular schedule of sacred services held for the congregation daily and on the Sabbaths and the set festivals.

The guild of musicians, with an eye always to the good of its members, no doubt took advantage of the king's approval to suggest he show his admiration in a practical manner, for during his father's reign the singers had fallen on lean times. Hezekiah took immediate steps to ensure them a better livelihood by ordering the people of Jerusalem to bring in the tithe that was traditionally their due.

The people responded willingly. Corn, wine, oil and honey, oxen and sheep quickly piled up in such quantities that the Levites were at a loss where to put them. The king had to order new storage chambers prepared, placing over them a corps of administrative officers. The guild also saw to it that his solicitude did not stop with the singers on duty in the Temple; the priests and Levites who were away tilling their fields in outlying suburbs also received a share of the people's contributions.

Such an assessment, ostensibly voluntary, actually represented a special tax, corresponding to a kind of church tax in today's sense. From this to the next stage, in which the Temple singers were supported by fiscal means, was but a step. It would not be long before the musicians were elevated to the privileged class of state functionaries.

Word of their artistry must have spread abroad, carrying the fame of Hebrew music and musicians far beyond the frontiers of Israel and Judah. In a fateful hour they were to render an unpremeditated service to Hebrew culture by helping to ransom the sacred city of David.

While Judah grew prosperous under Hezekiah, the predatory Assyrians under Sargon II swept down and carried off the ten tribes of Israel (722 B.C.), repopulating the northern kingdom with alien peoples from Mesopotamia who brought their gods with them. This was a staggering blow to the Hebrews, of whom there now remained only the tribe of Judah, the little tribe of Benjamin, and a remnant of Israel clustered loyally about the nucleus of Jerusalem.

A few years later (701 B.C.) Sargon's son, Sennacherib, threatened the cities of Judah. As his price for sparing Jerusalem he demanded a heavy tribute, the terms of which are still preserved in an Assyrian cuneiform inscription:

> Together with thirty talents of gold (and) eight hundred talents of silver, he (Hezekiah) sent to me to Nineveh, my chief city, precious stones, cosmetics . . . couches of ivory, elephant skins . . . all kinds of treasures in quantity, and his daughters and women of the palace, and male and female musicians.

The text does not make clear whether the musicians mentioned were Hezekiah's court singers or those of the sacred service. Probably the former, although it is not impossible that the Temple singers were meant, since their rigorous and specialized art was unique among the nations. At any rate, Sennacherib seized the opportunity to add to the luster of his own court, as a rare instance of an Oriental monarch foregoing the capture and pillage of a conquered capital for a musical consideration.

So, thanks partly to the fame of its musicians, Jerusalem was spared. But not for long. Sennacherib at last laid siege to the Golden City and sent a taunting letter to Hezekiah:

> "Do not let your God, on whom you rely, deceive you. You know what the kings of Assyria have done to all lands, destroying them utterly. And shall you be delivered?"

Hezekiah carried the letter into the Temple and spread it before the Lord. Then he went out and helped his people to adulterate the enemy's water supply. The Lord's answer came promptly by

the prophet Isaiah, who in the solemn half-sung chant reserved
for sacred matters intoned the Lord's scorching rebuke to Sennacherib:

> Whom have you mocked and reviled:
> Against whom have you raised your voice,
> And haughtily lifted your eyes?
> Against the Holy One of Israel!
>
> Have you not heard
> That I determined it long ago?
> I planned from days of old
> What now I bring to pass . . .

That night a mysterious plague raged through the enemy camp,
killing off a hundred and eighty-five thousand men. In the
morning the astonished Judeans beheld the enemy field strewn with
bodies, the flower of the Assyrian army, which had "melted like
snow in the glance of the Lord."

About this same time Hezekiah was himself sick to the point of
death. "Set your house in order," warned Isaiah, "for you shall not
recover." The king turned his face to the wall and prayed, weeping bitterly, for he was only thirty-nine.

Presently Isaiah returned. "Thus says the Lord, the God of
David your father," he chanted. " 'I have heard your prayer, I
have seen your tears. Behold, I will add fifteen years to your life.' "

Recovered, the grateful king wrote the song referred to earlier,
praising and thanking the Lord. Although it is not included in the
Psalter it is actually a psalm of thanksgiving. At the end Hezekiah
added the little postscript that gives us one of our clues to the fact
that musical instructions for all the psalms were customarily placed
at the end instead of at the beginning:

> The Lord was ready to save me; therefore we will sing to
> my stringed instruments all the days of our life in the house
> of the Lord.

Hezekiah lived out his fifteen added years in peace and well-
deserved happiness. But in his innocence of heart he made one
fatal error for his kingdom. When the prince of Babylon sent

presents congratulating him upon his recovery, Hezekiah took naïve pride in showing the messengers his entire store of treasures: the silver, the gold, the spices, the precious oils, and his whole armory.

Isaiah the prophet was horrified. "The day will come," he predicted, "when these same Babylonians will come and carry off everything you possess!"

"If it must be, it must," said the king. "But at least there is peace in our time."

Neither peace nor piety, however, marked the half century that followed Hezekiah's noble reign. His son, Manasseh, started off wickedly, dealing in witchcraft, sacrificing his own children, and setting up carved idols in the house of God. As punishment he was carried off in brass chains by the Assyrians. Ransomed and restored to his kingdom, he behaved much better, but when his successor showed signs of starting off in like fashion, the people lost patience. They gave him two years, then they slew him and made his little son, Josiah, king in his stead.

Josiah (639–609 B.C.) was only eight years old when he began to reign, and by the time he was grown the heathen images were pretty well cleared out of the groves and high places. The cult of Yahweh, in fact, appears to have prospered during the reign of child kings, no doubt because the priesthood formed a royal protectorate. Josiah turned his own attention to repairing the Temple, which was badly dilapidated by the vicissitudes of several centuries.

He sent his secretary, Shaphan the scribe, to Hilkiah the high priest. "Have him count the money in the Temple," ordered the king, "and give it to those who have the oversight of the sanctuary, to repair it."

"Those," of course, were the Levites, the singers and musicians, the scribes and other officers. Joyfully, because for many years they had not dared do so, they hired carpenters and bought quarried stone and stout timbers to reinforce the beams of the building. Once again the sound of psalms being rehearsed rang jubilantly from the singers' chambers, counterpointed by the sound of workmen's tools as the neglected sanctuary was systematically restored under the watchful eyes of the Temple musicians and their fellow Levites.

Many of the musical instruments had also suffered damage. These underwent a thorough restoration at the hands of the Levitical performers themselves, "all who were skilful with instruments of music."

The treasury coins were kept in large heavy jars, sometimes half as high as a man. Finding safe hiding places for these during the frequent lootings and threats of invasion over the years had been a recurrent concern of the priests and Levites. Some of the jars had been so carefully secreted in niches and behind walls that they had been forgotten.

It was while Hilkiah the high priest was searching through one of these forgotten jars that he came upon something that sent him trembling with awe and excitement to Shaphan, the king's secretary.

"I have found the Book of the Law of Moses," quavered Hilkiah. The two men gazed in wonder at the holy relic, which none of their generation had ever laid eyes on. For a century, perhaps two, it had lain where reverent hands had hidden it, against the imminent threat of defilement by any one of a dozen raiding parties—the Philistines perhaps, or the Arabs, the Syrians, the Edomites, or the Assyrians.

Swiftly Shaphan carried it to the palace, and before the gilded throne he carefully unrolled the brittle parchment. Laboriously he read to the king the faded antique writing, and as he read the words that Moses had set down nearly a thousand years before, the king rent his clothes and wept.

At once he bade his counselors inquire of the Lord concerning the scroll. "For great is the wrath of the Lord," he said, "because our fathers have not harkened unto the words of this book."

They went to the prophetess Huldah, whose husband was related to the keeper of the king's wardrobe. Huldah's oracle, doubtless delivered to some kind of music, was that greater evils than had ever yet befallen the land would shortly come upon it, but that King Josiah, because of his uprightness of heart, would not live to see them. The king no doubt received the news with mixed feelings.

To the Temple in a body went the elders, the prophets, the liturgical functionaries, and the king. There, before the entire congregation that had assembled in the courtyard, Josiah stood on the high dais of the kings while at his side a Levitical singer clearly and reverently chanted the words of the sacred scroll. When he was done, the king made everyone stand and take an oath to keep the Lord's commandments and the laws that were written in the book.

After this they made ready to celebrate the most elaborate Passover feast that had ever been held. As an essential part of the ceremonies the Levitical singers, "who taught all Israel and were holy to the Lord," were ordered to prepare themselves for regular service, after the traditional order of their courses, and to stand again in the holy place to utter psalms of praise and thanksgiving.

To maintain the musical accompaniment unbroken through the almost continuous service of offerings for seven days, the singers evidently followed a set order of rotation. Here again we have an instance of the continuing organization that preserved intact, over long stretches of time and wholly by oral means, a musical ritual that could resume in all details with fidelity to the ancient tradition.

Tradition was all-important to the sacred service, much of whose strength lay in the fact that it furnished a direct emotional link with the golden days of the early kings and the heroic age of Moses. As living repositories of the sacred tradition, the Levitical singers fell easily into the routine of their ancient office and took their appointed place as in all the generations past, "according to the command of David, and Asaph, and Heman, and Jeduthun the king's seer."

Throughout his entire reign Josiah was a solicitous patron of music and musicians. Unhappily for both, he met a hero's death at the age of thirty-nine, on the battlefield against the Pharaoh Neco. He was buried at Jerusalem in the tomb of his fathers, and all Judah and Jerusalem mourned for him. The Temple musicians had special reason to mourn the loss of a ruler who had been so sympathetic to their cause.

And all the singing men and singing women spoke of Josiah in their lamentations, unto this day; and they made them an ordinance in Israel.

The strongly organized Levitical guild was influential enough to arrange that a permanent national day of mourning was established for him. No other king has ever been honored in this way. Centuries later the memory of this music-minded monarch was still green, as we learn from the book of Jesus Sirach:

The memorial of Josiah is like the incense prepared by the work of the apothecary; it shall be sweet as honey in every mouth, and as music in a banquet of wine.

16

BY THE WATERS OF
BABYLON

During the next twenty years several puppet kings were whisked
across the throne alternately by Egypt and Babylonia. Then the
catastrophe the prophets had foretold fell upon the land of ancient
Israel.

Nebuchadnezzar, King of Chaldea, besieged the Holy City,
broke its walls, and burned the sacred Temple to the ground. The
flames of the sanctuary and the royal palace fed each other in a
furious orgy of crackling timbers and crashing stones, and writhed
upward symbolically merging the sacred and profane. On the
slopes below, flames from a score of lesser palaces lighted the scene
of devastation and death that shortly before had been the Golden
City of Jerusalem.

The slaughter, although great, was not indiscriminate. Israel's
reputation as a nation of sages and singers whose poetry proclaimed the omnipotence of a single moral God had long intrigued the rulers of countries less singularly committed. Along
with the spoil taken to Chaldea of gold and sacred treasures went
the flower of Israel; children of the royal family and youths from
the Levitical aristocracy were carried east to enhance the court of

Babylon. Craftsmen, scholars, and musicians were taken also to enrich the culture of their conquerors. Only the simplest farming class remained to work the fields of Judah for their new Chaldean overlords.

It looked as if the music of Israel were doomed to extinction, along with the rest of its culture. In Babylon the psalmists cried the grief of a stricken people too proud to entertain their conquerors with songs designed for the ear of God:

> On the willows we hung up our lyres,
>   For . . . our captors required of us songs,
> And our tormentors, mirth, saying:
>   "Sing us one of the songs of Zion!"

How shall we sing the Lord's song in a foreign land?

But music was too closely knit to the fabric of their lives for the Hebrews to reject it wholly. As throughout all of their history, music would be a solace and a safety valve for the emotions of a people smarting under alien rule. It helped unite the exiles in Babylon as it had once helped unite the captive children of Israel during their long Egyptian bondage.

Songs kept alive the memory of their homeland. At work the homesick toiler cheered himself by humming a scrap of Judean folksong. When his family gathered in the evening, songs remembered from happier days drew them together in indissoluble unity, reaffirming and preserving the ancient traditions. Customs that may once have seemed irksome or without meaning now came to be cherished for their new role as part of a shared inheritance.

If the Hebrew nation was forged under Egyptian bondage, it was tempered and annealed in the years of Babylonian captivity. Distance from their homeland lent perspective, and for the first time the people undertook to assess their heritage. The backslidings and apostasy that had scarred their covenant with the God of their fathers belonged to an age they would never again be part of. What prosperity and power and the imprecations of all the prophets had not been able to do, adversity now accomplished.

Alien and enslaved, a thousand miles from the Promised Land, the people of Israel entered into full recognition of their covenant

with the God of Abraham. From this time on, their adherence to
their faith was to be a steadfast, stubborn, and to the ages that
were to witness it, often infuriating instance of a total spiritual
commitment.

As an intimate part of their religious expression the sacred musical liturgy assumed a new role. So long as the Temple existed
music had served to embellish the sacrifice, which had continued
to be performed despite the growing disapproval of the later
prophets. It is probable that initially the sacrifice had been a concession to the customs of antiquity, which were too widespread
and too strongly entrenched for a young, revolutionary cult to
eliminate entirely.

The dedication of livestock designed largely for public feasts
or the sustenance of an ordained priesthood was intended to substitute for the practice of human sacrifice then universal among
early peoples. It was perhaps the single greatest step forward in the
ethical evolution of man.

In time, men of emancipated mind and sensitive spirit decried
even this concession to the dark reaches of the primal mind. A
hundred years before, the prophet Isaiah had sung:

> What to me is the multitude of your sacrifices?
>   Says the Lord;
> I have had enough of burnt offerings of rams,
>   And the fat of fed beasts;
> I do not delight in the blood of bulls,
>   Or of lambs, or of he-goats.
>
> When you come to appear before me,
>   Who requires of you
>   This trampling of my courts? . . .
> Come now, let us reason together,
>   Says the Lord.

It was not easy to uproot a tradition of such long standing. In
the enforced adjustment of their captivity, however, more than
one change had to be made. Over the centuries following the
exodus from Egypt the concept of Yahweh had developed from

that of a desert deity to the God of the land of Israel. But now the people were far from the land of Israel. The altar to their God was gone, the Temple also, and the holy vessels of the sacrifice. The physical trappings by which they had sought to contain or to woo him were no longer available to them.

But two things remained: their faith in him and the joy of song to exalt him. In the bonds of foreign slavery the people of Israel achieved the truest freedom: the realization that wherever they went they could take with them, invisibly and inviolably, the concept of a just and loving God. And with this realization the need for music to glorify his name became an even more passionate concern of the Levitical poets and singers.

Faithfully they continued to compose psalms and prayers, and to teach these to the people, openly when possible, in secret when necessary. It was during these stringent times that a great portion of the psalms in book four of the Psalter were probably written:

> Hear my prayer, O Lord . . .
> In the day of my distress!
>
> Thou wilt arise and have pity on Zion . . .
> For thy servants hold her stones dear.

Captivity is never an enviable condition, but it is not recorded that under their Chaldean captors the Hebrews were badly treated. The Euphrates basin had been the ancient cradle of the Hebrews themselves. Over the intervening centuries they had assimilated the customs of many other nations and had developed their own system of beliefs and habits, but the active commerce of the ancient Near East had kept alive many cultural ties.

Their accomplishments in the arts of poetry and music and the scholarly vision of their prophets must have struck a sympathetic chord among the Babylonians, who were themselves heirs to the rich culture of the Sumerians. Not only was their learning respected, but the Hebrews were permitted to take an active part in the country's political life, as we learn from the Book of Daniel.

Daniel and his three young friends, whom the Babylonians renamed Shadrach, Mesach, and Abednego, were among those taken captive to adorn the court of Babylon, "youths without blemish, handsome and skillful . . . endowed with . . . learning and competent to serve in the king's palace."

The lads proved so competent, in fact, that before long the king made Daniel ruler over the whole province of Babylon and appointed his three friends to administer its affairs.

Things were going well indeed. But then the king made a golden image a hundred feet high and reared it up on the plain outside of Babylon. He assembled his satraps and the officials of all the provinces to attend the dedication of the image. And when all were standing before it, the king's herald proclaimed: "You are commanded, O peoples, nations, and languages, that when you hear the sound of the *karna, mashrokita, kathros, sabbeka, pesanterin, sumponyah,* and every kind of music, you are to fall down and worship the golden image that King Nebuchadnezzar has set up; and whoever does not fall down and worship shall immediately be cast into a burning fiery furnace."

Thereafter, needless to say, the instant the people heard the sound of all these instruments they fell down and worshiped the golden image for their very lives. But certain Chaldeans who were jealous of the Hebrews reported to the king that Shadrach, Mesach, and Abednego were not worshiping the golden image.

In furious rage, Nebuchadnezzar commanded they be brought before him. "Is it true," he demanded, "that you do not serve my gods or worship the golden image that I have set up? Now if you are ready, when you hear the sound of the karna, mashrokita, kathros, sabbeka, pesanterin, sumponyah, and every kind of music, to fall down and worship the image that I have made, well and good; but if you do not worship, you shall immediately be cast into a burning fiery furnace; and who is the god that will deliver you out of my hands?"

"If it be so," replied the three youths, "if it be so that our God is able to deliver us, then he will do it. But if not, be it known to you, O king, that we still will not serve your gods or worship the golden image that you have set up."

Then Nebuchadnezzar, full of fury, ordered the furnace heated seven times hotter than usual, and the three lads were cast, mantles, tunics, hats, and all, into the burning fiery furnace. But then astonishment overwhelmed the king and his counselors. Nebuchad-

nezzar approached as near to the furnace door as was comfortable
and called: "Shadrach, Mesach, and Abednego, servants of the
Most High God, come forth and come here!"

And at this the three young men stepped out of the furnace as
handsome as ever and not a hair of their heads singed. To make up
for any inconvenience he may have caused them, Nebuchadnezzar
generously promoted all three lads and thereafter treated the Jews
with marked consideration.

But exactly what were the karna, mashrokita, kathros, sabbeka,
pesanterin, and sumponyah?

To this day, no one knows for sure. That the first five are the
names of musical instruments seems certain, and of the more than
a dozen versions of the Bible, each has made its own attempt to
identify them. They have been translated in the English versions as
cornet, flute, harp, sackbut, psaltery, and dulcimer; as horn, pipe,
lyre, trigon, harp, and bagpipe, among many combinations. Other
suggestions would include the trumpet, rote, guitar, double flute,
and hurdy-gurdy as possibilities.

None of them, however, takes dramatic considerations into account. Daniel and Nebuchadnezzar lived in the first half of the
sixth century B.C. The Book of Daniel was not written until the
middle of the second century B.C. Thus the events related took
place four centuries prior to their writing (about 165 B.C.). Portions
of the Book of Daniel, moreover, were originally written in Aramaic (verses 2:4 to 7:28), the language of Chaldea, where the
events occurred, and only later were translated into biblical Hebrew.

However, when the author of the Book of Daniel came to list
the instruments used at the ceremony before Nebuchadnezzar's
golden idol, he avoided both Hebrew and Aramaic names, wishing
apparently to stress the exotic, pagan character of an occasion that
must have been so repugnant to the Hebrews. None of the instruments he named is mentioned anywhere else in the Bible, indicating that they had no part in the music of the Hebrews, and were
quite likely unknown to them.

Where he got the names we cannot tell. Since he was writing in
the Hellenistic period some understandably show a Greek influence. Most, however, appear to be of Asiatic origin. After the fall

of Troy in the eleventh century B.C., or around the time of David, the Greeks colonized Asia Minor and took over certain of its instruments, improving and embellishing them. In time, these improved instruments found their way back to the country of their origin and were reintroduced there with new Greek names.

Hebrew instruments of biblical times had similar names in Aramaic. Thus karna, listed first among those of Nebuchadnezzar's orchestra, may have been the Aramaic equivalent of the Hebrew keren (neat horn). More probably it denoted a foreign instrument of the horn type, to convey the exotic effect the author sought.

From the sound of the word, early Greek translators took mashrokita to mean their own Pan's pipe, the syrinx, whose row of graduated pipes produced a kind of hissing sound. A similar Hebrew word, *sharak*, meaning to "hiss" or "whistle," likewise may have been the root of mashrokita, although this seems unlikely, since the Hebrews did not even know the instrument. Perhaps another Semitic root served, but the most plausible theory is that the Greeks were right and mashrokita was really the early Hellenic syrinx. All English Bibles translate it as either pipe or flute, thus missing the point of the story, in which the exotic character of the mashrokita is expressed by its very name.

The term kathros is less thorny. Everyone agrees it is a variation of the Greek word kithara (lyre). But this still does not tell us enough, for the kithara denoted a different type in as many countries. Was the kathros of Nebuchadnezzar's orchestra an Arabian lute? A long-necked guitar from Persia? A Nubian lyre? Or was it the Berber's guitar known to the Egyptians? We can at least assume that it was not the Hebrew kinnor, since the author's whole purpose was to stress the un-Hebrew character of the ceremony. English Bibles, early and modern, including the Jewish version, translate the word as "harp." Only Moffat and the Revised Standard Version render it appropriately as "lyre."

The sabbeka may originally have come from Asia, but it has been identified with the *sambyke* of the Greeks and the *sambuca* of the Romans, among both of whom it was a popular instrument at banquets. Roman writers describe it as triangular, with four strings and a rather harsh, high tone. Its high pitch made it a suitable accompaniment for the female voice, and this may have been one reason it was a favorite with girls of ill repute.

It seems likely that the sabbeka was some kind of horizontal angular harp, similar to the triangular sambyke of the Greeks. Among English Bibles, the Jewish and Revised Standard Versions approximate it as "trigon." The Authorized and other principal versions use "sackbut," an instrument that would correspond to today's trombone. Only the similarity of the terms could have caused such gratuitous reasoning, for the sackbut did not make its appearance until the late Renaissance.

The similarity between Nebuchadnezzar's pesanterin and the Greek word for harp, psalterion, has also led many to think them different words for the same instrument. However, the root of pesanterin would seem to be *santir*, which is the name of the Arabian dulcimer. In Arabian, *pi-santir* means "small santir," or small dulcimer, and this is the term that was taken over into the Chaldean (Aramaic) language.

A carving of one such instrument found in the ruins of Nineveh shows it to have been apparently square, with ten strings, held horizontally before the player and struck with small sticks. That it was not the Greek psalterion is proved by the fact that the early Church fathers described this as having its sounding body on the upper part, which would have been impossible for the Arabian santir. Again, Bible versions differ. Moffat uses "lute," the Revised Standard Version "harp." Most versions use "psaltery."

None of the mysterious terms has caused more speculation than sumponyah. The modern Italian word for bagpipe is *sampugna*, whose resemblance to *samponia*, the word for an ancient Syrian-Greek instrument, has convinced many that the sumponyah of Nebuchadnezzar's orchestra was a bagpipe. The bagpipe, however, was not yet in existence when Daniel and his friends were captives in Babylon.

Sumponyah may not mean a musical instrument at all; it may have been an adaptation of the Greek word *symphonia*, meaning to perform together concordantly. Following the usual order of biblical chronicling, the instruments of the Babylon orchestra were grouped according to their species: first the wind instruments (karna, mashrokita), then the strings (kathros, sabbeka, pesanterin), and lastly sumponyah, with "every kind of music."

This reflects the procedure of Oriental musical performances, in which the solo instruments first play singly, joining forces at the end of a piece in what might be called a symphonia, a playing in ensemble. Finally, "every kind of music" suggests that to the instruments already mentioned there were added drums, cymbals, sistrums and the other percussion instruments that were never lacking in Oriental performances.

We might, therefore, translate the command of Nebuchadnezzar something like this: "At what time you hear the sound of the horn, syrinx, lyre, and trigon playing together with every kind of instrument, etc."

Despite all evidence to the contrary, the controversy as to whether sumponyah was a bagpipe has continued into recent times. Most English Bibles interpret it as a musical instrument, the Authorized and American Versions as a dulcimer. Douay translates it as "symphony." Moffat, the Jewish Version, and the Revised Standard Version stand firm on "bagpipe."

Whatever the instruments at the court of Nebuchadnezzar may have been, their very ambiguity is revealing. It proves that the captive Hebrews were as determined to keep the alien musical practices of their captors out of their own zealously guarded musical liturgy as they were to keep the pagan gods of Babylon out of their religion.

That they succeeded in both was due in great measure to an institution that came into its own in the alien climate of Babylon. This was the synagogue. In Judah and Israel the synagogue had started out humbly enough as a convenience for those who were too far from Jerusalem or were unable for one reason or another to visit the Holy City. Utilitarian, designed for the studious, and with none of the glamor and sacred trappings of the Temple, it had played a prosy part in the everyday life of the people.

But for the exiles in Babylon the synagogue took on new meaning. Nothing could take the place of their destroyed Temple, but so long as they could gather together to reaffirm their ancient faith through the prayers and sacred psalms of their liturgy, they could remain a unified people in the midst of whatever alien surroundings.

By providing such a place the synagogue quickly became the nucleus of Hebrew religious life in exile. Without fanfare, so as not to arouse the ill will of their captors, the Hebrews took to meeting regularly, perhaps in some modest shelter, perhaps in one or another private home in their several communities. Unlike the Temple, which could be destroyed, the synagogue might exist wherever a group of the faithful met to pray. That the psalms, with their beauty of imagery and song, here played a vital part in creating an atmosphere of reverence and of hope in the Almighty can scarcely be doubted.

Designed to accompany the elaborate and complicated ritual of the sacrifice, Levitical singing now came to symbolize the entire ceremony in a way that Samuel himself must have hoped it one day might. Soberly, supplicating now, the psalms filled the little houses of prayer, coloring the meager furbishings of exile with some of the glory of past observances.

To a generation growing up with no memory of Temple tradition, the reading and singing of psalms commemorating some historic event or expressing some aspect of devotion was an educational process that kept the seeds of Hebrew culture vigorously alive. For half a century the indefatigable efforts of the Levitical musicians and scribes continued to make this possible. Then, as if in answer to the ceaseless outpouring of songful prayers, deliverance came to the captive Hebrews.

17

RESTORING AN ANCIENT
HOMELAND

IN THE YEAR 529 B.C. Cyrus, King of Persia, overthrew Babylon. The conquerors of the Hebrews were now themselves the conquered, as the prophet Jeremiah had long ago foreseen:

> Hark! a cry from Babylon!
> The noise of great destruction from
> The land of the Chaldeans! . . .

> Her images are put to shame,
> Her idols are dismayed. . . .

> Her bulwarks have fallen,
> Her walls are thrown down.

It was a fateful hour for the Hebrew people and for their music. Both might easily have vanished and left no trace, absorbed into the culture of a conqueror like countless other nations of the ancient world. If this had happened, the entire course of Western thought would have been far different.

But it did not happen. The Persian king's sympathetic interest in the captive Hebrews is one of the nobler pages in the annals of antiquity. No doubt the Levitical orders, the poets and the sages, turned their considerable powers of eloquence to persuading the new ruler to let them return to their homeland. Persia itself had a lofty culture, and Cyrus must have felt a certain affinity of spirit as he listened to the exalted sentiments of the psalms:

> For the Lord is a great God,
> And a great King above all gods.
> In his hand are the depths of the earth;
> The heights of the mountains are his also.
> The sea is his, for he made it . . .
> His hands formed the dry land.
>
> O come, let us worship and bow down,
> Let us kneel before the Lord, our Maker!

Did the Levite choirs choose for the king's ear psalms calculated to rouse in him compassion, awe, or simply the reflection that it might be wise to have the goodwill of this "King above all gods?" At any rate, Cyrus of Persia listened, and was moved. He made a proclamation throughout the land and, with curious prescience, even took the trouble to put it in writing.

> The Lord, the God of Heaven, has given me all the king-doms of the earth, and he has charged me to build him a house at Jerusalem, which is in Judah. Whoever is among you of all his people, may his God be with him, and let him go up to Jerusalem . . . and rebuild the house of the Lord.

Then, with rare generosity, he brought out from the pagan temples the holy vessels that Nebuchadnezzar had carried away from Jerusalem—more than five thousand gold and silver basins and bowls and censers—and gave them to the returning Hebrews.

Cyrus further charged that each returning pilgrim should receive all practical assistance for his journey, in addition to any freewill offerings for the new temple. Thereupon, the heads of the Hebrew families, with the priests and Levites who were minded to return to

Jerusalem, made ready to set out, amply provisioned with household goods, money, and beasts of burden by their friends and relatives. It was the first of several such caravans that would make the long overland journey to the Holy Land during the following century.

But not all of the Hebrews elected to return. Many who had been born in Babylon considered it their home. Many others were too old to make the long hazardous trip, despite their longing to see once more the land they had known as children. Still others held high offices throughout the provinces of Chaldea, like Daniel, who continued to prosper under the Persians as he had under the Chaldeans. Such persons were not minded to leave a land that had treated them so well, to return to a country they knew largely from stories told by their elders.

Moreover, the admirable tolerance of the new Persian king guaranteed that they could continue their faith and its traditions with as much freedom as in their original homeland—and with more security, for their religious fortunes had varied too cruelly under their own kings not to have left thought-provoking memories.

Under the benign reign of Cyrus many of the older scholars and sages chose to remain in Babylon. There they would compile a body of Hebrew teachings that would become the Babylonian Talmud, the most comprehensive commentary on Hebrew law. Some of the priests and Levites also remained in Babylon, serving a tradition that was to preserve to our own day many of their national and religious customs, as well as the character of psalmody in much the same form as it was instituted by David.

But if many Hebrews chose to remain behind, enough burned with a zeal for repatriation to make up an assembly of some 50,000 people who set off with high resolve to reclaim the land of their fathers. That many journeymen and artisans were among them goes without saying, but the only professional group mentioned is "two hundred male and female singers." These were evidently secular musicians, for the Levitical singers, the sons of Asaph, are listed elsewhere as one hundred and twenty-eight.

Since the Levitical singers were an essential part of the returning party, they perhaps warranted special mention, particularly when we consider that their order chronicled many of the events of Hebrew history and was naturally quick to point out the extent to which its own members participated.

But such a pioneering group would seem to have scant need for the luxury of so many secular singers. Their inclusion in the ranks of those dedicated to restoring a devastated land proves the essential role music played in the life of the people wherever they might be, and the mention of professional musicians in a chronicling so chary of more crucial details proves the high regard in which their art was held.

The journey over mountain and wasteland took several months, but the road was well traveled by the trading caravans that plied constantly between the Mediterranean and the Euphrates. It was not without its dangers, however, from raiding parties of Arab nomads or sudden ambushes by hostile tribes. The caravan stayed close together, traveling by day and at nightfall setting up a city of tents, lighted by thousands of campfires.

In some ways it was not unlike the earlier journey taken by their ancestors. coming up from Egypt to the young, sweet land of Canaan. They too had camped at nightfall, marching through mountain passes and over the arid plains on their way to claim a homeland they had never seen. Now their descendants were marching westward to reclaim that homeland, which most of them had never seen either.

But they were a much older people than the raw, untempered Hebrew tribes who had fought and clawed their way through a wilderness to the glory of an empire. They had a history now, with its burden of memories—splendid ones, and shameful ones as well. They had pitted their strength of arm and mind against a dozen nations. They had built a city to the Lord and they had served him in his Temple. Their singers had preached the glory of God, and their prophets the need for humility before him. They had a treasury of song and a literature that would live while the earth endured. They had the will to pursue their far and curious destiny.

Turning homeward after a lifetime spent in exile, they went forward joyfully but slowly, for there were many little ones among them. Slowly they climbed the rising slopes above the Jordan plain, and as they climbed they sang.

Was it perhaps one of the Songs of Ascent, uttered in gladness and hope as they looked across the Kidron Valley toward the crest where the Temple of Solomon once had stood?

> When the Lord returned us to Zion,
> We were like those who dream.
> Then our mouth was filled with laughter,
> And our tongue with shouts of joy . . .

> The Lord has done great things for us;
> We are glad.

Or was it a plea for divine help in the difficult task they were about to undertake?

> Do good to Zion in thy good pleasure;
> Rebuild the walls of Jerusalem.

They would need help. They had not expected that it would be easy. But in wealthy Babylon, with its handsome buildings and material comforts, they had not envisioned the desolation they would find. Before their eyes the land of their fathers lay waste and stricken, the fields untilled, the orchards a tangle of untrimmed branches. The majority of those who had been spared by their captors to work the land had risen years before against their foreign overlords and fled to the dubious sanctuary of Egypt. Only where a poverty-stricken few scratched a meager living from the soil could an occasional patch of green be spotted amid the brown dust.

It was a disheartening view. But the remembered prediction of Isaiah may have given them fresh courage:

> For the Lord will comfort Zion . . .
> Joy and gladness will be found in her,
> Thanksgiving and the voice of song . . .

> Instead of the thorn shall come up the cypress,
> Instead of the brier . . . the myrtle.

Buoyed by such thoughts perhaps, the weary repatriates separated to find what might remain of the towns and villages they had once called home.

It soon became clear that the devastation was spiritual as well as economic. The local population, lacking all intellectual leadership, had turned utterly to the alien religions of the area. In the northern province now lived the Samaritans, a people only half Hebrew, who followed the gods and customs of the lands from which the Assyrians had brought them.

On every side the return of the exiles was viewed with suspicion and resentment. Uneasy in the face of so much hostility, they met together in Jerusalem at the Passover season and built an altar to the Lord. The foundations of the Temple were not yet laid, but the need for some cementing agency was imperative.

In Babylon, where the best minds of Jewry had operated, they had foregone the traditional acts of sacrifice. But here in Judah they had to reckon with the local remnants of their people who had reverted to superstition and idolatry. To reclaim them, if possible, was a moral duty, and restoring the awesomeness of the ancient ritual may have seemed the surest way to impress them.

Or perhaps the land itself exerted its own dark potency. At any rate, the continuous ceremonies of burnt offerings once more resumed on the altar built to Yahweh, and the hundred and twenty-eight Levitical singers took up their hereditary task of accompanying these with song.

That the traditional psalms and their antiphonal manner of delivery had been carefully preserved during the half century in Babylon now became clear. When the builders laid the foundation of the Temple, the priests in their vestments came forward with their silver trumpets, and the singers, "with their brethren over against them," lifted their voices to praise and give thanks, according to the ordinance of David.

And as the divided choirs sang the familiar refrain of faith and thanksgiving, "For he is good, for his steadfast love endures forever toward Israel," a great shout went up from the thousands of people unable to contain their emotion. But while the younger ones shouted for joy, many of the old men who remembered the glory of the First Temple broke into loud weeping, so that one could hardly distinguish between the shouts of joy and the sounds of weeping.

Their hopes, however, were premature. The neighboring peoples did everything they could to hinder the Temple's progress. The Samaritans wrote to Cyrus' successor, warning him that if the walls of Jerusalem, "that rebellious and wicked city," were allowed to go up, he might look for no further tribute from the Hebrews and could expect to lose possession of the entire province.

Back came a decree "that these men be made to cease and that this city be not rebuilt. Why should damage grow to the hurt of the king?"

Triumphantly their enemies hastened to Jerusalem and forced the Hebrews to leave off working on the Temple. For nearly two decades it lay unfinished. Thorns grew up among the piled timbers and small gray lizards confidently sunned themselves on the gray stones. Once again it looked as if the songs of praise would never again resound in the house of the Lord.

But one thing ancient Israel could always count on—the tongue-lashings of its prophets. Meager harvests and a threatening drought gave point to the counsel of Haggai:

You have looked for much, and lo, it came to little. Why? says the Lord of hosts. Because of my house that lies in ruins, while you busy yourselves each with his own house. Therefore the heavens above you have withheld the dew, and the earth has withheld its produce.

Stung to remorseful activity, the people returned to work on the Temple. When the Persian vice-regent asked, "Who gave you a decree to finish this structure?" they stoutly answered, "Cyrus!" And they refused to budge from their labors.

To see if such a decree existed, the vice-regent wrote to the king of Persia, this time a king named Darius. Darius ordered a search among the royal archives, and there, to be sure, was found a scroll recording the decree of Cyrus: "Let the house be rebuilt . . . and let the cost be paid from the royal treasury."

"Now, therefore," wrote back Darius, "keep away."

Let the work on this house of God alone; let the governor of the Jews and the elders of the Jews rebuild this house of

God on its site. Moreover . . . the cost is to be paid to these men in full and without delay from the royal revenue, the tribute of (your own) province.

And whatever . . . the priests may require, let it be given to them day by day without fail, that they may offer pleasing sacrifices to this God of heaven, and pray for the life of the king and his sons.

The benevolent Darius further decreed that out of "the king's goods" the Temple functionaries, including the singers, should receive "expenses . . . and that which they have need of."

Thereafter the work of the Temple went forward so fast that four years later it was completed.

It was less grandiose than the First Temple. There was little to suggest the early glory that had shaken the courts of Solomon with rapturous song. If any of the old men were still alive who remembered the First Temple, their tears might well have flowed afresh with regret for a magnificence that would not be again.

For them it could not be. Wood and stone could not again command the glory of a sanctuary that had become transfigured by the tears and prayers of exile. But for the younger people it was an hour of triumph. They had built their own Temple to the Lord, with strong and willing hands. Its dedication was celebrated joyfully and with all the pomp their frugal circumstances could provide.

One attribute at least remained in undiminished splendor, the beautiful voices of the sacred choirs, lifted purely to heaven in the Thirtieth Psalm:

> I will extol thee, O Lord, for thou hast drawn me up,
> And hast not let my foes rejoice over me.

> Thou hast turned for me my mourning into dancing,
> Thou hast loosed my sackcloth and girded me with gladness.

Nonetheless, the task of restoring unity to the land proved beyond their powers. Too many alien influences had been too long at work. The religious renaissance they had sought to achieve did not come about, and without this there could be no hope of political independence. Some strong organizing intellect was needed to consolidate their sturdy pioneer labors.

Such an intellect was being honed in scholarly sessions in the synagogues of Babylon. Ezra the priest, the scribe, had set his heart to study the Law of the Lord and to teach it throughout Israel. Grieved by reports of disharmony in his homeland, he persuaded the reigning king, Artaxerxes I, to grant him full plenipotentiary powers to go to Jerusalem. With him he took some 1,500 of his people, many singers and musical instruments for the Temple, and an unlimited drawing account on the royal treasury.

A man of remarkable attainments, Ezra the scribe arrived in Jerusalem with full authority to enforce obedience to the Mosaic Law throughout the entire province. This meant that the Temple services would now have to accommodate many more worshipers and that the Levitical singers would go on an even more active schedule.

Ezra also brought from his sovereign a veritable magna charta of new privileges for the singers. Their fees were now expressly stipulated, and as his crowning benefaction the Persian monarch granted to them, along with the other Temple officeholders, complete exemption from taxes:

> Also we announce to you, that touching any of the priests and Levites, the singers, porters, Nethinim, or servants of this house of God, it shall not be lawful to impose tribute, impost, or toll upon them.

From now on the singers were not only state functionaries but tax-exempt ministers of the sanctuary—a still further advance in their gradually rising status in the life of ancient Israel.

18

A MUSICAL RENAISSANCE IN JUDAH

EZRA DID what he had set out to do. He rallied the people to a new sense of nationhood and a renewed allegiance to the faith of their fathers.

His efforts were aided greatly by the arrival of a man who would back up with military acumen Ezra's zeal to consolidate the Hebrews in the ethical and intellectual sphere.

This was Nehemiah, a young Hebrew who had been cupbearer to King Artaxerxes. Nehemiah had been born in Babylon, but when he heard that his brothers in Jerusalem were actively menaced by the neighboring peoples, he fell to such prolonged weeping and fasting that the king inquired the reason.

Impressed by the young man's depth of feeling, the king appointed him governor of the province of Judah and sent him with a contingent of soldiers to rebuild the wall around Jerusalem. Nehemiah had as high a sense of purpose as Ezra, but he had in addition a flair for the dramatic, which could turn an act of drudgery for a people into a passionate dedication.

Arrived in Jerusalem, he told no one what he had come to do. Quietly one night he rode off by himself and inspected the broken boundaries of the city. He saw the desolation that had bent the people's spirit. He saw the gates, which had been destroyed by fire, and the blackened stones of the wall lying weedgrown in the moonlight.

The next day he called the people together. He did not say that he was empowered to make them rebuild the wall. He spoke of their ancient pride and of the ruins of their holy city lying exposed to the sneers of hostile neighbors. He spoke of many things, and at the end he spoke of what was uppermost in his heart. And when he had finished, there was not a son of Israel who was not ready to roll up his sleeves and begin the task.

Grouping themselves by crafts and by families, they made each group responsible for a section of the wall. Next to the priests worked the men of Jericho; next to the goldsmiths, the perfumers. The merchants, the servants, the district rulers, the Levites, formed a circle of workers around the city. And not only the men. Side by side with their husbands and brothers worked the women, reclaiming from the weeds and rubble whatever stones were not too blackened or broken for reuse.

The jeers of their enemies kept pace with the work. "If a fox goes up on it, he will break down their stone wall!" scoffed Tobiah the Ammonite. Tobiah had power and high connections, but his offer to help had been snubbed because he could not prove his Hebrew lineage.

In spite of everything the wall rose steadily, and presently it was joined together to half its height. With this their enemies grew concerned, and they conspired together to attack the Hebrews. When Nehemiah learned of this he stationed the people by their families in low areas behind the wall, with their swords, spears, and bows. "Now fight," he said, "for your sons, your daughters, your wives, and your homes!"

So they frustrated the enemy's plan, but when they returned to work on the wall, "each with one hand labored on the work, and with the other held his weapon." Atop the wall at Nehemiah's side constantly stood a man with a shofar, ready at any moment to sound an alarm. For, as Nehemiah told the people, "The work is great and widely spread, and we are separated on the wall, far from one another. In the place where you hear the sound of the trumpet, rally to us there. Our God will fight for us."

At his order also, those working on the wall remained in the city at night to form a guard. Every day from early dawn until the stars came out they labored on the wall, weapon in hand. The governor himself stood vigil throughout, never removing his clothes until, at the end of fifty-two days, the last stone had been laid in place and the many gates made secure.

In the gala ceremonies that celebrated the wall's completion the Levitical singers throughout Judah took a prominent part. Messengers were dispatched who ". . . sought the Levites in all their places, to bring them to Jerusalem to celebrate the dedication with gladness, with thanksgiving and with singing, with cymbals, harps, and lyres."

All the sons of the ancient tradition of sacred singing gathered together from the suburbs around Jerusalem, where the singers had rebuilt their former villages. Much preliminary rehearsal must have taken place to prepare them for an event that would involve their entire forces as well as most of the population of Judah. Nehemiah's flair for the dramatic was in full swing.

On the appointed day the governor, in his official regalia, brought the princes of Judah upon the wall and divided all the people into two great companies to march in procession around it singing psalms of thanksgiving. To the right upon the wall went half the princes of Judah, the priests with trumpets, and the singers and musicians "with the musical instruments of David the man of God." Before them, as befitted his high standing, went Ezra the scribe. At the Fountain Gate they climbed the city stairs where the wall ascended above the onetime house of David, to the Water Gate on the east.

The other company went with Nehemiah to the left, marching past the Old Gate and the Fish Gate and the three tall watchtowers, and coming to a halt at the Gate of the Guard. Then the two companies, still singing, met at the Temple, where the singers, led by Jezrahiah, "sang one to another" (i.e., antiphonally) psalms of praise to accompany the many offerings. There was much singing, "for God had made them rejoice with great joy."

The chronicle mentions that the women and children also rejoiced, suggesting that whereas they may not have accompanied the men on their procession atop the walls, they took their usual active part in other festivities entailing music and especially dancing.

That such a multitude was able to join in all of the songs as they marched around the wall was owing to the principle of the makam, the melodic kernels upon which their music was based. Backed by a host of trained Temple singers, the marching nobles and officials confidently lifted their voices with the heartiness of men who have done a job fraternally and well.

For such a large open-air occasion many additional musical instruments were needed, so we can assume that substantial orchestral groups accompanied each of the two marching companies. Although pipes are not mentioned, they must have been included on an occasion so patently festive, for their bright piercing timbre was better suited than strings to the outdoor celebration. So universal was the music-making, in any case, that "the joy of Jerusalem was heard afar off."

Once the new walls made the city and the sanctuary safe from attack, the resumption and reorganization of the national and religious institutions were easier. The people cast lots to bring one out of every ten to live in the Holy City, to build up its population and form a protective guard for the Temple and its treasures.

At the Passover season all the people gathered in the square before the Water Gate, for Ezra was about to read to them from the Torah, the book of the Law, which Moses had codified. In an impressive procession, attended by the priests and the Temple singers, Ezra the scribe brought the sacred book before the congregation. Although there is no mention of music here, the carrying of the scroll of the Law was undoubtedly accompanied by sacred songs, as in earlier religious ceremonies of the kind.

High above them on a large wooden platform especially built for the occasion, Ezra stood so that all the people could see him clearly. On either side were ranked the priests and singers. When he opened the sacred book, all the people stood. Then Ezra and the singers took turns reading from the book, carefully and distinctly, so that all might understand the meaning of the various laws that Moses had received from the Lord.

The Levitical singers, long trained in the art of transmitting the nobler, utterances of Hebrew literature, projected the commands in the form best calculated to impress the people and stay firmly in their minds. The Bible stresses the fact that "they read in the book distinctly and caused them to understand the reading." This is regarded by many as the first direct allusion to the cantillation of the Torah, the distinct manner, half chanted, half sung, in which it is still delivered today in Jewish synagogues.

From early morning until noon the singers chanted clearly from the book, and that they succeeded in reaching the hearts of their listeners we know, "for all the people wept when they heard the words of the Law," so that Nehemiah and Ezra "and the Levites who taught the people" had to reassure them.

"Do not be grieved," they were told, "for this day is holy to the Lord. Go your way, eat the fat and drink sweet wine, and send portions to him for whom nothing is prepared, for the joy of the Lord is your strength."

Another reform that Ezra brought about was received with less enthusiasm. After their return from exile the Israelites had intermarried freely with the peoples of the land. Leading men, including many priests, had taken wives of Ammonite or Moabite stock. This was contrary to the injunction of Moses, but no one had enforced it until Ezra arrived with a zealot's determination to restore the cult of Yahweh to its pristine estate.

Armed with full legal powers, he demanded that all who had married outside of the cult must put away their foreign wives or be banned from the congregation and stripped of their possessions.

Dutifully the people assembled in sackcloth and with ashes upon their heads to separate themselves from all foreigners and to confess their sins. Among the defectors eager to make amends were six Levites and one singer, a man named Eliashib. Upon the stairs of the Levites stood eight Temple singers, calling the Lord (i.e., singing) with a loud voice. When they had finished, they ordered the assembly to stand and bless the Lord, while the singers chanted the long litany of the people's sins from the days of Abraham.

At the end of it they made a covenant to walk in God's law as given by Moses, to pay all tithes required by the Temple and its functionaries, to desist from all commerce on the Sabbath, and never again to marry foreign women.

Under the leadership of Ezra and Nehemiah the religion of Yahweh once more began to flourish. Ezra had been a leading scholar among the priest-scribes in Babylon, where recording and preserving the chronicles of Hebrew history in written form had been a passionate concern of the exiles. By his time many of the biblical books had presumably been written, among them the Pentateuch, the first five books of the Old Testament, traditionally attributed to Moses, which Hebrews call the Torah.

But many of the other books that are now in the biblical canon were still waiting to be transferred from their ancient oral form to a more stable record on parchment. Ezra's most lasting service was to form a council of some 100 scribes, the *soferim*, which became known as the Great Assembly. Working carefully from various versions, partly written, partly oral, Ezra and his fellow scholars formulated an official religious and civil code for the repatriates, as well as committing to writing several books of the prophets and certain historical accounts covering the period down to their own day. By their efforts also the great Jewish credo, *Sh'ma Yisrael* (Hear, O Israel, the Lord thy God is one God), was formulated, along with such other important parts of the Hebrew ritual as the *Kedusha* (Sanctification) and the *Shemone Esre* (the eighteen Benedictions).

As part of this cultural renaissance music and song were again cultivated. The voices of the Levites in rehearsal resounded once more beside the Gate of Singing. The literary activity sparked by the Great Assembly spilled over into the lyric sphere to join with music in a new outflowering of sacred psalms. It was presumably during this period that a majority of those in the fifth and final book of the Psalter were written.

Within the Temple enclosure an active schedule of devotional offerings kept the singers occupied day and night, for David's ordinance had been that within the sanctuary songs of praise and thanksgiving should mount upward to the Lord without ceasing. In the chronicles of this period the names of two chief singers have been preserved: Jezrahiah, who led the singers at the dedication of the wall, and Mattaniah, of Asaph's progeny, who at some time was "the leader to begin the thanksgiving in prayer," with Bakbukiah as the second soloist, and Abda, of the house of Jeduthun, as the third. Mattaniah apparently played a prominent part in the Levitical order, for his name is mentioned several times.

Since their return more than a century before, the people had been frugal of everything that was not essential to their pioneer estate. Musical instruments fine enough to be consecrated to Yahweh's service were not so abundant as in the days of Solomon, and over the course of years they had lessened in importance as the role of singing increased.

Instruments were now restricted to the bare minimum necessary for an open courtyard, and their numbers were strictly prescribed. In weekday services, according to rabbinic accounts, the trumpeters blew "never less than twenty-one blasts . . . and never more than forty-eight" during the course of the day. Two to six harps were permitted, and when pipes were in order, from two to twelve of these. Pipes might be played before the altar only on the first and second days of Passover, on the festival day of Pentecost, and on the eight days of the Feast of Tabernacles.

On the Sabbaths and the New Year instruments were increased, and trumpets then might run to any number. There were never fewer than nine lyres, and they might be increased "without end." But for percussion only a single pair of cymbals was permitted. The showy character of Solomon's Temple music was exchanged for a sober dignity more in keeping with the venerable institution it had become.

Every effort was made to carry out the ritual precisely as it had originally been ordained. Both Ezra and Nehemiah were sticklers for tradition, and the learned assembly of scribes threw the weight of its scholarly research on the side of historical fidelity.

The reestablishment of sacred music in the Temple began a new era of musical culture that in some respects even surpassed that of Solomon's time. In this new flourishing the Levitical musicians played a paramount role, with a corresponding rise in both their social and artistic standing.

As in earlier days they formed a professional organization that jealously watched over the interests of its members. They occupied a special status in Temple hierarchy, and in any enumeration of Temple officeholders they are always mentioned as a particular group. Their services and their dues were precisely defined, and like the priests they had servants, Nethinim, at their disposal.

According to a register drafted by Nehemiah, the number of Levites living in Jerusalem at the time was 284. Of these "the sons of Asaph, the singers, were over the work of the house of God." Their salary was largely in natural products: "And all Israel . . . in the days of Nehemiah, gave the daily portions for the singers and the gatekeepers."

These were tributes that the people, according to a special assessment, brought regularly to the Temple:

> The tithes of grain, wine, and oil, which were given by commandment to the Levites, singers and gatekeepers.

Further, the Levites received a daily salary from the king's treasury:

> For there was a commandment from the king concerning them, and a settled provision for the singers, as every day required.

The tribute was stored in special chambers situated around the Temple court, and in a position of trust over these Nehemiah placed the priest Eliashib.

Nehemiah had now been in Jerusalem twelve years, and it was time for him to return to Susa and make a personal report to his kindly sovereign. The king must have been pleased with it, for Nehemiah remained at court some little while, no doubt enjoying the city's cosmopolitanism after the stringent years in Jerusalem.

But his heart was still in the Judean highlands, and as soon as he was able, he left the Persian capital behind him and beheld once more the strong-walled citadel of Zion rising proudly upon its tawny hill and crowned by the holy Temple of the Lord.

But as he approached the sanctuary he heard no sound of singing from the rehearsal chambers. Entering the large courtyard he found no people worshiping, no service taking place, no Levites chorusing songs of praise to heaven. The very walls were chill with silence.

Incredulous and horrified, Nehemiah descended on the sons of Aaron.

"Why is the house of God forsaken?" he demanded.

They told him why.

The singers had gone on strike. To a man, they had walked out, with the rest of the Temple Levites, and "were fled every one to his field."

Nehemiah went straight to the root of the matter, and there he found Eliashib the priest. Eliashib had been an unfaithful steward over the tribute chambers. One of the largest he had emptied of its holy vessels, cereal offerings, and frankincense, along with the tithes of grain, oil, and wine belonging to the Levites.

Then Eliashib had moved into it all the household furnishings of a relative by marriage—none other, it developed, than the odious Tobiah, who had earlier intrigued against the building of the wall and even against the governor's life.

Nehemiah, in a passion of anger, promptly threw out Tobiah's stuff, bag and baggage, cleansed the profaned chamber, and brought back the dedicated offerings. But the Levites' provisions of grain, wine, and oil had all been embezzled by Eliashib and Tobiah. It was obvious that the musicians, their complaints unanswered, had taken a strike vote and walked off the job for nonpayment of salary.

Nehemiah persuaded them to return to their Temple duties. To restore the deficit he appealed for voluntary contributions, and the people, glad that the holy service was reestablished, promptly reprovisioned the storage chambers. Eliashib and his accomplices were deposed and new treasurers, who "were counted faithful," were appointed.

Although on the surface the reason for the singers' walkout seems self-evident, it scarcely justifies their jeopardizing the sacred service, which was their hereditary trust. We must suspect a more deep-seated grievance. Their action probably represented a long-standing and bitter contest of power between themselves and the priesthood. The obvious abuses carried on by Eliashib, apparently in connivance with his priestly colleagues, brought matters to a head. Staging the world's first strike, the singers in the house of God provided a precedent for organized labor for all time to come.

What no other class might dare, the Levitical musicians, backed by a solidly organized fraternity, were able to bring off triumphantly. The guild protected its members from any untoward consequences, while their unshakable solidarity obviated any possible strikebreaking. Thus it could only end in the complete victory of the Levites and singers over the powerful caste of the priesthood.

The incident, dramatically told in Nehemiah's own narrative, represents the first recorded struggle of workmen in the history of mankind. All the conventional factors are present: unredressed grievances, union solidarity, protection against reprisals, and finally the appointment of trustees to prevent future abuses. That the musicians of ancient Israel, who had never heard of collective bargaining, managed to gain their end demonstrates both the external and internal strength of their professional organization.

That strength was due to several things: their high artistry, their deep-rooted place in the community, their strong class loyalty, and not least, their own recognition of their practical worth.

19

WOMEN'S ROLE IN ANCIENT
HEBREW MUSIC

THUS FAR THE role of men in the music of ancient Israel seems to have far exceeded that of women. But women's part in both sacred and secular music throughout the ancient Orient is amply documented by any number of written records, as well as by wall paintings and stone carvings—all testifying to their activities as dancers, singers, and instrumentalists.

In Egypt, for instance, music in worship was largely relegated to priestesses. In the New Kingdom almost every woman of noble birth took part as a singer in one or another temple, performing songs "before the beautiful face of god" to the metallic tinkle of the sistrum.

In the music of Assyria and Babylonia women also took an active part in worship as well as in social life. Female singers and musicians are shown in many pictured records, the most beautiful of which is perhaps the bas-relief found in the excavated royal palace at Kuyundchik, showing the triumphal reception of the victorious Assyrian king, Ashurbanipal, entering Susiana (Elam). Here we see a group of musicians, consisting of five men, six women, and nine singing boys, with harps, double oboes, psaltery (a kind of zither), and a hand drum.

But if we were to judge solely from biblical sources, women's role in Hebrew music would appear to have been uncontested only in the dance. As singers, they have been given little importance, and as instrumentalists their contribution is so scant that they would appear to have been actively discouraged from this or, worse, to have shown no aptitude for it.

But there are at least two explanations for the curious reticence of biblical scribes regarding women's part in the musical ritual of the time. One is the editorial playing down of anything confirming the precult paganism of the Hebrews, in which women had played an active role. Another is that a developing antifeminine bias among the priestly caste finally reached such intensity that women were displaced from all ritual functions. Consequently, any allusions to women's participation in these had also to be deleted. Only faint vestiges of them slipped by the keen editorial eyes to remain obscurely tucked away here and there in the Scriptures.

On the other hand, the priestly scribes were not concerned with the role of women in secular music, so that many references to their talents as popular dancers and singers were left intact.

Still another reason for their minimizing the musical ability of women may have been the self-conceit and narrow party spirit of the Levitical music guild. That women also belonged originally to this is apparent from the official mourning for King Josiah, in which "all the singing men and singing women" lamented him by ordinance. Sheer self-preservation may have prompted the Levites to eliminate such dangerous competitors as women from Temple ritual and from the guild as well.

But if the Bible gives us no direct proof of women's participation in the sacred service, we still can find a few indirect scriptural allusions to their part in it. Among these is the statement that in the early sanctuary erected by Moses in the desert, women, like the Levites, regularly assembled at the east side of the tent to perform certain ritual functions. Such functions were not menial, for those were assigned to the Nethinim, the servants of the Levites.

And (Moses) made the laver of bronze . . . from the mirrors of the ministering women who ministered at the door of the tent of meeting.

These mirrors (of polished brass), like the metal mirrors that would adorn the Court of the Women in the Temple of Herod, testify to women's role in religious dances. Both the east side of the desert tent and the specially appointed Court of the Women of the later sanctuary provided a "dressing room" where the dancers for the divine service could don their showy attire, arrange a special headdress, and adorn themselves with the heavy makeup of the Orient.

Apart from dancing, women's role in the cult may have been identical with that of the male musicians. Up to the time of David, women were predominant in the lyric arts. Clues for the participation of female singers in worship are found in the very earliest period of Hebrew history. It is said of Noah's wife: "Naamah was a woman of a different stamp, for the name denotes that she sang to the timbrel in honor of idolatry." Naamah's songs, in this case roundelays, evidently served pagan rites. However, the motive was no different between her songs and later ones performed in honor of Yahweh.

Of the women who took part in early Hebrew rites, Miriam "the prophetess, the sister of Aaron," is the prototype. Here the meaning of "prophetess" is still that of the early heroic age, when the prophet meant a singer-musician, a folk bard, and not, as in later times, the divinely inspired messenger of God. Miriam not only led the women in their song and dance by the Red Sea, but she, or some other woman, would have led the songful ceremonies around the desert well, since this sort of celebration was commonly the function of women.

Like Miriam, the prophetess Deborah was so called because of her talent as a minstrel. Deborah was also a judge, which in Israel at that time meant one of the elected leaders and chief magistrates of the nation. She is remembered for her paean of triumph when the Israelite forces overthrew the Canaanite chief Sisera.

At great national victories such songs of triumph, intoned mostly by women, gushed forth spontaneously. Deborah's paean was such a song. Even though the victorious general, Barak, also took part in it, Deborah was the real leader, being urged by the people: "Awake, awake, Deborah; awake, utter a song." And Deborah herself said, "I, unto the Lord will I sing."

Such victory celebrations all had a definite religious character, further proof that women took part in early ritual acts. The psalmist corroborates the fact that this was a musical function assigned mainly to women:

> The Lord giveth the word (of victory); the women that proclaim the tidings are a great host.

This was the case as well upon the return of Saul and David from their victory over the Philistines:

> The women came out of all the cities of Israel singing and dancing, to meet king Saul with timbrels, with songs of joy, and with instruments of music. And the women sang to one another (i.e., antiphonally) as they made merry.

A heroine of early Israel whose tale is told in the Apocrypha was Judith, a young widow of commanding beauty who lived during the time the Assyrians were besieging Jerusalem. Dissuading the desperate elders from surrendering the city, Judith made her way to the camp of Holofernes, the Assyrian general, and captured not only his heart but his head, which she promptly bore home in a satchel.

Judith's song of triumph is not inferior to earlier models, either in inspiration or poetic loftiness:

> Begin to my God with timbrels,
> Sing unto my Lord with cymbals:
> Tune unto him a new psalm.

The fact that the Book of Judith is a late product and lies outside the Old Testament canon does not lessen the importance of this song. The poem is imbued with the same antique vitality that distinguishes the paean of Deborah. Although both may have been sung as simple unsophisticated folksongs, as was usual among ancient peoples, both are enlivened by the same power of expression, figurative speech and heroic impulsion.

Compared with these powerful songs, Hannah's song of praise, "My heart exults in the Lord; my soul is exalted in the Lord," may appear pale. It is also surpassed by the poetic transport of many a psalm. Nonetheless, it is a remarkable example of early hymnic Hebrew poetry, which was to develop into the luxuriant outgrowth of the Psalter. The *Magnificat* of the Christian liturgy is closely modeled on it.

After Miriam and Deborah no prophetess is mentioned for several centuries, and then with nothing like the drama of those early figures. One such was Isaiah's wife, who is thought by some to have been a folk bard in the ancient tradition.

In the accounts of both Ezra and Nehemiah, "singing women" are mentioned along with "singing men" as part of the first group of Hebrews returning to their homeland. These were probably secular singers who went along to help lighten the hardships of the long journey. Songs had always accompanied the Hebrews on their many pilgrimages. More than most people they had reason to appreciate the power of song to lift the spirit and kindle fresh courage under adversity.

However, the chronicling Levites were primarily concerned with matters affecting the religious cult, and their reference to such a group of singers suggests that these may have been drawn from extra-Levitical reserves for the sacred service, prepared in Babylon against the possibility that the sons of Asaph might not survive the exile in sufficient number.

If this were the case, then the statements of Ezra and Nehemiah would support the theory that women participated in the Levitical choirs from the beginning, and even, for a time at least, in the Second Temple.

A somewhat obscure reference by Amos also seems to allude to women singers in the Temple. Foreseeing dire punishment for Jerusalem, the thorny old herdsman from the Tekoian hills declared, "And the songs of the Temple shall become wailings in that day."

Since wailing at funerals was the special province of women, his meaning seems clear. But it is possible to translate the passage even more explicitly. Vowels were a later addition to the Hebrew text, and the latitude this gave its translators was one of the reasons for its many varying versions. The Hebrew word *shirot*, meaning "songs," can also be read *sharot*, meaning "female singers," in which case the passage might best be translated, "Then will the women singers in the Temple wail." This seems to be another of those passages in which the priestly zealots tried to obscure an allusion to women's part in the cult.

Not before the eighteenth century did biblical expositors concede the probability that women, aside from their role of dancers, had been admitted into the Temple service as singers and instrumentalists. One of the first was the French scholar, Augustin Calmet:

> In the Temple and in religious ceremonies, female musicians were found as well as male musicians. As a rule, these were the Levites' daughters. . . . The Chaldean version of Ecclesiastes, in which Solomon says that *He got for himself men singers and women singers*, indicates female musicians in the Temple.

Attempts to prove that there may have been separate music schools for women, however, fail for lack of evidence. In the heroic period women received their music instruction from male and female folk bards, who were then the legitimate protagonists and carriers of musical art. In subsequent times, women, along with men, were educated musically in the Levitical school. As members of the Levitical music guild they had the same claim to music instruction as men.

In early times women seem to have served merely part time in the sanctuary. Later the custom developed that young women, but especially widows, devoted themselves permanently to the sacred service. These were usually recruited from the wives and daughters of the Levitical singers, although some were from priestly families as well.

Besides their participation in the Temple choir, women had another important function in the sanctuary. This, although it is not

mentioned in the Bible, was indispensable for certain liturgical ceremonies.

At the three great religious festivals, and even on minor festive
occasions, the thousands of pilgrims converging on the Temple
participated in large numbers in the divine services. After the day's
devotions the festivity was climaxed by a popular entertainment in
which dances were the main feature.

These were performed, according to ancient custom, by the sexes
separately or by women alone. To lead the many women from the
provinces who would take part in these, there must have been certain ones skilled in this who were officially attached to the sanctuary. It seems logical to assume that they were the same ones who
daily performed the sacred music there.

We know much more about women's role in secular music. They
participated in all social entertainments—weddings, banquets,
popular festivals; they solaced the bereaved, published glad tidings,
and enlivened the work of harvest with their songs.

At all times, male and female singers were part of the retinue of
an Oriental royal court. In David's entourage they were an important part of that music-loving monarch's household staff. The pleasure they furnished is made clear in Barzillai's moving reply to
David's offer that he return with him to Jerusalem as the king's
guest. David owed him much, for the wealthy old Gileadite had
provisioned the king's forces during his flight from Absalom. But
Barzillai thought it best to decline:

> I am this day eighty years old; can I discern what is pleas-
> ant and what is not? Can your servant taste what he eats or
> what he drinks? Can I still listen to the voice of singing men
> and singing women? Why then should your servant be an
> added burden to my lord the king?

But if old Barzillai chose not to submit his failing senses to the
dazzlement of a royal court, a later and less temperate man would
find the "singing men and singing women" of Jerusalem sufficiently tempting to forego his pillage of the Holy City. This was
Sennacherib, who, as we have seen, listed them among his ransom demands of King Hezekiah.

In biblical times, at least one musical field belonged exclusively to the distaff side, that of wailing women at funerals. These could not be just any women connected with the mourning ceremonies, but only those possessing certain prescribed skills in which they had been specially trained. They were called "wise women," "cunning women," "skillful women," or women "well skilled in dirges."

Some of them must have been especially well versed in their craft, able to impart a highly emotional character to the ceremonies. For a man who had died they cried *hoi ahi*, "Ah, my brother!" And for a woman, *hoi ahot*, "Ah, my sister!" For a nobleman or prince, the mourning expression was "Ah, lord!" or "Ah, his glory!"

Their work was not restricted to mere routine functions, but constituted a real art. The kinah, or lamentation, was an actual song, based on lyrics of logical content, written in poetic form and performed in a musical context. Specialized though their art was, however, it would be stretching the point too far to call such women poets, even though the characteristic metrical pattern of their threnodies warrants their classification as poetry. Undoubtedly the profession of wailing women entailed a certain training, but the *kinot* (lamenting songs) used were, as a rule, traditional threnodies that any woman might learn.

To strike up wailing or lament was called *anah*, "to sing" or "to intone." The form was either responsorial (when one began and the rest responded) or antiphonal (when two groups alternated). Rabbinic sages of later times made a distinction between lamentation and wailing. In the first, all sang together. In wailing, one woman began the song, and the rest responded after her.

Wailing women accompanied the entire funeral procession and used various songs during the ceremonies. Every step in the ritual had its prescribed kinah; the Talmud quotes the texts of eight such songs. Apart from singing, they had to perform some additional functions connected with music, but these more properly belong to the section on the dance.

Professional wailing women were a universal institution throughout the ancient Orient. In Egypt the implements destined for the tomb were carried in a solemn procession, followed by priests and wailing women. The Israelites must have taken over the custom of

wailing women from the Egyptians and found it equally adhered
to by the Babylonians during the exile. The Greeks too had wailing
women at funerals.

Their presence on such occasions was mandatory among all peoples. If not enough "skilled women" were available in any one
place, they were fetched from other cities. In Greece, the Carian
wailing women were so much in favor that they were frequently
brought from Asia Minor for funerals of aristocrats.

Singing and the playing of certain instruments also belonged to
the profession of prostitutes who, after the custom of the ancient
Orient, plied their trade to the accompaniment of small triangular
harps, or psalteries, which they sometimes mastered. Syrian girls, as
we saw earlier, used as the trademark of their profession the *abub*
(a Syrian pipe), from which the Romans called them *ambubaiae*.

Their presence was a familiar feature of all city life, to judge
from the imprecations of the prophets and by Isaiah's prophecy
that "Tyre shall sing as a harlot":

> Take a harp, go about the city,
>   O forgotten harlot!
>
> Make sweet melody, sing many songs,
>   That you may be remembered.

20

MUSIC AND SUPERSTITION

FROM EARLIEST TIMES, music and magic went hand in hand with religion. Nor were the ancient Hebrews unique in this. Early religion has everywhere used acts of magic, spells, and incantations in its rites. Through magic, man established contact with the invisible world, a world of forces that he identified as spirits or demons and that filled him with superstitious fear.

These forces he sought to propitiate or to coerce by magical acts, and in these music was a potent agent. The cultural history of all peoples furnishes innumerable examples of their use of music to chase away demons, heal madness, and invigorate acts of magic in religious rites.

Even the early Hebrew religion, with its emancipated concept of a universe governed by divine law, had to struggle with a host of superstitious beliefs before—and to a great extent after—attaining its spiritual maturity. Such beliefs were tacitly tolerated by priests and prophets, who were powerless to expel them from the people's thinking. Once the threads of magic had been woven, however subtly, into the fabric of their religion, it was almost impossible to eliminate them.

Many references to such acts of magic and sorcery remain in the biblical text. Earlier drafts doubtless contained many more, but countless editors, whose hand can be discerned throughout the Old Testament, either deleted these or altered them greatly. Even after the Hebrew religion became consolidated as a cult, the belief in magic remained strongly rooted in Jewish minds. As late as talmudic times the cult was still tinted with ancient beliefs in magic, as confirmed by any number of references in rabbinic writings.

When the Israelites took possession of the Promised Land they found it teeming with pagan magical practices, all of which were irreconcilable with their own religious laws. Moses, according to legend, had sternly admonished his people against any form of idolatry, sorcery, or divination:

> When you come into the land which the Lord your God gives you, you shall not learn to follow the abominable practices of those nations. There shall not be found among you anyone who burns his son or his daughter as an offering, anyone who practices divination, a soothsayer, or an augur, or a sorcerer, or a charmer, or a medium, or a wizard, or a necromancer.
>
> For whoever does these things is an abomination to the Lord, and because of these abominable practices the Lord your God is driving them out before you.

Despite all religious prohibitions, however, idolatry, superstition, and magic flourished among the Hebrews not only before but also long after the conquest of their new homeland. During Saul's reign, magic and divination apparently reached such proportions that the king was forced to expel from the country all the diviners and soothsayers.

This, however, did not prevent the king himself from consulting one, the woman of En-dor, when he was hard pressed by the Philistines. Music is not mentioned as part of this nocturnal escapade, but it is almost certain that some form of chanting at least was used to conjure up the spirit of the departed Samuel. In all such ceremonies music assisted the enchanter; it created the necessary psychological state, enabling the participants to believe in the *reality* of the magic act.

Another pagan superstition was the use of teraphim, large or small portable household idols corresponding to the Roman lares and penates (household gods) of later times. In ancient Israel they could be found in practically every home and were still worshiped —no doubt with accessory music—even during the period of the early kings, when the religion of Yahweh was at its peak and the theocratic state regulated with an iron hand the entire spiritual and intellectual life of the nation.

Their use in David's household is shown by the fact that his wife, Michal, in order to mislead Saul's messengers, "took an image and laid it in the bed, and put a pillow of goathair at its head, and covered it with the clothes."

It is surprising that at a time when the true faith seemed firmly established there should have been idols in the house of David, the standard-bearer of the Hebrew religion, and that the biblical chronicler did not hesitate to report the fact. The cult of the teraphim must have been alarmingly widespread also in the eighth century B.C., as we learn from Hosea:

> For the children of Israel shall dwell many days without king or prince, without sacrifice or pillar, without ephod or teraphim.

Some two hundred years later their use was still common, as the prophet Zechariah scornfully observed: "For the teraphim utter nonsense, and the diviners see lies."

Even Solomon the wise seems to have encouraged, or at least tolerated, superstition and idolatry, for he "went after Ashteroth, the goddess of the Sidonians, and after Milcom, the abomination of the Ammonites." Further, he built "a high place for Chemosh, the abomination of Moab, and for Moloch, the abomination of the Ammonites . . . so he did for all his foreign wives, who burned incense and sacrificed to their gods."

The chronicle implies that the aging Solomon merely winked at such practices to indulge his womenfolk. Yet where idolatry exists there is also superstition, and the entire people must have been strongly influenced by it, despite the severe proscriptions of the Mosaic Law. Little wonder, then, that other cults, especially that of the Queen of Heaven, the Babylonian Ishtar, widespread in Canaan, was once adopted and perpetuated by the Hebrews, regardless of the prophet Jeremiah's fiery condemnation.

With the worship of alien deities the music of their various pagan rites was bound to be introduced anew into Hebrew life, if only sporadically. It must have formed a strange contrast to the dignified Temple music, which in its final form was one of the great and enduring achievements of King Solomon.

Many centuries were required for the Hebrew cult to evolve from its earliest stage of worshiping spirits and demons until it was ready to give the world the first concept of a sole, eternal God. The primitive rites and beliefs of many other peoples had to be adopted and sublimated. Much earlier belief in magic's power to abrogate the will of the gods had to give way before the stubborn determination of the Hebrew prophets to proclaim an ethical universe.

The schism between magic and devotion is nowhere more evident than in the sacrifice. Magic was an attempt to confuse and outwit the supernatural forces that menaced primitive man on every side. It implied that with his fear went a certain sly cunning and a nascent contempt for gods who might be thus foolishly tricked. The sacrifice, on the other hand, was an attempt to woo God, to confess man's humility in the presence of forces he acknowledged were greater than himself. As developed by the Hebrews, its basis was reverent, its form austere, its purpose ethical.

In its primitive stage, however, it reflected the character and purpose of similar rites among neighboring cults. Although the Hebrews addressed their prayers to the invisible Yahweh, the accompanying ceremonies were largely of ancient pagan origin. To these music was thought to add its own magical properties, and many traces of this attitude were preserved throughout the later, more enlightened periods of the Hebrew religion.

Invoking the deity with a loud voice or with noisy instruments was common to all primitive religions. It was the original form of prayer. One did not talk to God, but "invoked" him, "shouted" to him, or "exalted" him. When Hannah, the mother of Samuel, prayed silently in the sanctuary, this appeared to the high priest as something extraordinary. Seeing only her lips moving silently, he supposed her to be drunken. The silent prayer, the invocation of God in the secrecy of the soul ("I have been pouring out my soul before the Lord," in Hannah's words), evolved later, along with a more refined conception of God.

But in primitive religions the rule for invoking the deity was: the louder, the better! When the human voice was not powerful enough, musical instruments were resorted to. Most Oriental peoples used percussive ones for this, but the Hebrews used an instrument whose sound was closest to the human shrieking voice, the shofar.

In secular use the call of the shofar had a wholly practical purpose. Whether it assembled the warriors or encouraged them for battle, enlivened a popular festival or announced some impending disaster, its aim was always utilitarian. There was nothing mysterious or magical about it.

Things were different, however, when it was used in religious rites, or when its sound was the accompaniment or symbol of some supernatural occurrence. Often it was used to imitate the sounds of nature; at rites it was designed to compel the forces of nature.

At the rite of water libation, the pitcher of water drawn from the pond of Siloam was brought under shofar blasts into the Temple, where the water was poured solemnly into the spouts of the altar. Traditionally the aim of this water libation was to insure rain for the coming year—an instance of sympathetic rain magic common among all primitive cultures. The needed rainfall was to be brought about by imitating it on a smaller scale, since the essence of imitative magic is to substitute a symbolic action for the fact itself and to assume that a real connection exists between the two.

During this ceremony the shofar's task was to reproduce the sounds of nature: the howling of the wind, the rumble of thunder, and other heralds of a good, soil-drenching rain. At the Beth-ha-Sheuba the playing of pipes was also an important feature. On the surface such piping merely furnished an accompaniment for the dancers, whose performances usually were a part of the festivity. Apart from this, however, the pipes served a hidden magical purpose.

The "men of good works," or "men of might," who performed the dances were expected to exercise through their prayers, songs, and dances the "power" of rain. The pipes' sharp, exciting sound was meant to send them into the necessary state of transport to work the rain magic.

At this festival also, the use of burning torches in the dance had a purpose besides the obvious one of lighting the Temple court. Superstition held that burning lights chased away demons, and thus these were a favorite protection against all hostile spirits. Similar customs were preserved among the Jews until the late medieval era. At daytime weddings young men customarily proceeded the bridal procession throwing lighted torches or candles into the air. Noisy and often cacophonous music betrayed the real purpose: to chase away the demons.

Ancient Israel celebrated the new moon with loud blasts of the horn:

> . . . in your new moons you shall blow with trumpets over your burnt offerings, and over the sacrifices of your peace offerings.

The horn's real purpose was to frighten away the darkness by the magic power of sound, a common practice among many peoples. Even today we usher in the New Year by a cacophony of whistles, rattles, and automobile horns, as can be verified every year in Times Square. Hebrew tradition also ordered that the shofar must be blown on New Year's Eve, in order to thwart the evil powers that would try to prevent the sun's rising on the New Year. Certain allusions in rabbinic writings indicate that this Hebrew custom was primevally related to the ancient worship of the sun.

At the New Year service the shofar was blown twice during the standing prayers, and once sitting. The reason was "to confuse Satan." In rabbinic thinking, the second and third series of shofar blasts were intended to bewilder and stagger the Evil One, who, supposing the first series to be a mere compliance with the Law, is surprised by the second series, assuming that it announces the advent of the Messiah. Hearing the third series, Satan fears that the Resurrection is about to take place, with which his power over the

Jews will cease. Like other such uses, this was connected with the power of sound to confuse and outwit evil spirits.

An important role was ascribed to the shofar in the fight against the enemies of Israel and the cult of Yahweh. According to the belief of the antique Orient the enemy was assisted in battle by malevolent spirits and demons. It seemed logical, therefore, to vanquish the enemy by dispersing these with loud horn blasts. Thus the shofar served a magical purpose before and during the battle, quite apart from its use as a signal instrument.

In the vivid imagination of the prophets the shofar is sometimes even blown by the Lord himself, in order to demoralize his enemies or to lead the scattered host of the faithful back to his sanctuary:

And the Lord will blow the horn, and will go with whirlwinds of the south.

God blowing the shofar—what an apocalyptic picture of the divine grandeur!

In the magic lore of all peoples, numbers play an important part. The ancient Orient especially endowed them with magical properties. Those attributed to certain numerals empowered them to destroy men or lend them supernatural aid. Any incantation against evil spirits, to be effective, had to be repeated a specified number of times.

The numeral three, universally used in magic practices, is also represented in all religions. It manifests itself, for example, in the trinity of God, or of the gods, common to many religions; in the Hebrew conception of three archangels, three holy cities, three biblical festivals.

Next to the number three, seven was the favorite mystic figure in the ancient Orient. Throughout the ages the numeral seven has had an esoteric relationship with music. The seven notes of the diatonic scale were identified with the tones of the seven planets, the differences of pitch being produced by the different periods and speeds of revolution of the planets. This is the Harmony of the Spheres, a notion often found in the literature of antiquity and the Middle Ages.

In Hebrew thinking the number seven had a predominant role. According to Genesis, the universe was created in seven days. After seven times seven years, in the seventh month, the Year of Jubilee had to be announced with the blowing of the "great horn." When Elijah went up to Mount Carmel to bring rain, he sent his servant seven times to the summit before the rain-bringing cloud was sighted on the horizon. On the seventh day of the Feast of Tabernacles, the altar had to be encircled seven times by the priests and congregation, an act that must also have been reflected in some sevenfold musical accompaniment.

The number seven had a particular significance at the conquest of Jericho, the eastern fortress of the land of Canaan:

> And the Lord said to Joshua, "You shall march around the city, all the men of war going around the city once. Thus shall you do for six days. And seven priests shall bear seven trumpets of rams' horns before the Ark; and on the seventh day you shall march around the city seven times, the priests blowing the trumpets.
>
> "And when they make a long blast with the rams' horn, as soon as you hear the sound of the trumpet, then all the people shall shout with a great shout; and the wall of the city will fall down flat, and the people shall go up every man straight before him."

A similar use of the numeral seven occurs in the Dead Sea Scrolls, preserved for some 2,000 years in various caves near Jericho and uncovered in 1947. One of these describes an apocalyptic contest, *The War Between the Sons of Light and the Sons of Darkness*, which was to be carried on for forty years and in which the number seven, applied to the most diverse objects and actions, played a decisive role in subduing the forces of evil.

Each front line must be seven deep, the spears seven cubits long. Seven hundred cavalry on either side flank the seven battle lines drawn up. Seven priests arrive, one to encourage the troops, the others with trumpets for calling to arms and for sounding the charge—trumpets of pursuit and of recall, and memorial trumpets.

Accompanying the priests are seven Levites bearing seven rams' horns of jubilee. While the trumpets sound, the first squadron seven times hurls seven spears against the enemy. After thus attacking seven times the combatants reform their lines, and so on. In this rule of battle, based wholly on the mystique of some armchair strategist of ancient times, every action, repeated a magical number of times, is bent toward a supernatural efficacy, as in the legend of Jericho.

In late talmudic times the number seven still retained its magic associations. It was customary, for example, for mourners returning from a funeral to stop and sit down seven times. In later days verse 11 of Psalm 91 was then recited; this in Hebrew had seven words, and at every halt one word was added. All knew the reason for the custom—to confuse and shake off the evil spirits that followed the mourners.

Even in our own day the association of magic with the number seven can be found in Jewish customs. At the funeral rites for Sephardic Jews, the bier is encircled seven times, while the mourners recite or chant seven supplications. In today's Jewish weddings seven blessings are chanted by the cantor.

In primitive stages the borderline between music and noise is often hazy. Especially when musical elements are made part of the magico-religious act is it hard to tell where noise leaves off and music begins.

Among primitive peoples both are used for purposes other than invoking the gods. They are used to protect man against the wrath of the gods and against acts of revenge by offended demons. Loud music and certain noises presumably cannot be endured by these, and therefore form a safeguard against them.

One such protective sound was furnished by the tiny bells on the robe of the Hebrew high priest. According to Scripture this was in order that "the sound thereof shall be heard when he goeth in unto the holy place before the Lord, and when he cometh out, that he die not." Evil spirits traditionally like to frequent sanctuaries and thresholds; therefore it was essential that he be protected "when he goeth in . . . and when he cometh out." The bells also protected him from another danger.

Hebrew religious law emphatically forbade any attempt to look upon the deity. Whoever ventured to do so must die. Only an exceptional figure, such as Moses, was privileged to communicate face to face with the Creator. The high priest was thus put in jeopardy, for in carrying out his duties he had sometimes to enter the holy of holies, God's own dwelling. Thus he might have chanced, inadvertently, upon the sight of God, which would have instantly meant death. The bells around his garment's hem served to forewarn the deity of a mortal's presence in his sanctum.

The early Jewish historian, Philo, refers to another expedient designed to prevent profane eyes from chancing upon the sight of God in the sanctuary:

> All inside is unseen except by the high priest alone, and indeed he, though charged with the duty of entering once a year, gets no view of anything. For he takes with him a brazier full of lighted coals and incense, and the great quantity of vapor which this naturally gives forth covers everything around it, beclouds the eyesight, and prevents it from being able to penetrate to any distance.

Similar safeguards were used in the Greek religion. Those consulting the oracle at Delphi were allowed to enter Apollo's sanctuary only with their heads covered and to the accompaniment of loud music, in order not to see or hear things forbidden to mortal knowledge.

As the Hebrew religion developed, the primitive function of the priestly bells was forgotten and they were regarded merely as ornaments. But bells or clappers to keep evil spirits away from useful domestic animals long continued to be hung around the necks of horses and cattle. Larger and made of base metals, they were in common use throughout the Orient. An Assyrian bas-relief shows horses wearing little bells with clappers around their necks, while an Assyrian carving in the British Museum shows two horses drawing a carriage, each wearing around its neck six bells of various sizes. The original purpose of children's toy clappers may have been to protect the child from envious demons.

For the use of noise-making instruments to frighten off hostile spirits there are any number of examples in ancient and modern times. The Egyptian sistrum was used for this as well as to draw the attention of both deity and worshipers to the sacred act. At Bacchic festivals and the Roman feasts of the Saturnalia and Lupercalia, processions were always well supplied with cymbals, bells, sistrums, and other noise-making instruments to banish mischievous demons that could have rendered ineffective the ceremonies aimed at fertility.

The ancient Chinese beat tamtams, clanked chains, and set off firecrackers at eclipses of the sun or moon to drive away the dragon that threatened to devour the brightness of the celestial body. Among the Abyssinian Christians the sistrum was used against demons, and even in the Catholic Church vestiges remain of the ancient superstition. A liturgical formula used at the consecration of church bells has its origin in this fear. In the Catholic services of Maundy Thursday and Good Friday the bells normally used in the ritual are exchanged for wooden clappers, as more effective in warding off malevolent spirits.

Nowhere in the Bible is music's power to exorcize evil spirits more explicit than in the report of David's playing the lyre to restore the ailing Saul. By the time this tale was set down in written form, music had long lost its primitive function as an element in magic. Yet the carry-over was still strong enough for Saul's relief to be attributed to music's magic power.

Ancient belief held that music not only had a sedative effect but was able to bring the morbid impulse to a climax, after which the afflicted one might recover. In Saul's case, music not only drove out the demon but acted as a healing agent, thus combining the offices of magic and medicine, as even today among primitive peoples for whom the priest is at once magician and medicine man.

The idea of music's healing power was widespread among the Jews until late talmudic times. We find in the Talmud mention of a song that was thought to provide protection in times of epidemic.

In ancient Israel, Mosaic Law decreed death to all sorcerers. Nonetheless the prophets bear witness that they existed throughout. Jeremiah considered them enemies of the true faith. Ezekiel described their evil influence upon the credulous. Nahum ranked them among the social evils of his time. Malachi, writing after the return from Babylonian exile, linked them with adulterers, perjurers, and inhumane employers. Since music in some form was an essential part of all such practices, the prophets implicitly condemned all the musical trickery used in their ceremonies.

Magic and sorcery in ancient Israel, therefore, were not only religious but also social problems, which the nation's leaders had to take into account. At the summit of religious power, God's protection was considered the best safeguard against the mischief of demons and spirits. But for all this, the ancient magic customs were never entirely abolished.

The priests, in fact, deliberately permitted certain deeply ingrained pagan notions to survive, investing these with the proper moralizing force to serve the new religion. Thus throughout the early phase of Hebrew life we find references to holy cities, sacred trees and stones, high places (former pagan sites of worship), teraphim (idols), and ephods (amulets and other objects to protect against evil influences).

In times of danger and distress the Jews sought to obtain God's aid through prayers. But they continued to believe also in the effectiveness of magic incantations, especially if the musical background was sufficiently impressive. Even the sacred ritual itself was permeated with magic, since certain psalms sung in the rites were thought to possess preventive or antimagic power. The sacred silver trumpets were used in pairs, in accordance with an ancient belief in the power of symmetry.

In postbiblical literature, evidence for the fear of demons and for magical action against their influence is even more pronounced than in the Bible. Talmudic superstition was so strong and sincere that even the most pious teachers shared the belief, common to the Middle Ages, that the air was full of spirits hostile to man, which were lying in wait to destroy him. As a result, all sorts of antidemoniac practices, along with their musical concomitant, flourished during this period as never before.

21

THE DANCE
IN ANCIENT ISRAEL

DANCE IS CERTAINLY as old as music. By the time we find it in
civilized cultures, however, it has long since clothed its primitive
directness with symbolic functions in the service of religion and the
state.

In Sumeria's early period the sacred dance had various forms. In
one, a procession of singers moved soberly, perhaps around the altar, to liturgies played on flutes. In another, prostrations before the
altar or sacred object were part of a danced supplication accompanied by the lyre.

An inscription on a rock from around 2000 B.C., found in Cap-
padocia, tells us something also about the ritual dance of the ancient Hittites. Centered in the carving are gods and goddesses,
toward whom from either side a procession of dancing men and
women advance in what is evidently a sacred dance in honor of
the deities.

In Assyrian excavations many scenes of dancing men and women
have been found, dealing with both the religious and popular
life of the country. At the victory reception of Ashurbanipal we
see a procession led by men playing harps. Some are obviously

dancing. They are followed by a group of women whose raised arms indicate that they too are taking part in this, while a group of children are clapping hands, a common form of rhythmic accompaniment in the Orient. The group represents a band of musicians, singers, and dancers in their characteristic threefold duties at an ancient Oriental court.

The Phoenicians had a special god of the dance. He was called Baal Markod (Lord of Dancing), either because he was believed to have created the dance or because he was the deity most hallowed by it, particularly in bacchantic dances performed in his honor.

Like the Phoenicians, the Egyptians believed the dance was of divine origin. For them its deity was Hathor, a cow-headed divinity who was also the goddess of love and of music. She is commonly shown attended by a small boy who shakes a sistrum before her. Her priests are usually depicted dancing and clattering castanets.

Like other ancient peoples, the Egyptians gave the dance an essential role in their religious rites. Large temples maintained a special class of male and female dancers, and numerous pictures show these performing ritual steps, either solemnly, with arms uplifted in prayer, or dancing in wild abandon, their bodies sinisterly contorted. A scene frequently reproduced on the doors of Egyptian temples is of the king performing a ritual dance while offering sacrificial gifts to the deity.

Apart from religious observances in the temples, Egypt had many secular feasts at which dancing was general. Particularly at the yearly inundation of the Nile the people offered thanks to their god Ptah with fertility dances, striking small sticks together to mark the rhythm.

All such customs must have been witnessed times without number by the Hebrews during their four centuries in Egypt. Small wonder, then, that the Egyptian dance left an indelible imprint on the early Israelites. Like the Egyptians, they too honored their God with dances. David's ecstatic dance before the Ark is akin to the sacrificial dance of the Egyptian pharaoh, even though the ritual dance of the Hebrew cult developed along the more sedate lines of the classical period of Egypt's religion.

All other characteristics of the sacred as well as the secular dance of the Egyptians can be found almost without change in Hebrew customs. In both religions, processional forms were used in ritual ceremonies. National festivals alike included popular dancing. The harvest festival was celebrated by both peoples with fertility dances, the husbandman of Israel rejoicing, like the Egyptian, with palm and willow branches. In both countries dance was never lacking at any festivity of the nobility or the wealthy. Even the Egyptian belief that their gods themselves indulged in dancing had its parallel in a conception of the Hebrews.

All such commonly shared traits indicate that the dance of the Israelites was not only decisively influenced by the Egyptians but was perhaps taken over entirely from them.

The ancient Hebrews must have danced on every possible occasion. We find countless passages in the Bible mentioning dance in the daily life of the people. Biblical Hebrew has no less than twelve verbs to express the act of dancing. When we add to these the many terms found in rabbinic literature, we can only conclude that no other ancient language possesses such a wealth of expressions describing its various aspects.

The Hebrew word most often used is *hul*, or *hil*, meaning "to whirl." From this comes the noun for dance, *mahol*. The girl's name, Mahelah, or more modernly, Mahalia, is derived from this. And at least two psalms, 53 and 88, have in their headings the instruction, al mahalath, giving us reason to suppose that they were meant to be performed with some kind of dance.

Another term is especially interesting to anyone who enjoys probing the source of a language, the word *pasah*. This comes from a Hebrew root whose proper meaning is "to pass over," "to spare," in the sense that the Lord spared, or "passed over," the Hebrew firstborn during the plagues in Egypt. A second meaning of pasah is "to limp," consequently also "to dance in a limping fashion." This suggests a religious ceremony, perhaps a limping ritual dance from primitive times. (The pagan priests of Baal on Mount Carmel "limped about the altar.") This has led some biblical scholars to believe that Pesah, the Feast of the Passover, owes its name to the peculiar limping dance that may once have been performed at the spring festival of the early Hebrew religion.

In contrast to secular life, religious dance is so little mentioned in the Old Testament that we might suppose it played only

a minor role in the ritual. Actually, religious dance occurs very
early in biblical tales. When Moses' sister, Miriam, "took a timbrel
. . . and all the women went out after her . . . with dances,"
this was a ritual action, even though it was spontaneous and the
strict formalism of an organized sacred service was still a long way
in the future.

The dance in honor of God had, even at this stage of the Hebrew religion, a definite ritual purpose, originating in similar sacred
ceremonies of Egypt. As the Hebrew devotional service gradually
developed, other ritual acts, such as sacrifices, benedictions, songs
of praise, took precedence, but without ever completely obscur-
ing dancing.

The dance by the Red Sea was combined with song, both spring-
ing from the same impulse, and is our earliest biblical example of a
ritual song for dancing, or a religious hymn accompanied by dancing. For all its joyful character, it doubtless was performed with
dignity, especially as against the next example mentioned, the
pagan dance performed around the golden calf. The biblical narrator carefully points out the unrestrained nature of this to em-
phasize the sacrilege of idolatry that the people committed in
Moses' absence.

The best known example of sacred dance in Hebrew history is
that of David when he brought the Ark to Jerusalem. David's
dance was a ritual act, manifesting his adoration of God. The expression, "with all his might," suggests a degree of rapture bordering on religious ecstasy. What no music, not even singing, was
able to express became reality through the elemental power of
David's exalted dance. At that moment, rising above all things
mundane, David the king represented the concentrated religious
feeling of the entire Hebrew people. In its deepest sense it implied
a merging of Self with the Infinite, as David understood when he
replied to Michal, "And I will abase myself still further."

This self-abasement before his God shows also in the king's strip-
ping himself of his royal raiment and presenting himself girded
only with a linen ephod, the priestly garment of God's ministers.
At this moment David is not the crowned king but the humble
servant, unadorned, bare of his royal trappings, absorbed completely in adoration.

As ritual dances developed, however, under the austere regulation of the sacred service, they were likely confined to symbolically suggestive forms. We must imagine the sacred dance as a rather solemn display, with rhythmical gestures and pantomimic motions of arms and body, as reproduced in numerous Egyptian wall paintings. The Hebrew sacred dance, as an element of the ritual, must have been radically different from David's ecstatic dance, where such rapture was justified by the extraordinary circumstances.

In other Old Testament passages, dance as an element of the sacred ceremonial is mentioned only obliquely, as if the biblical editors felt it was unsuited to the sacred character of the text. But despite their zeal a few allusions remain to prove beyond doubt the survival of ancient dance rites in the sacred service. Especially is this true of the Psalter, which underwent less editorial purging.

The Psalter mentions the dance of worshipers around the altar:

> I wash my hands in innocence,
> And go about thy altar, O Lord,
> Singing aloud a song of thanksgiving.

Also the solemn approach to it: "Order the festival procession with boughs, even to the horns of the altar."

Other verses refer directly to the sacred dance: "Take up the melody, and sound the timbrel," the timbrel here pointing unmistakably to ritual dance accompanying song.

> Thy solemn processions are seen, O God, the processions of
> my God, my King, into the sanctuary—the singers in front,
> the minstrels last, between them maidens playing timbrels.

The two psalms concluding the Psalter point directly to the sacred dance: "Let them praise his name with dancing, making melody to him with timbrel and lyre!" and, "Praise him with timbrel and dance."

There seems little doubt that dance played an even greater role in the ritual than the few allusions in the Psalter suggest. Certain early Christian writers declared that David performed psalms with dancing and singing groups. The Christian Codex Kosmas, an early sixth-century manuscript preserved in the Vatican, contains the statement that the psalms were "sung, played, and danced." The frontispiece of this relic shows a picture of six dance groups that alternately performed such choral songs with pantomimic progressions.

The psalms, indeed, might easily have qualified as "lyric dances." Such dances, in classical antiquity, represented the fusion of three arts: poetry, music, and mime. They were performed by choirs, accompanied by instruments, enlivened pantomimically.

We find an analogy for this in Egypt, where certain stylized postures, called "dance tours," were customary when two or more dancers were involved. Such postures, and/or motions, expressed specific ideas and thus had special names. One such tour was called "column." Others might represent images as widely varied as the wind sweeping through trees and bending reeds, or the abduction of a beautiful woman.

It is conceivable that certain psalm headings might refer to such a standardized "dance tour," meant to facilitate their danced performance. The Greeks, for example, performed something called a "lily dance." Psalms 45 and 80 have in their headings "according to Lilies," which might possibly be a dance instruction.

Such lyric dances must have flourished before the exile, reaching their fullest expression in the sumptuous religious festivities of David and Solomon, and the great religious renaissance of Hezekiah's reign. During the exile any such lyric dances must have been discontinued along with other institutions not directly connected with the ritual.

The devotional dance itself, separated from the sacred service, survived for several centuries, perhaps in a changed form, as proven by postbiblical sources.

In any event, we may safely assume that some of the psalms were both sung *and* danced. If, as some believe, certain ones were also used for purposes of expiation, purification, and healing, such dancing progressions may have made them more effective, since in primitive religions the sacred dance is, among other things, an appeal to the pity of the god.

A hallowed object might be encircled with dancing, as in the case even of a newly sprung well. All ancient Semitic peoples had such a custom. When nomadic Arabs found a well, they celebrated it with songs and dances. A similar celebration doubtless took place when Moses led the Israelites, desperate with thirst, to the well in the desert. This was so important an event that the biblical chronicle even quotes the Well-digging song, but the accompanying dance was either considered self-evident or was later excised.

The custom of ritual processions around a holy place or object survived biblical times. We recall that on the Feast of Tabernacles, following the sacrifices, the priests walked in procession around the altar while the Levites sang. The "band of prophets" that Saul met as they filed down from the "hill of God" singing were doubtless either dancing as they went along or had been dancing around the altar, inasmuch as a hand drum was among their musical instruments.

Singing as an accompaniment to dancing was so self-evident that this is seldom mentioned, aside from such exceptions as Miriam's dance with the women at the Red Sea, the welcome of Saul and David, and a few others. On all such occasions the people danced in groups, just as the singing was general or by choirs. Infrequently a solo singer might accompany this, with a special song for the dance.

As in other ritual acts, men and women were customarily separated in religious dances. A signal exception to this was their joint dancing around the golden calf, further evidencing its un-Hebrew, pagan character.

Originally the sacrificial dance, the expiatory dance, the dance at celebrations of victory, at weddings and funerals, the harvest festival—all were of sacred character. However, as the cult developed, only those that were incorporated directly or indirectly into the ritual were preserved. The rest gradually became part of popular customs.

Among secular festivities it was the wedding at which, because of its joyous nature, dance was most prominent. Rabbinic writers repeatedly state that "they dance before her (the bride); they play before her," while the scribes lovingly detail how such dances, with appropriate songs and recitations, were performed in rabbinic times.

The bridal party danced all the way to the house of the wedding. Dignified rabbis were not above dancing before the bridal couple, with myrtle and olive branches, singing praises to the bride's loveliness, which ran something like this: "No powder and no paint and no waving of the hair, and still a graceful gazelle!" The idea being, evidently, to stress her unspoiled loveliness in a day when such artifices had long been common.

The dance before a person or an object had the ancient ritual intent of honoring them. One danced before people of standing, just as one sang or played for them.

The bride herself took part in certain of the dances, perhaps with her girl companions. Or perhaps a dance similar to one performed on Arabian wedding nights when the bride, in all her wedding finery, would perform a traditional sword dance. The wedding, in any case, appears to have challenged all Near Eastern brides to a remarkable show of energy. According to the Midrash, pharaoh's daughter performed eighty dances on her wedding night with King Solomon.

The Song of Songs contains a reference to a rustic bride's wedding festivities, which on the surface appears to make little sense:

> Why will ye look upon the Shulammite
> As upon the dance of Mahanaim?

Various Bible versions translate Mahanaim accurately enough as "two camps" or "two armies" or "two companies." But this leaves matters even more confused, for who, watching a lovely young girl perform her dance, is put in mind of military matters?

Turning, however, to Genesis and Jacob's parting from his father-in-law, we learn that "Jacob went on his way, and the angels of God met him. And Jacob . . . called the name of that place Mahanaim (two companies)."

What Jacob saw in his vision were two groups of angels hovering in air and swaying rhythmically in a sort of "antiphonal" dance. Knowing this, we read the erotic Hebrew verses with a different eye:

> Why will ye look upon the Shulammite
> As upon the dance of Mahanaim?

How beautiful are thy feet in sandals,
O prince's daughter!
The joints of thy thighs are like jewels,
The work of the hands of a cunning workman.

Thy navel is like a round goblet,
Wherein no mingled wine is wanting;
Thy belly is like a heap of wheat
Set about with lilies.

Thy two breasts are like two fawns
That are twins of a doe.

The dance of Mahanaim clearly is conjured up for the beholder by the breasts of the Shulammite maiden, which are swaying rhythmically in her dance like the two groups of angels in Jacob's vision!

Whatever its musical background, the secular dance in ancient Israel was nearly always accompanied by clapping hands, striking the thigh, or stamping the feet. If no musicians were available for the wedding, a sturdy rhythm for dancing could always be supplied by such means.

But on the Sabbath all secular music and dancing were forbidden, and with them all such folklike rhythmic efforts. And in certain times of national catastrophe, such as the disastrous War of Vespasian (A.D. 69), dancing even at weddings was prohibited.

In the life of the husbandman, dance was also prominent. At the harvest festival, at the vintage, and other happy events in the yearly cycle of fertility, dancing always crowned the celebration. Apart from their overt purpose of thanking the Lord for his bounty, such dances had a veiled magic significance. As a rule they were performed with green branches, by which the carrier, according to ancient belief, became the symbol of fertility.

In the time of the Judges it was a custom during the Feast of the Lord for the maidens of Shiloh to go out into the vineyards, where they performed round dances as part of the general harvest merrymaking.

Now it once happened that the tribe of Benjamin had committed a great evil some while before, and as part of the resulting bad feeling the men of Israel had sworn before God that none of them should ever give his daughters in marriage to any man of Benjamin.

But after a while the elders held counsel and decided to forgive the Benjaminites, who were now in a bad fix, since there was nowhere they might find wives among their own people. The elders decided that, in spite of everything, they must not allow a tribe to be blotted out from Israel.

"Yet," they argued, "we cannot give them our daughters for wife." For the people of Israel had sworn, "Cursed be he who gives a wife to Benjamin."

The problem seemed insoluble. Then in a stroke of inspiration came the thought of the yearly Feast of the Lord at Shiloh.

The elders of Israel gave the Benjaminite youths the benefit of their sage advice. Seldom has youth accepted the counsel of age so eagerly. As the feast got under way the young men hid themselves, as instructed, among the heavy leaves of the grapevines that dotted the rolling acres around Shiloh. And presently into the clearing trooped the bevies of young girls, laughing and singing, and with garlands of summer flowers in their hair.

Clasping hands, they formed large circles, dotting the ancient vineyard floor with dancing rings of lovely young virgins. Circling now to the right, now to the left, to bouncing folk rhythms, they wove the rustic patterns that were already old and that would keep their charm down all the ages.

Was it by a prearranged signal, or did one of the girls spy a pair of forbidden eyes among the grapevines and with a pretty shriek give the alarm? Or did some lad of Benjamin fasten his heart upon a certain damsel and rush to claim her before another should?

Suddenly, at any rate, the singing turned to girlish screams and the dancing circles dissolved before the onrush of the young men of Benjamin, who each picked himself a bride and carried her off triumphantly to his own country in the south.

When the fathers and brothers of the girls rushed to the elders to protest, they received a soft answer. True, it had indeed been a most deplorable affair. But no one could say that they had given their daughters willingly or had broken their oath to God. And after all, were not the Benjaminites their own blood brethren? Perhaps it would be best to accept the matter as it stood.

So they concluded the feast and all the people of Israel went home, everyone to his own tribe and family, and with no hard feelings.

The custom of dancing in the vineyards continued until well into talmudic times, and there were no happier days in Judah than when the daughters of Jerusalem went forth in virginal white to "dance in the dances." In time this became combined with the wood-gathering ceremony, which brought the local youths also into the fields to gather the year's supply of firewood for the Temple altar. Certain processional rites lent a properly religious overtone, but actually the two midsummer days devoted to dancing in the vineyards were days of matchmaking among the young people. Perhaps the Benjaminite lads had started the tradition, but more likely it was part of the ancient Canaanite harvest festival, which the Israelites incorporated into their own tradition.

Now, however, it was well supervised, for the family, or house, was the economic unit of the nation, and a man's stature increased in proportion to the number of sons and grandsons belonging to his house. The yearly vineyard dances gave all the marriageable girls a chance to be looked over by the eligible youths in a setting calculated to encourage romantic ardor and enlivened still further by the fruit of the wine harvest.

All the girls wore freshly laundered white garments, and none wore her own, for it was the custom that all the dresses worn on this occasion must be borrowed, so that none should have to forego the traditional dancing for want of suitable raiment. As they danced they sang an admonitory ditty that showed the stamp of parental care:

> Young man, lift up your eyes
> And see what you would choose for yourself.
> Set not your eyes on beauty,
> But set your eyes on family.

We are not told whether the Hebrew lads heeded the advice.

Such vineyard dances were not only ancient but widespread throughout Israel. The birthplace of the prophet Elisha was known

as Abel Meholah (the field of dancing) and may have been an
ancient site of such annual events.

In late talmudic times the nocturnal festivities connected with
the rite of water libation brought out the dancing skill of more
than one distinguished rabbi. One such must have been an expert
juggler as well, for he is reported to have performed a dance with
eight lighted torches, all of which he kept in the air, allowing none
to touch the ground while he prostrated himself, touched the
ground with his fingertips, kissed it, and leaped up again.

The Talmud tells of several sages whose juggling skills high-
lighted this and other happy occasions. One performed with eight
knives, one with eight glasses of wine (spilling none), and one
with eight eggs (presumably breaking none).

The war dance, or dance preceding battle, customarily performed by Oriental peoples had a double aim: to gear up the warriors' courage and to terrify the enemy by a demonstration of
strength and ferocity. Originally, however, the war dance was
motivated by magic considerations—to appease the souls of the
slain or ward off the spirits protecting them.

The Old Testament does not mention war dances. But among
all Semitic peoples the act of war could usually summon up an
ostensibly religious motive; thus we read in Isaiah that the warriors "consecrate themselves" before the battle. To "prepare
oneself" had the meaning of sanctifying or consecrating the war.
Before battle, burnt offerings and peace offerings were made,
and afterward a portion of the spoil was consecrated or dedicated to the Lord.

What form the consecration of the warriors took is not related,
except that they participated in a sacrificial ceremony to induce
God to support their cause. We can be certain that dancing was
part of this.

The dance played a small but tragic part in one episode connected with such a prebattle ceremony. During the time of the
Judges, in Israel's early days, the Ammonites declared war and
encamped against Gilead. The men of Gilead sought out a valiant
fighter named Jephthah to lead their forces.

Jephthah performed the customary prebattle rites. But he

wanted to make doubly certain of victory, for they had promised, if he won, to make him chief over Gilead. Rashly he made a
vow to God: "Grant me victory, and whatsoever first comes forth
from my house to meet me when I return, I will offer up as a
burnt offering."

Jephthah returned victorious, a man with the world in his pocket.
Proudly he rode up the hill to his home. And out of the door, eager
to be first to greet her father with timbrel and dancing, rushed his
lovely young daughter.

Jephthah rent his garments in agony of soul. "Alas, my daughter," he wept, "you have caused me bitter anguish." And he told
her the terrible thing that he had vowed to do.

"My father," she replied, "if you have vowed this thing, then
you must do it. I ask but one thing. Give me two months that I
may go and wander on the mountains and bewail my virginity, I
and my companions."

Jephthah gave her leave, and she departed with her girl companions. At the appointed time she returned to her father, who
did with her according to the vow that he had made. And it became a custom in Israel that its young women went annually to
lament the daughter of Jephthah the Gileadite four days in the
year.

There is no mention in the Old Testament of dances at funerals.
However, we can safely assume that the Israelites honored not only
their living but also their dead with dances.

In Egypt, dances in honor of the deceased were an ancient custom; dancing and singing girls as well as wailing women were
never lacking at Egyptian funerals.

Here again, dancing at such occasions originally had a magic
motivation. In primitive cultures the spirit of the deceased was
thought to harbor a hostile attitude toward the survivors. Funeral
ceremonies, including the dance, were intended to appease this
hostility and if possible convert it into benevolence.

The dance was also thought to be an effective means of restrain-
ing the spirit of the deceased from going astray. Many ancient peoples believed that a person newly dead was surrounded by every
sort of evil demon seeking to get hold of him or of his spirit.

Dances to ward off such malevolent forces were performed in the
form of a circle, the "magic circle," designed to protect not only
the deceased but the participants from evil spirits.

The silence about funeral dances on the part of biblical
chroniclers may be due to the fact that these, like many other
common practices, were such an accepted part of ancient folk
life that their mention seemed superfluous. Another reason, of
course, may have been that such ritual dances pointed to the fact
of ancient pagan rites, and were therefore purged from the sacred
text.

For all this, certain hints remain in Scripture, and these, added
to traces of the ancient custom still found in late rabbinic times,
tell us something about it. For one thing, the two musical instruments essential for the ceremony, the pipe and drum, were
both instruments of the dance.

Originally they must have accompanied an actual funeral
dance, which in time was reduced to the merest suggestion of
physical movement, in that the mourners clapped their hands and
rhythmically beat their thighs and limbs. During festival days and
certain others in the Jewish calendar, the wailing women were
forbidden even to clap their hands. As soon as the corpse was
buried, anything remotely suggestive of dancing had to cease,
along with the wailing.

In talmudic times and later, the custom degenerated into nothing more than the mourners' monotonous rhythmic stamping of
the ground during the entire funeral oration. This was evidently a
residual form of what had once been a genuine dance in honor
of the deceased, continued as a stubborn adherence to some ancient funeral rite, long forgotten. That such stamping was actually
a dancing ceremony, however, is betrayed by the fact that it was
performed by the entire funeral gathering, as was customary among
other peoples also.

Whereas among the Hebrews the sexes were commonly separated
at dances, during funeral ceremonies both men and women performed these vestigial dancing steps together, in addition to certain pantomimic motions of hands and fingers.

Apart from such collective honoring of the dead, there may also
have been individual dances of mourning, for we find in rabbinic

literature a reference to a woman who performed such a dance before the portrait of her dead son.

The modern Sephardim (Spanish and Portuguese Jews) still cling to a peculiar custom at their funeral rites that strongly recalls a processional dance. This is their act of walking seven times around the bier, during which seven short prayers are recited or chanted, each ending with the words: "And continually may he walk in the land of life, and may his soul rest in the bond of life."

Such a procession is apparently a remnant of an ancient funeral dance whose direct purpose of warding off evil demons through the power of the magic circle has fallen into disuse and merely its external form survived. Imitative magic may also be implied in the act of *walking* around the bier, and the mourners' prayer that the deceased may *walk* in the land of life.

Curiously this custom has entirely disappeared from Western Jewry and can be found only among the Eastern Hasidim. But it offers living proof that dancing at funerals was a primeval custom that, however transmuted, still survives into our own time.

22

PEACE
UNDER PERSIAN RULE

UNDER PERSIA'S TOLERANT rule the Jews were contented enough in their restored homeland. But the spirit of their younger, adventurous years was gone. In its place was a disciplined conformity to the teachings and customs that tradition had hallowed.

In exile they had learned to live with dignity as a subject people. Returned to their own soil but still a subject people, they maintained that dignity by making paramount the one area in which they retained full autonomy, the area of faith.

Gone forever was the grinding imperative to carve or to preserve an empire. During their lifetime as a people, they had seen the two greatest empires of the ancient world disintegrate—Egypt by a slow internal bleeding, Assyria by a sudden death thrust to the heart in Babylon. They had seen the kingdom of Mitanni crumble before the onslaught of the Hittites, and the Hittite Empire fall before the Philistines. They had themselves dispatched more than one of the ancient tribes of Canaan, and ten of their own tribes had vanished utterly from human knowledge.

Their faith in the staying power of earthly glory was understandably diminished. Now they were content to cultivate their

fields and carry on a modest commerce in their towns, which offered few luxuries to the travelers passing through with tales of
the rising commercial power of Greece across the Great Sea to the
west.

The Temple priests had every reason to be satisfied with a suze-
rainty that treated them so generously. And although the common
people did not enjoy the same exemption from taxes, it mattered
little whether the king to whom these were paid received them in
Jerusalem or in Susa; they got nothing in return in either case.

Judah, politically though not fraternally linked with the
northern province, now called Samaria, was poor and remained
poor. Its people owned nothing for others to covet. But from Dan
to Beersheba they were free to utter songs of prayer and praise to
their God, and this became, to an extent unparalleled among
peoples of any age, the prime cementing factor of their society.

Turning their back on the outside world and its politically
changing fortunes, they concerned themselves with only one thing,
the consolidation of their religious heritage. They had been a people, and then they had been a nation, and now they were again a
people. But before anything else they had been a Faith. To preserve this last possession against all future vicissitudes became the
commanding passion of their scholars as it had once been of their
prophets.

Study and interpretation of the Law of Moses was made a universal feature of daily life. Ezra the scribe had dedicated himself
to bringing this about, and the fruits of his labor lived after him.
From now on wherever Jews were scattered—in Babylonia, in
Egypt, or in other lands throughout the ancient Near East—the
spiritual focus for them would be Jerusalem.

Its religious ordinances and observances were honored at the
same hour and in the same way by Jews wherever they might
live. We have a message, dated 419 B.C., from the king of Persia
to a Jewish military post near what is now the Aswan Dam, de-
tailing how the Feast of the Passover should be celebrated. The
music of the Passover psalms had been heard in Babylon, and now
it was heard in Egypt.

In the Holy City the scholars and scribes of the Great Assembly continued their noble work of transcribing the sacred texts. But
even more important for the time was the grass-roots flourishing

of an institution that had proved its worth during the exile in
Babylon.

The synagogue, which had sustained the people through those
difficult years, returned home with them and took firm root. In
every community throughout Judah a local house of study sprang
up, where men of scholarly mind met regularly to peruse and to
ponder the first five books of the Old Testament, the Torah.

How far back into Hebrew history this custom may have gone
we do not know. Although rabbinic tradition holds that it began in
Mosaic times with the elders appointed by Moses to help him administer law in the desert, historical records of it date only from
the final years of the Second Temple, when such meetings already
represented the central form of Jewish worship. Because at first
these were held only on the Sabbath the meeting places came to
be called "houses of Sabbath," and later by the Greek word
synagoge, meaning "house of assembly."

Their original purpose, in any case, had not been divine worship
but study of the Law. The synagogue had no altar; therefore no
sacrifices could be performed there. But as the people had learned
in Babylon, the psalms lost none of their spiritual power by being
sung independently of these. After the return from exile the sober
weekly readings of the Law alone must have struck the congregation as needlessly ascetic. Even Ezra must have been forced to
concede that not everyone is a scholar.

Soon the synagogue expanded its role of study hall into a place
for worship and prayer. Psalm-singing, with its stimulus to the
spirit, gradually crept into the service; first mere portions, then
entire psalms were added to the lections, benedictions, and prayers.

Singing followed the traditional form the people had learned
at the Temple. The Levitical singers may themselves have sometimes furnished the musical portion at services in their home communities during their weeks off duty. Nor were all the Levites who
had been trained for song qualified for the rigorous Temple duties. In every community there would have been no dearth of able
singers.

Qualified instrumentalists would have been harder to come by.
But since theirs was merely an accompanying role, their scarcity,

or even complete absence, would not materially have affected the character of psalm-singing. Certainly instrumentalists able to accompany the most complex psalms were available in the larger cities.

Music's importance in the synagogue becomes even clearer when we consider the multitude of such houses of Sabbath that grew up over the next few centuries in every city throughout the Near East that contained a Jewish population. The larger ones had many synagogues. Jews from such cities, especially where the vernacular was Greek, maintained their own houses of prayer in Jerusalem. Every trade and profession had its own synagogue where its members met for services.

Rabbinic lore declares that Jerusalem, at the time of its destruction by the Romans in A.D. 70, had 394 or 480 synagogues. Either figure is of course grossly exaggerated. Still, Jerusalem must have had a great number, for the increasing population of the city and its suburbs would have made the Temple inadequate for the multitude of pilgrims who now visited the Holy City.

The heightened religious devotion of the postexilic centuries was shared by Jews in every country. Where once pilgrims to the holy feasts had come merely from Judah and Israel, now the yearly celebrations brought additional thousands from other countries.

During the High Holidays the Temple was put primarily at the service of such distant visitors, while the Jerusalem citizens, like good hosts, observed what ceremonies they might in their neighborhood synagogues. Even the Levites had their own house of study, a small court of squared stones within the Temple enclosure, where they might pray and receive daily instruction. In later days it was known as "the little sanctuary of God," and that it played an active part in the life of the Levitical singers is indicated by a talmudic description of their working schedule on a festival day.

On the Festival of Water-drawing, according to the Talmud, the first hour was occupied with the daily morning sacrifice. From there the singers proceeded to prayers, then to performance of the noon sacrifice, and after that to the house of study. Later they joined in the general feast, following this with afternoon prayers. Then came the daily evening sacrifice, and after that the official rejoicing at the Beth ha-Sheuba.

According to rabbinic tradition, every synagogue in Jerusalem was provided with a grammar school as well as one for higher learning, where young people were instructed in the Law and the poetical books of the Scriptures. This may also have held, in lesser degree, for the many synagogues in the provinces.

Teaching the sacred text was always done by singing it. There were traditionally two reasons for this. Chanting of the scriptural text was considered essential for clarity of diction and meaning, as well as for investing it with proper emotional weight. Also, centuries of oral teaching had proved chanting to be immensely more effective than the spoken word for memorizing lengthy passages.

Fidelity to the tradition of Temple singing was easy enough to maintain in the synagogues of Jerusalem and its immediate neighborhood. But how was this tradition to be implanted in distant communities and kept alive there?

The answer was found in the Anshe Maamad. Maamad means "place of standing," and it refers to an organization of delegates from twenty-four remote districts throughout Judah, the towns of which sent representatives twice a year to Jerusalem to attend the Temple services and participate in the sacrificial rites. On each visit the delegates stayed a week, during which they were expected to familiarize themselves with all details of the liturgy. Returned home, they would see to it that in their local synagogues the songs and benedictions were performed correctly. Such twice-yearly practical instruction, amounting to regular refresher courses, spread the knowledge of the sacred routine and materially helped to safeguard the tradition.

The Temple priests, who probably conceived the idea, seem to have had a keen sense of public relations. They contrived to make the visits so attractive that the delegates felt it a privilege and an honor to undertake the long twice-yearly trips, which were agreeably timed to coincide with the two liveliest festivals, the offering of first fruits in the spring and the harvest thanksgiving in the fall.

In Jerusalem the delegates were received with ceremonies designed to make them feel they were men of standing who were there on an important official mission. No burgher from the prov-

inces would willingly forego the opportunity to be so honored by
the sacred priesthood and the citizens of the Holy City.

The journey, accompanied by music and singing, had the appearance of a religious pilgrimage. The evening before, delegates
from the district villages gathered in the town of the Maamad and
spent the night in the open square. Before setting out early next
morning, their leader intoned the lines from Jeremiah: "Arise ye,
and let us go up to Zion, unto the Lord our God."

With them they took offerings from the current harvest. At the
festival of first fruits those from villages nearer Jerusalem carried
fresh figs and grapes, while those from more distant communities
took along dried figs and raisins. Before them, its gilded horns cir-
cled with an olive wreath, they drove an ox, which would be sacrificed as a peace offering and later provide a feast for the assembly.
All along the route the cheery sound of the pipe preceded them.
Approaching the Holy City, they sent messengers ahead to announce their arrival, and while resting they arranged their offerings of first fruits.

A welcoming delegation of Temple officials came to escort them,
each according to rank, up the long slope to the Temple. Along
the way tradesmen of Jerusalem rose at their approach with a formal greeting: "Brethren, men of (such-and-such a place), ye are
welcome." Following the piper to the Temple mount, they entered
with other dignitaries into the great courtyard, whereupon the
waiting Levitical singers took up their musical duties, beginning
with Psalm 30.

Since the twenty-four districts corresponded to the twenty-four
groups of Temple singers, each choral group probably made itself
responsible for the delegates from a particular district, who thus
took part in all the services involving that group.

In the beginning the visiting delegates were supposed to come
prepared to recite from memory the words prescribed for their part
in the service. This was not only rather long but required a special
mode of cantillation, and it finally became evident that not all the
delegates were up to it.

Unwilling to shame themselves before such august company, an
increasing number began to find one excuse or another for not
bringing in their twice-yearly offering, and the tradition of the
Anshe Maamad was in danger of being lost.

Not only the words of the liturgical text but its proper cantillation was considered very important. To insure uniformity as well as to make it easier for the provincial visitors, it was decreed that all the delegates should repeat after the priest the entire text exactly as he cantillated it, verse by verse. Thus every correct intonation and inflection would be impressed upon their memory, and, taken home to their own districts, would help keep the ritual uniform throughout the many synagogues.

The Anshe Maamad performed an inestimable service in disseminating and preserving Jewish sacred song. By means of it the psalms of the Temple were carried to the farthest Jewish communities. Even if the melodies may not have been everywhere transmitted with flawless fidelity, the Maamad, while they flourished, stood as legitimate guardians of the sacred musical tradition.

23

SPREAD OF HELLENISTIC INFLUENCE

FOR TWO CENTURIES the Hebrews lived uneventfully in their home-land, untroubled by the shaping forces of the West, which were to challenge the Orient's long dominance of human thought. Their indifference was not uncalculated. It opposed a negative form of resistance to a new attitude of mind now radiating from Greece across all countries of the Mediterranean.

To an almost unparalleled degree the Hebrews throughout their history had been quick to accept from other cultures whatever features were compatible with their own religious institutions. From Egypt had come the sense of organization by which they had survived. The provinces of Canaan had enriched their folk cus-toms, and Babylon's teeming intellectual life had stretched the minds of their scholars.

But whether they accepted or rejected a custom, it had always been part of a cultural complex with which they were familiar. All their habits of thought and of action were oriented to the East. They understood its patterns, and as they shaped their own they knew what to cut away and what to keep. The result was a religion, a social fabric, and a musical art that were uniquely their own, and they asked only to keep these as they were.

Shortly, however, all three were to undergo their severest testing since the early days in Canaan.

The Eastern rule that had allowed the Hebrews to dream of ancient glories amid their sheltering hills came to an end with the victory of Alexander the Great over Darius III of Persia. This in itself posed no threat to Hebrew customs. Like his Persian foe, Alexander was a man of learning, with the cultivated mind's respect for other men's beliefs.

It is reported that he even visited Jerusalem and attended divine services at the Temple, where we may assume that the Levitical singers made every effort to surpass themselves. A pagan, he paid his respects to the Hebrew God with perhaps something more than lip service, for the spiritual basis of the Jewish cult must have intrigued this visitor from a country where an incestuous household of gods and goddesses whored and quarreled with prodigious enterprise.

Alexander's conquest, however, made Greece the dominant power of the ancient world. The Greek tongue replaced Aramaic as the international language of commerce and learning. In Egypt the city of Alexandria, named for its founder, quickly became the great intellectual center of the age.

Descendants of Jews who had fled there during the captivity now prospered with the full status of citizens. To them gravitated many thousands of younger Jews from Jerusalem and its environs, attracted by the greater social and intellectual freedom of the city on the Nile delta. There they would speak Greek. To enable them to understand the Jewish services in the synagogues of Alexandria the sacred Torah was translated into Greek. The seventy-two Hebrew scholars who performed this task gave the new Greek version its title: the Septuagint, or "Translation of the Seventy."

When the Jews of Alexandria visited Jerusalem at the festival seasons they now attended their own synagogues where services were held in Greek. The tradition of holy pilgrimage, which had been designed to preserve the ancient ways, now threatened to bring alien customs into the City of David with every incoming wave of worshipers.

Among these customs none was subtler or more to be feared than the strange new music that had sprung up in the West. To the Hebrew sages it represented everything that was alien to their cherished traditions. These were especially vulnerable because music was so closely interwoven with the entire Hebrew social and religious life.

Greek music was a rigid theoretical discipline, reflecting the Greek mistrust of intuition and the Greek genius for speculative thought. The basis of Hebrew music, on the other hand, was emotion and not intellectuality, just as the cornerstone of the Hebrew religion was faith and not rational inquiry.

Whatever challenged this musical attitude, they felt, struck at the very heart of the sacred Mosaic teachings. Indifference was a luxury they could no longer afford. Adding to their alarm was the fact that Greek music came quickly to be associated with the Sybaritic revels that were now a common feature among the wealthier circles of Alexandria.

Against such relaxed moral standards the Hebrew sages hurled anathemas, as the Hebrew prophets had once railed against the sins of their ancestors. The Jews spearheading the fight were called the Hasidim, or "devout ones." Rabbinic literature, which on the whole extols music's role in every sphere, including the celestial, bears manifold witness to the censure the Hasidim now levied against such Hellenistic practices, and since music was always a part of the pagan revels, against secular music as well.

In the Talmud we find such declarations as: "When there is a (secular) song in a house, there is destruction on its threshold." "Whoever drinks (wine) to the accompaniment of four musical instruments, brings five punishments on the world." The four instruments generally found at feasts were "the harp and the psaltery," to accompany singing, and "the tabret and the pipe," indicating that the songs usually wound up in some kind of bacchanalian dance. One rabbi was so incensed at the state of affairs that he opined: "An ear that listens to (secular) song should be torn off."

In the desperate battle the sensuous charm of the female voice was castigated with special fervor: "Listening to a woman's voice (song) is a sexual excitement." "When men sing and women join in, it is licentiousness; when women sing and men join in, it is like fire in tow."

Rabbinical scorn was particularly fierce against any of their own ranks who defected to Hellenism, as in the case of one talmudic scholar, Elisha ben Abuya, who succumbed to the beauties of Greek music along with its literature. His apostasy was attributed by his fellows to the fact that "Greek song did not cease from his mouth." Official contempt for him went so far that he came to be referred to only as "the other one," or someone whose very name it was sinful to utter. The anathema pronounced against him included another talmudic teacher whose sin seems to have been merely that he had "learned tradition at the mouth of Elisha." Even Elisha's daughter was denied religious comfort upon his death.

Overzealous village rabbis sometimes carried matters to extremes, in illustration of which a tale, no doubt apocryphal, is related in the Babylonian Talmud:

A certain rabbi, it appears, forbade all secular singing in his village. As a result all social life came to an abrupt halt. There were no private feasts, no weddings, no bar mitzvahs, no festivities that the people would normally have celebrated, for without music social activity of any sort was unthinkable.

In no time at all the village was in the grip of an economic crisis. Merchants sold no goods, workers were laid off, all the symptoms of a local depression were felt. Prices of the most essential commodities fell to an all-time low. "A hundred geese were priced at a zuz (a silver denarius), and a hundred seahs of wheat (a dry measure) at the same low figure, yet even so there were no takers."

Happily, the rabbi who succeeded the zealot rescinded the ban against song, and prosperity was at once restored. The pendulum swung the other way. Now a single goose was priced at a zuz, but there were not enough to meet the demand in the sudden flurry of feasts and celebrations that took place.

For all their striving, the Hasidim could not prevent Greek music, along with other Hellenistic influences, from permeating to some extent the life of Jews in other countries, especially in large cities where they came into permanent contact with Greek customs.

It was possible, however, to retard the spread of such influences in the provinces of Judea, and to a considerable extent in the Holy City.

Here their concerted efforts turned toward keeping alien music out of their religious rituals, and in this they were wholly successful. To do so they were forced to draw a sharp line between secular and sacred music. Jews who yielded to the lure of Greek popular songs could take their chances with perdition, but under no circumstances was the Temple music to be profaned by outside influences.

To ensure this, no changes of any sort were permitted in the ancient formulas by which the psalms were sung. No new psalms might be accepted, no new settings rehearsed. To the congregation acquainted with the more sophisticated Greek modes, the ancient songs as sung by the Temple choir must have sounded increasingly old-fashioned. This very quality protected them. It was too late to affect materially the Hebrew sacred music. By the time the Hellenes arrived on the stage of history Hebrew music was already codified, and its characteristics were so idiomatic that Greek influence was unable to penetrate it.

The Temple priests and Levites carried their conservatism into still another area. The idea that a woman's song might be a sexual stimulus appears to have given them the opportunity they had long been seeking. We do not know just when antifeminine feelings first arose in Temple circles, but they may well have been building up over the centuries. Now the Levites were able to argue that Greek moral laxity had a potential fifth column within the very walls of the holy sanctuary itself.

Even though the women of Greece no longer enjoyed the freedom they once had, by the Eastern standards of the Hebrews they displayed an appalling boldness of thought and conduct. This, the Levites may have contended, could easily rub off on the women Temple singers and in time demoralize the entire sacred organization.

The hetaerae, or professional courtesans, were an openly accepted fact of Greek social life. These were often brilliant and cultivated women, and their accomplishments, which naturally included music and singing, were an inexpendable feature of the private banquets that formed a major Greek diversion. In secular life, therefore, the Hellenistic attitude toward "woman's song" could only be construed by the Hebrews as an influence of incalculable harm. Moreover, even the Greek religion embraced a view of female behavior that, as exemplified by its goddesses, left something to be desired.

Aided by the ranting of the aroused sages and rabbis, the Temple priests and Levites would appear to have pressed their advantage. Women were eased out of any official status in the sacred choir. In their place the sons of the Levitical singers seem to have been admitted, at least for special occasions. These were not permitted to play their own accompaniment, being insufficiently skilled for this, although they were no doubt already undergoing the intensive training by which the singers were groomed for Temple service.

The boys' only role, we are told, was that of choristers, "to add spice to the music." They were called the Levites' "helpers," and sometimes their "tormentors." Below the platform holding the regular choral group, the lads stood with their heads just reaching the feet of the twelve adult singers. While these accompanied themselves on harps and lyres the bright, sweet voices of the choir boys evidently doubled the melody in the upper range, where their pitch level was that of the female voice.

Implacably the sages continued their resistance against the Hellenes for more than a century, but at best it was no more than a holding operation. The balance of forces that had maintained Alexander's empire after his early death now shifted in a direction that actively threatened to overthrow Hebrew culture altogether.

Antiochus IV, surnamed Epiphanes, took over that portion of the empire that held the little theocracy of Judah, now called by the Greeks Judea. Determined to Hellenize it in short order, he applied pressure on a main artery, the ruling caste of the priesthood. An accommodating Jew named Jason saw his political ambitions realized by being made High Priest. Serving his Greek masters, the second book of Maccabees tells us, "he forthwith brought his own nation to the Greekish fashion."

He went about this with devilish simplicity. Under the very shadow of the Temple tower he built a sports stadium where games of skill, especially discus-throwing, were encouraged after the Greek manner. Now the pilgrims wending upward with sanctuary offerings could not avoid the sight of vigorous young athletes openly enjoying themselves in the sunny valley below the somber Temple. To their ears rose the chaff and laughter of friendly contest, along with the pulse-stirring rhythms of Greek music.

Inside the Temple court the familiar sight of the Levitical singers, ranked stiffly in their traditional robes, must have struck the younger people as more than a trifle stuffy when they thought of the merry exercises going on outside. The time-hallowed intonation of the psalms, broken by perfunctory responses from the congregation, must have sounded curiously antiquated to youthful ears still ringing with the spirited melodies of the Greeks.

Before long even the priests themselves began to find their chores irksome, and envious looks were increasingly cast toward the valley stadium. Encouraged by Jason, the sons of Aaron soon joined the youth of Jerusalem in the forbidden pastime.

> Now such was the height of Greek fashions . . . that the priests had no courage to serve anymore at the altar, but despising the Temple, and neglecting the sacrifices, hastened to . . . the place of exercise, after the game of discus.

As a fad, the game's encouragement so near holy ground was a calculated affront to the Hebrews. But as those responsible were well aware, it was more than a fad. In two ways it struck directly at the foundations of the Hebrew religion itself. After the fashion of Greek athletes the contending youths wore nothing but a thin coating of oil. To the Hebrews this amounted to moral degeneracy, for nakedness was counted a sin in the Orient.

But even less tolerable was the fact that the music and songs performed before and during the games were addressed to the pagan gods of Greece, Zeus and Apollo, thus bringing the worship of alien deities to the very doorstep of the Temple of the Lord.

Devout Hebrews were ready to take up arms. And before long they had even better reason to do so.

Antiochus IV, losing patience with the Orient, pillaged the Holy City, plundered the Temple, and replaced its sacred treasures with a statue of Olympian Zeus. All ceremonies honoring Yahweh

—festivals, sacrifices, singing of sacred psalms—were forbidden the Jews on pain of death. The synagogues were shut up, the people ordered to follow the Greek religion and to sacrifice to its pantheon of pagan gods.

Jerusalem was crushed. But in a nearby village the fire of the ancient faith burned high in an aged priest named Mattathias. Refusing to obey the edict, he and his five stout sons spearheaded a guerrilla rebellion in the Judean highlands and after four years of heroic fighting liberated the Holy City.

> But when they saw the sanctuary desolate, and the altar profaned, and the gates burned up, and shrubs growing in the courts as in a forest . . . they made great lamentation . . . and blew an alarm with the trumpets and cried toward heaven.

While the battle still raged they cleansed the sanctuary, built a new altar, and made new holy vessels. And when all was done, they dedicated it "with songs, and harps and lyres and cymbals."

Mattathias' son, Judas Maccabaeus, carried on the fight until full religious liberty was regained throughout the province. His successors, continuing the Wars of the Maccabees, restored the ancient frontiers of their country and wrested complete political independence from their gradually weakening adversary.

Once again the ancient land of the Israelites had its own rulers, who now were priests as well as kings, combining spiritual and temporal powers in an alliance that was at last wholly theocratic. Thus doubly assured, the services of the Second Temple successfully weathered the political upheavals and internecine struggles for power of the next hundred years.

The sacred musical ritual continued to be performed faithfully, but the times themselves wrought certain changes in it. One of these had to do with the nasal quality of tone characteristic of Oriental singing, which must have prevailed in ancient Israel from the first. Another was related to the use of a vocal tremolo, which for the Temple singers had probably always been a part of their vocal technique.

Now, however, both devices began to be exploited for their own sake. Efforts by musical leaders to keep the form and expression of singing simple and dignified failed to prevent vocal abuses from creeping into the liturgical performances, even to the point of imperiling their devotional character. The original purpose of the sacred psalms seemed likely to be forgotten in the singers' growing concern with vocal virtuosity, as reflected in their affectedly nasal tones, exaggerated tremolo, and other devices calculated to demonstrate their artistry.

Inasmuch as these were Oriental in source, the Greeks could scarcely be blamed for them. However, the emphasis on individual virtuosity that prompted such vocal extravagances could be traced directly to the new awareness of self that was spreading throughout the sphere of Hellenistic influence.

In a wider context, though, such changes were part of a general development in musical life itself. Over the centuries music had undergone a functional evolution. In its primitive stage it had been utility music, filling some social or environmental need. It served religion, lightened labor, was an organizing element in all communal gatherings. At this stage it was strictly a cooperative activity. One performed music or assisted in its performance, if only by clapping hands. One never merely passively listened to it.

Many centuries and much exposure to music were needed for the listening faculty to become independent of any muscular involvement in music-making, so that music, freed at last from its utilitarian role, could be enjoyed purely as an aesthetic experience.

That it had become an autonomous art form and that the people were eager to accept it as such became increasingly clear with the public encouragement of such displays of individual virtuosity as certain Levitical singers now offered.

In time the popularity of sundry leading soloists led them into even further excesses, in which the cadenzalike portions of the psalms became merely an excuse for a display of exaggerated trills and other vocal ornamentation. The congregation picked its favorites among the soloists and a spirit of partisanship developed. Responding to the adulation of their public, the singers strove to outshine one another and a fierce rivalry for the spotlight ensued, especially during the public festivals when great numbers of visitors from other countries could be expected.

Their rivalry also took other forms. The Talmud tells of a certain Hygros ben Levi, apparently a famous singer-virtuoso of his time, who was thought to have invented a new technique by which he was able to produce a succession of beautifully trilled tones. He violated all fraternal rules by refusing to share his secret with anyone.

The best his fellow singers could do was try to watch how he accomplished the feat, and every Levitical eye must have been on him whenever he opened up on a cadenza. But all they could see was that "when he tuned his voice to a trill, he put his thumb in his mouth and placed his finger in the middle of his moustache." What resulted, it appears, was a trill so piercing that it staggered those nearby.

Hygros ben Levi kept his secret and the mystery was never penetrated. His refusal to divulge his technique enraged the singers, so that "his memory was kept in dishonor."

Such excesses were confined to the Jerusalem Temple and perhaps to some of the larger synagogues of Alexandria. They did not have time to spread to the provinces, for while the drama of Hebrew music was by no means ended, the curtain was slowly lowering on the thousand-year-old performance of the Temple singers.

24

DISASTER UNDER ROMAN RULE

Across the Mediterranean the military power of Rome had made it undisputed master of the West. In 63 b.c. the Romans entered Judea, besieged and took its capital. But before the lights of the Holy City were extinguished in a final holocaust a few more scenes had yet to be played across the space of the next hundred years.

By the Romans the area incorporating Judea was now called Palestine, after the Hebrews' hereditary enemies, the Philistines. Permitted religious freedom and freedom from military service, the Jews made out at least as well as they had under Hellenistic rule. Roman music, showy and eclectic, held no attraction for them and consequently posed no threat to their traditions. Local tetrarchs were appointed to govern Judea, and during the rule of one named Herod a Jewish girl of the house of David gave birth to a man-child whose influence on Western thought would materially help to preserve the Hebrew psalms.

But it was impossible for the Jews to accept the fact of once more being a subject people. Incited by nationalist factions, they refused to get along with their Roman masters. Herod they hated

as one who professed Judaism while serving the adopted Hellenism
of his Roman protectors. Shrewd and ambitious, he undertook to
conciliate his subjects by building a magnificent new Temple on
the site of the old one.

On its white marble dais the Temple of Herod overlooked a series of huge courtyards leading up to it by terraces. The outer one
was known as the Court of the Gentiles, since everyone might
share it, but beyond this a stone lattice admitted only Hebrews. A
small terrace, broken by nine gates, led to a main forecourt,
divided on the west into the Court of the Israelites (i.e., male Hebrews) and on the east into the Court of the Women, where an
enclosing balcony allowed them to watch the torchlight festivities
of the Festival of Water-drawing. Immediately before the Temple
was the Court of the Priests, with the great brazen altar beside
which the Levitical choir sang.

The Jews may have hated Herod and most of his successors, but
they were immensely proud of their new Temple, which, still un-
completed, was ready for use in 10 B.C. In their handsome new setting the Levitical singers basked even more fulsomely in the admiration their artistry evoked. Conscious of their drawing power
and filled with an exorbitant self-esteem, they undertook to become equal in rank and in attire with the immediate ministers of
God, the priests. They petitioned Herod's grandson, Agrippa, for
the privilege of wearing the priestly white linen garments during
the sacred service.

Violent resistance came from the priesthood, which viewed the
suggestion as a flouting of the divine order. Class differences between priests and Levites, and even between the various categories
of Levites, must have been very marked at the time. According to a
talmudic account, a young Levitical singer once offered to help
with closing the Temple gates but was waved back by an older
Levite gatekeeper with the words, "Turn back, my son, for thou
belongst to the class of singers."

Expecting strong resistance the singers moved cautiously, flattering Agrippa "that this would be a work worthy the times of his
government, that he might have a memorial of such novelty as
being his doing." To be sure, their request had to be approved by
the Sanhedrin, the legislative tribunal of Judea, but the authority

of that body was already considerably reduced. At the king's insistence it granted the petition.

Encouraged by this, the lowliest class of Levites, the menial helpers in the sacrifices, now asked to be instructed in Levitical music and promoted into the Temple choir. Although this completely abrogated the hereditary nature of choir membership, their request was also granted by Agrippa, so that even the lowest Levitical orders might aspire to wear the distinguishing white garments on an equal sartorial plane with the priesthood.

The Temple musicians had reached the peak of their social position, equal to the highest rank in the sacred hierarchy. Admired and flattered, free from economic worries, they savored their triumph—for a little while.

The priests had to bow to the royal decree. But they struck back at the singers by withholding their livelihood, the public tithes, virtually impoverishing the singers. These complained to the Sanhedrin, but that assembly, perhaps still smarting, took no action. Generations later, the singers of the Hebrew liturgy would still be trying unsuccessfully to restore the ancient privilege.

The unsettled times and the distance of many Jews from the nucleus of their religion gave rise to a number of sectarian religious groups, two of which, lasting into the Christian era, we know about from Greek and Jewish writings of the period.

One, known as the Essenes, was a community of men, mostly of mature age, who renounced all worldly possessions and led an ascetic life based on strict observance of the rigid Mosaic laws.

Their day, according to Josephus, started with prayers and hymns:

> Before sunrise they speak not a word about profane matters, but offer up certain prayers [to the sun] which they had from their forefathers, as if supplicating it to rise. After breakfast, when the priest has a second time offered up supplication, they again praise God in hymns.

Although this group did not admit women into membership, Josephus states that "there is another order of Essenes, who, in their way of living, customs, and laws, exactly agree with the others, excepting only that they differ from them about marriage."

The discovery in 1947 of a number of ancient Hebrew scrolls in several caves beside the Dead Sea brought to light the fact that a monastic Jewish community had lived in the area anywhere from 100 B.C. to A.D. 68. It is referred to as the "Qumran Sect," after the site of the ruins, some seven and a half miles south of Jericho. The sect is also known as the Zadokites, inasmuch as it was directed by priestlike leaders who called themselves the sons of Zadok, after David's high priest.

This sect shows such distinct affinities with the Essenes that some scholars consider them to be one and the same. Their musical practices would thus have been identical, but unfortunately the scrolls tell us little about these.

One contains the treatise, *The War Between the Sons of Light and the Sons of Darkness,* mentioned in the chapter on superstition. Another treatise, *The Manual of Discipline,* minutely details the rules of the brotherhood. At the end stands what was presumably a hymn chanted by the initiants upon being admitted into the community. A literal translation reveals its use of musical terms:

> I will sing with knowledge,
>   And all my singing will be to the glory of God,
> And the lyre and my harp
>   For his perfect holiness.
> And I will raise the flute of my lips
>   In the chord of his judgment.

A third treatise, titled *Psalms* (or Hymns) *of Thanksgiving,* also contains references to music,

> They thundered abuse of me
>   To the tune of the harp,
> And in jingles chorused their jeers.

Musical metaphors also occur, "A song was I unto transgressors." In still another treatise, *The Book of Jubilees* (or Seasons), the

opening line declares, "I shall chant the Ordinance," thus telling
us how the daily prayers were rendered.

Another Jewish sect about which we have a contemporary account was known as the Therapeutae (lit., "the Healers"). Its
members also lived a pious life, shared by the women of the group.
Although both sects in general followed the tradition of Temple
and synagogue, they adapted to religious use a ceremony known to
the Greeks as the agape, the friendship or love feast.

Philo of Alexandria, a Jewish writer of the time, describes vividly
such an agape of the sect, which formed a large community near
his native city at the beginning of the first century. He informs us
that the members spent six days of the week isolated from one another, assembling on the Sabbath in the common praying hall,
where, following the custom of the synagogue, men and women
occupied separate places.

After prayers a passage of Scripture was expounded.

> Then the speaker rises and sings a hymn to God, either a
> new one of his own composition or an old one by poets of an
> earlier day who have left behind them hymns in many meas-
> ures and melodies . . . suitable for processions, or libations
> at the altar, or for the lyric dance, with meters to fit the vari-
> ous progressions.
>
> After him the others take their proper turn, while the rest
> listen in silence, except when they must chant the closing
> lines or refrains, for then they all lift up their voices, men and
> women alike.

After sharing a frugal supper,

> they hold the sacred vigil, which is conducted in the follow-
> ing way: They rise up all together and standing in the middle
> of the refectory form two choirs, one of men and one of
> women . . .
>
> Then they sing hymns to God, composed of many meas-
> ures and set to many melodies, sometimes taking up the bur-
> den antiphonally, hands and feet keeping time in accompani-

ment. Rapt with enthusiasm, they reproduce sometimes the
lyrics of the procession, sometimes of the halt, and of the
wheeling and counterwheeling of a choice dance.

Then when each choir has separately done its own part in
the feast . . . they mix and become a single choir, the bass
of the men blending with the treble of the women, note in response to note and voice to voice, creating a harmonious con-
cord of music in the truest sense.

Continuing thus until dawn, they then faced the sunrise and
lifted their hands to heaven in prayer, after which each returned
to his locked cell.

Still another mixed group of Jewish sectarians arose in the first
century A.D., in whose devotional rites music was similarly stressed.
Inasmuch as they considered themselves nothing other than devout
members of the Jewish faith they naturally continued to sing the
songs of the Jewish liturgy.

These first Judeo-Christians held their services in the Temple or
in the synagogue. At the close of the Sabbath they gathered together in their houses for the agape. Throughout the night they
kept watch, reading the Scriptures, praying and singing psalms. In
the early hours of dawn they celebrated the Mass, after which the
faithful proceeded to the Temple to assist at the sacrificial offerings.

After the death of Agrippa (A.D. 44), who had been popular
during his brief three years' reign, Judea lost its semiautonomy.
Resentment against the Romans mounted. Heavy taxes and the
concentration of wealth by Jewish landholders who controlled the
priesthood played into the hands of an extremist element, known
as Zealots, who took over the hierarchy and viciously agitated for
civil revolt. Oppressive legislation by Nero exploded the powder
keg and rebellion spread like wildfire.

In A.D. 67 General Vespasian led 50,000 Roman troops into
northern Judea, and quickly put down the insurgent provinces.
Josephus, who had led the Jewish forces in Galilee, was carried off
in chains. But behind its 250-foot-high walls Jerusalem spat de-
fiance. Nero's death and Vespasian's ascension to the throne de-

layed the inevitable clash, which was left to Vespasian's son, Titus, to bring about.

During the Passover week of A.D. 70 the Holy City was asurge with thousands of pilgrims. While Jewish factions pursued a bloody intramural strife, four Roman legions took up positions outside the walls. Not until siege engines and stone throwers began to crack the heavily fortified north wall did the quarreling Jewish factions unite against the common foe.

Titus, reluctant to destroy so beautiful a city, suspended the attack and sought to impress the Jews with a show of military strength. For four days 80,000 Roman soldiers, horse and foot, paraded in their splendid uniforms to loud trumpet blasts. When this had no effect, he sent their countryman Josephus to the city walls to beg the Jews to surrender.

Josephus' impassioned appeal, as we read it in his *History of the Wars of the Jews,* might well have melted the stone walls themselves. It was powerless against the obdurate forces now in control of the city. For its own part, imperial Rome could not afford to be outfaced by tiny Jerusalem; Titus had no choice but to press the attack.

Through the suburbs and up the streets to the mount of Zion slowly pressed the war engines of the Romans. As fast as they built scaffoldings for these, insurrectionist torches sent them up in flames. To build more, orchards were leveled, vineyards stripped for wood. The Mount of Olives, bare of its ancient gnarled trees, overlooked an area denuded of all vegetation.

But now a new kind of forest sprang up outside the city walls— a forest of crosses, on which Jews caught trying to escape to safety were crucified by the Romans, often 500 in a single day, according to Josephus, until the shortage of wood ended the gruesome practice.

Besieged, Jerusalem could not support its thousands of Passover visitors, which according to Tacitus swelled the population to 600,000. Famine raged, unspeakable acts of madness were committed, and the people died like flies. Intransigent, the defenders made a fortress of the Temple itself.

The rain of catapults failed to halt the regular daily sacrifice, which went on as in all the ages past. Frail against the noise of bat-

tle rose the sacred psalms. It was not the first time they had cho-
rused heavenward while battle raged around the sanctuary; Hebrew history had been full of such crises. Not until three weeks before the Temple itself fell did the sound of the psalms within its
walls grow still. Starvation and siege had done their work. No singers remained to fill the sacred office.

Titus, loath to demolish either the Temple or the considerable
wealth it contained, again urged the Zealots to surrender. When
they refused, he fired the wooden gates but ordered that the sanctuary be left intact. The frenzy of imminent victory, however, and
the hope of spoil, fanned the soldiers' hatred of a subject people
who for six months had mocked the military strength of mighty
Rome. The battle was joined. Nothing could have stayed the savage onslaught of Roman against Jew.

In the fighting, a lighted torch flung through a window set the
sanctuary ablaze. Titus himself rushed to save it. Failing, he res-
cued the altar, the seven-branched candelabrum, and the two sacred silver trumpets, whose replica in Rome still adorns the Arch of
Titus erected to his triumph.

Leveled to the ground, the Holy City was forbidden both Jew
and Christian upon pain of death. The Jews, dispersed and sold
into slavery by hundreds of thousands throughout the Near East,
struggled as always under adversity to preserve their heritage. In
place of the Levitical hierarchy, rabbis (teachers) now assumed the
task of perpetuating the ancient Hebrew faith. In Jabneh of southern Palestine some of these formed an academy that would furnish
the body of doctrine and commentary eventually collected in the
Mishnah and the Palestinian Talmud.

All Jewish energies were now directed toward religious and spiritual survival. In the struggle, music—cherished by the Hebrews
above all arts—suffered a singular fate. To the rabbis' long an-
imadversion against music as a profaning influence there now was
added all too tragic reason for silencing it. Decreeing national
mourning for the Jews' triple bereavement—the loss of their freedom, their Temple, and their nationhood—the rabbis sought to
prohibit music in every form.

Their interdict extended even to music in the synagogue,
where, as in the Babylonian exile, devotional services now cen-

tered. But they reckoned without the Jewish people's passionate need for song, especially in matters so intimately woven into their spiritual and social life as the synagogal devotions. Song had become inextricable from these. Chanting of the sacred writings throughout the centuries had forged a tradition that the Babylonian Talmud was to confirm, that to read the Torah without melody was to show disregard for its laws and teachings.

Earnest attempts to restore the lost Temple psalmody were largely annulled by regional folk influences and the precarious conditions of Jewish life. Instead of a hereditary Temple choir, the precentor of the synagogue now filled an honorary office as the leading singer-reader of the service, and the reluctance of the Levites to impart any trade secrets to a non-Levite helped seal the doom of the traditional musical ritual. Of the elaborate Temple music all passed from oral memory—that is, all but the more familiar chants in Palestinian folk modes, but even these underwent change by long exposure to alien styles.

Many factors contributed to the penetration of these into the ancient Hebrew melodies. In the sixth century all talmudic teaching in the synagogue was forbidden by the Emperor Justinian, and to circumvent this the Jews added to their liturgy new hymns and prayers designed to instruct, but in terms obscure enough to deceive their Byzantine oppressors. This opened the way for contemporary additions to the ancient liturgy, and when a century later Arabian conquests throughout the Near East liberated the Jews, they continued their poetic output, but on Arabian models.

Equally attractive were the melodious, metrical hymn-tunes of the Christians, so much livelier than their own cheerless synagogue worship, where music, having nothing joyful to express, was retained only as a necessary function in the ritual. Further, the oppressive conditions of Jewish life during the Middle Ages often made it impossible to fill the honorary post of precentor with qualified men. Increasingly the role fell to the hazzan, the caretaker (beadle) of the synagogue, who, being always present, was in the best position to familiarize himself with all details of the ritual. In time these evolved into a highly skilled professional class of singers, chosen for their beauty of voice and their ability to weave free vocal fantasies, often of an extremely virtuoso character, upon the musical motives of the prayers. Ultimately, as the

Renaissance lifted the spirits of Western Europe, such solo ex-
travaganzas came increasingly to color the music of Hebrew worship, as the florid improvisations of the Roman Church liturgy
overlaid that of Christian worship.

At the beginning of the Dispersion the ancient system of manual
signs (called *cheironomy*) had still served for the musical cantillation in the synagogues. For this a helper stood at the precentor's
right, to cue him, by the rise or fall of a finger or stretching of the
palm, as to the direction the melody was supposed to take. This
highly fallible method, subject to the variable memory of local
officials, had served well enough so long as the Temple provided a
stable central authority, but now the dislocation of thousands of
Jews made the need imperative for a more precise means of preserving the tradition of both song and literature.

Ancient Hebrew scribes, following the custom of antiquity, had
inscribed onto their clay or parchment records only the consonants
of a text, leaving it to the reader to supply the missing vowels. Errors in interpreting the sacred text were thus all too easy in a system that—to use an English illustration—permitted a word written as ht to be construed as hit, hot, hat, heat, or hate. Accordingly,
as other peoples were doing during the first thousand years A.D.,
the Hebrew scholars of Babylon and Palestine devised a system of
dots and dashes, added above or below a consonant, to indicate the
vowel to follow. A dot below meant that the consonant was to be
followed by I; a dot above, that it was to be followed by O.

The vowels indicated by a sign beneath were thus referred to as
low; those by a sign above, as high—the direct opposite to our
Western conception of the same vowels. In the same way, the
Semitic Orient still holds exactly opposite views to ours about the
highness or lowness of a tone. The lowest lute string is considered
the highest, the original meaning of "higher" for them being
"taller" or "longer," and the longer lute strings, of course, produced the lower tones. For them a man's voice is considered high,
a woman's low, while they "jump up" to a lower note in singing,
or "drop down" to a higher one.

Scarcely less important than correct punctuation of the Hebrew
text was its proper intonation. In any language words uttered in a
rising tone of voice take on a coloring different from the usual.

"You are going?" means something quite other than "You are going!" Some kind of written symbols was needed to insure correct melodizing of the text once the oral tradition, then fast fading, had wholly disappeared, and for these there was adopted in the eighth century a system of further dots, dashes, and hooks specifically adjusted to the text.

The scholars devising both systems were called the Masoretes, from the Hebrew word *masora* (tradition), and the signs they chose are still used today as the *ta'amim*, the Masoretic accents of the Bible. Each accent was designed to express a motive, through the connection of which a mode was produced. As a system of notation, however, it was limited, being useful only to one already familiar with the motives and characteristics of a mode. Oral tradition thus forfeited little of its importance, and as late as the eleventh century the ancient hand signs continued to be used by Palestinian precentors in chanting the Pentateuch.

In the life of the common people song was too deeply ingrained to be permanently silenced, despite the severe restrictions imposed upon all secular musical activity. This was officially countenanced only at such validly joyful occasions as weddings, and even here the gaiety was not allowed to become too extravagant. During the talmudic period it was told of certain prominent sages that when the festivities grew too pronounced they would suddenly break the most costly dishes, to shock the guests into remembering the need for perpetually mourning the destroyed Temple. Similarly they would begin to sing a sobering hymn, in which the guests must perforce join, dealing with death and the earnestness of life.

Within the family, songs for the Sabbath and the Hallel Psalms of the Passover meal, with their hopeful message of deliverance, continued to be sung at the family table through all the centuries. But although singing as a profound expression of Jewish feeling could be eradicated neither from the synagogue nor from daily life, the fate of instrumental music was sealed forever.

The unsavory association of musical instruments with pagan debaucheries made them, in the thinking of the Hebrew sages, unsuited to the devotions of a people who had suffered such crushing misfortune. No instruments of any kind were permitted to accompany singing in the synagogue, and their ban from public use caused their eventual disappearance from Hebrew life.

Only the shofar, with its ancient religious associations, escaped the interdict. This primitive instrument, easily made and easily mastered, still held in the Jewish subconscious a vestige of its early magical properties. National despair, clutching at any symbol of hope, now invested the instrument with a certain messianic significance that served to retain it in the synagogue service, so that of all the instruments of ancient Israel the shofar alone survives.

Within the span of two or three generations the once-flourishing instrumental music of the Jews was irretrievably lost, the technique of playing was forgotten, and musical terms once generally familiar became incomprehensible.

25

THE HEBREW PSALMS IN
CHRISTIAN LITURGY

But was the sacred music of Solomon's Temple utterly lost to history? Today we know the answer.

Even before the fall of Jerusalem the music of ancient Israel had begun to split into two forks, branching from the parent stream and pursuing a course so divergent and often so obscure that nearly 2,000 years were to pass before scholars would recognize their common source.

One branch, as we have seen, supplied the liturgy of the early Christians, in whose devotions psalm-singing was preeminent. Let us follow this branch for a while, tracing its progress through the many writings left us by early Church fathers.

For the first Judeo-Christians the rich tradition of song that for centuries had been part of their Hebrew heritage became the foremost vehicle by which they expressed the new spiritual force uniting them. Psalms and hymns known to every pious Jew from childhood formed the music of their gatherings. We have it on the authority of the apostle Matthew, himself a Jew, that the singing of a hymn concluded the Last Supper. This was held on the first evening of the Passover, since the Hebrew day started at dusk. Jesus and his companions celebrated the traditional meal at the house of a friend in Jerusalem, as Jews throughout the known world gathered at the same hour to commemorate the exodus from Egypt. A traditional observance, it required the traditional songs, and for centuries those chanted at the paschal table had been the Hallel psalms (113 to 118). Matthew, like Jesus, must have heard these sung at every Passover feast of his life; he knew their ritual importance. "And when they had sung a hymn they went out to the Mount of Olives."

The fact that for Jesus himself the singing of psalms had constituted a final act of worship endowed them for his followers with an aura of special holiness. The use of psalms in family devotions would continue among the early Christians, as among the Jews, for many centuries. Christian prayer meetings, of which the vigil celebration, adopted from Jewish holy day observances, was the oldest form, combined prayers with songs of praise in close imitation of the synagogue.

The songs were traditional synagogue chants that everyone knew by heart, or were based on Jewish tunes that would remain essentially unchanged in form and substance for centuries. Even the various languages in which they might be sung, such as Syriac, Greek, and later, Latin, would be unable to alter substantially the character of their Hebrew melodies. Since the psalms had a flexible meter, the melodic pattern of their singing could easily adapt to the rhythm of other languages.

By the middle of the first century A.D., psalm-singing was already common throughout the Christian communities of Asia Minor, following the simplest form of synagogue practice in which one person intoned the entire psalm, half verse by half verse, and the congregation responded after each in unison with a refrain or an acclamation. According to Socrates of Constantinople (fifth century), it was St. Ignatius, a pupil of the apostle John, who introduced into the primitive Church the ancient Hebrew usage of singing hymns and psalms antiphonally. (Ignatius, who was Bishop of Antioch, was later martyred by the Romans by being thrown to the lions.)

Theodoret, in his *History of the Church*, names two Greco-Syrian monks, Flavian of Antioch and Diodor of Tarsus, as being "the first to teach the antiphonal singing of Davidic hymns, the choir of the singers being divided into (two) parts." In his message to the Christian colony of Ephesus, the apostle Paul confirms the practice of antiphonal psalm-singing:

> Be filled with the Spirit; speaking one to another in psalms and hymns and spiritual songs, singing and making melody with your hearts to the Lord.

The term hymn, at first used for all songs in praise of God, later became identified with certain new songs that arose in response to the needs of the new faith. Some of these were provided by the New Testament, but the majority were taken from earlier Scripture and given a Christian interpretation, as in the case of the *Sanctus* (the ancient Hebrew *Kedusha*), which echoes the antiphonal song of the seraphim in Isaiah 6:3:

> Holy, holy, holy, is the Lord of Hosts;
> The whole earth is full of his glory.

These words, absorbed into Church liturgy, would become associated in the Holy Communion with the *Benedictus Qui Venit* ("Blessed is he that cometh in the name of the Lord"), taken from Psalm 118 and traditionally thought to have welcomed Jesus' entry into Jerusalem.

Another Old Testament canticle:

> O all ye works of the Lord, bless ye the Lord;
> Praise him and magnify him forever,

and reputedly sung by Shadrach, Mesach, and Abednego when they were thrown into the fiery furnace by Nebuchadnezzar, would become known as the *Benedicite*.

The joyful Hebrew exclamation, hallelujah (Praise the Lord), was very early adopted from the Jewish ritual and would be sung, as alleluia, through all the centuries of the Church's existence. St. Jerome, the editor of the Vulgate, tells us that in his time (fourth century) the very ceilings of houses of worship were "shaken with the reverberating hallelujahs."

In addition, communal singing among the early Christians was sometimes marked by spontaneous outbursts of praise, as one or another worshiper gave vent to the collective feeling in an improvised chant. The spiritually charged temper of the times caused such spontaneous outpourings to be regarded by the members as inspired and their texts were carefully written down, to serve along with the traditional Hebrew psalms and other Scriptural canticles as a basis for the primitive Christian liturgy.

Tertullian, the early Western Church father, tells us in the second century that during vigil-celebrations in the Christian community in North Africa:

> After the bringing of lights, each is asked to stand forth and sing, as he can, a hymn to God, either one of the holy Scriptures or one of his own composing.

Sometimes the psalms themselves were adapted to new melodies. Eusebius Pamphilius of Caesarea (c. A.D. 260–340) records in his *History of the Church:*

> When someone had started to sing a psalm to a soft melody the congregation, at first, would listen in silence, and only sing in chorus the last verses of the hymn.

These were ". . . the new songs, the songs of the Levites, with their eternal strain that bears the name of God, and which gives order and harmony to the universe," in the words of Clement of Alexandria (c. A.D. 170–215), who also calls them "at the same time psalmodic and prophetic."

But not all such new songs were acceptable to the early Church —only those that conformed to the ancient Jewish spirit. In the vigorous Christian community of Syria, where the services were most faithfully modeled on the Jewish liturgy, many new lyrics sprang up in the ancient Syrian tongue, which was closely akin to the Aramaic dialect then common in Palestine. But whereas orthodox Christian psalmody was based on the musical forms of Jewish worship, these new creations, written in the strict meters of the pagan world, reflected the beliefs of the many heretical sects then challenging the young Christian Church.

Antioch and Constantinople were centers of such hymn-writing activity. The prolific output in the second century by a Gnostic teacher named Bardesanes and his son, Harmonios, gave such heretical hymns wide currency. Between them they created a complete Gnostic Psalter, a collection of 150 metrical paraphrases of the psalms, designed to be sung to the lyre between the verses of the traditional psalms, and whose tuneful melodies succeeded in winning many orthodox Christians to the Gnostic doctrine. Observing their success, the Arians and other heretical sects likewise drew upon the persuasive powers of music to spread their own religious tenets, to similar purpose.

It was perhaps in reaction to such heretical hymns that Sts. Paul and Stephen early set up certain rules for the monks of their time:

> Nobody may either meditate upon or recite responses and antiphons in the congregation which are sung by some to their own musical setting and which are not taken from canonical Scripture.

All songs contrary to the essence of Jewish tradition were branded heretical by the early Church fathers, at least one of whom, Paul of Samosata, "abolished (in his congregation) the singing of hymns . . . which had been written recently by composers of the day," and reinstituted the ancient Hebrew usage. Athanasius (c. A.D. 298–373), while Bishop of Alexandria, disapproved of the "exquisite heretical songs," and his contemporary, Epiphanius, condemned "the heretic psalms . . . which do not conform to the ancient (i.e., Jewish) tradition."

Still, it was not until the fourth century, when such tuneful heresies seriously threatened the unity of the Church, that steps were taken to eradicate them. After the Council of Nicaea (A.D. 325), the Syrian liturgy was purged of them, at least officially, and a half century later the spontaneous improvisations, which by then had become a heretic feature, were also proscribed at the Council of Laodicea:

> Besides the appointed singers who mount the ambo and sing from the book, others shall not sing in the Church.

The ambo was the pulpit from which the scriptural lessons of
the Mass were read, separated by psalms. The singer stood on the
step, *gradus*, of the pulpit, from which the first psalmody after the
lesson became known as the Gradual. In the beginning only one
singer chanted the psalmody, but later two or three were used,
their elevated place on the step harking back to Hebrew Temple
practice, in which the Levites sang psalms while standing on the
fifteen steps of the sanctuary.

The fourth-century reforms in the Eastern Church cleared the
way for a resurgence of the traditional psalms, which thereafter
were officially commended over all other forms and texts. In addition to their devotional purpose, their salutary effect upon the
singer was generally proclaimed:

> . . . they calm carnal passions . . . evil inclinations, chase
> demons away . . . they strengthen the pious fighters for the
> sufferance of terrible ordeals . . . they heal the wounds that
> life has struck . . .

Within the same century St. John Chrysostom introduced into
the Church at Constantinople the ancient Hebrew form of antiphonal singing between two choirs, which was to become the most
important and enduring form of psalmodic chant in the Christian
ritual.

While the battle against heresy still raged in Asia Minor, the new
Church, along with the psalms of David, swept westward throughout the Roman Empire. The psalms at first were sung in Greek, for
Latin had not yet come into popular use and the Greek tongue, or
dialects of it, was still the universal language of the West. Neither
was Rome as yet creative in Church music. It would appear that
hymns were first introduced into Rome by St. Hilary of Gaul, who
reportedly heard them being sung while under a six-year banishment to Asia Minor by the Emperor Constantine in A.D. 356. St.
Hilary returned with some of the Eastern hymns and later wrote
others of his own in Latin, as did his contemporary, Pope Damasus I.

It was left, however, for St. Ambrose, as Bishop of Milan, to
characterize the Church music of the fourth century. Bitter con-

flicts with the heretical Arian sect still raged throughout Christendom and as a countermeasure Ambrose undertook to make Latin psalmody more attractive to the common people by introducing congregational singing into the churches of Milan. Psalms and hymns that previously had been recited by a single functionary, often a mere clerk, now recaptured the ancient Hebrew drama of a solo figure intoning portions of a sacred text, balanced against short choral refrains by the massed congregation.

This *cantus responsorius* necessitated, as it had for the Jews, a trained soloist whose chant quickly became overlaid with ornamentation. Neither was it long before the refrains as well became highly elaborated. Too difficult now for the congregation, the responses were taken over by a trained chorus and considerably lengthened by the Oriental device of melisms—long vocal passages sung to one syllable—while the number of verses was correspondingly reduced.

Under Ambrose also the second form of Hebrew psalmody, choral singing, now attained new prominence. Following traditional Jewish usage this developed into two half choruses, a male choir and one composed of women or boys, which alternated the verses in their respective vocal range. To this was soon added a short introductory piece called the antiphon, taken usually from the psalm itself and repeated throughout as a refrain, again following the pattern of the refrain psalms sung in the Hebrew Temple.

Ambrose not only brought to early Church music a new sense of order, including a primitive attempt at musical notation, but he also wrote many hymns and encouraged the writing of others. (His own great *Te Deum Laudamus* bears startling melodic resemblance to the ancient Jewish chanting from the Prophet Zechariah, "Rejoice greatly, O daughter of Zion.") From all such, along with the traditional Hebrew psalms and certain Greek adaptations, was evolved a type of modal plainsong known as Ambrosian Chant, whose metered but easily flowing stanzas became immediately popular.

That its sweetness and solemnity as well as its strongly rhythmical character were able to generate great emotional power we know from the writings of St. Augustine, perhaps the greatest of the Church fathers, who came to Milan in A.D. 384 as a teacher of oratory. Moved by the eloquence of Ambrose's sermons, he re-

mained to become the most famous of his converts, and in his
Confessions he has recorded for us the deep spiritual impact made
upon him by the sound of Ambrosian hymns being chanted in the
Milan basilica:

> How abundantly did I weep to hear those hymns and can-
> ticles of thine, being touched to the very quick by the voice
> of the sweet Church song . . .
> Those sounds flowed into my ears, and the truth streamed
> into my heart; so that my feelings of devotion overflowed,
> and the tears ran from my eyes, and I was happy in them.
> It was only a little while before that the church in Milan
> had begun to practice this kind of consolation and exultation
> . . . singing psalms and hymns after the manner of the East-
> ern churches. . . . The custom has been retained from that
> day to this, and has been imitated by many, indeed, in almost
> all congregations throughout the world.

Antiphonally borne, the psalms quickly spread to other Latin
churches, in Gaul, in Spain, in southern Italy. That the Latin
Church fathers fully appreciated the spiritual and moral values of
Jewish sacred song is evident from their writings, which are filled
with praise for psalm-singing in the ancient Davidic style.

Eusebius, the great fourth-century churchman and himself of
Palestine, describes:

> the divine mission of the apostolic men . . . who were, it ap-
> pears, of Hebrew origin, and thus still preserved most of the
> ancient customs in a strictly Jewish manner.

His contemporary, Augustine, also speaks of the old (i.e., Jewish) usage of singing in the Church and declares that "hymns and
psalms should be sung according to the Oriental custom."

A clinging to old customs and traditional practices was axio-
matic in the early Christian Church. Jesus himself had said, "I am
not come to destroy, but to fulfill." Consequently, everything the
early fathers had to say about the liturgical music of the first Christian centuries sheds light on ancient Jewish music, and especially

on Jewish song, which lived on practically unchanged in early Christian liturgy.

How important a place this held in the early Church may be deduced from the *Apostolic Constitutions*, a compendium of Christian liturgies and ordinances that probably originated in the fourth century in Syria but whose traditions date from at least a century earlier, and in which we find several adjurations:

> Sing the psalms of David . . . and peruse diligently the Gospel. . . . If thou desirest something to sing, thou hast the psalms . . . assemble yourselves together every day, morning and evening, singing psalms and praying in the Lord's house.

No exhortations were necessary to encourage the practice of psalm-singing. Among the early Christians it formed one of the strongest stimulants for the religious exaltation so characteristic of the age. Augustine speaks of "the great delight of the brethren, singing together with both voice and hearts." Eusebius reports:

> Throughout the whole world, in towns and villages and in the fields also, in short, in the whole Church, the people . . . sing to the one God . . . hymns and psalms with a loud voice, so that the psalm-singers are heard by those standing outside.

That these were ancient Jewish psalms is attested by Pope Leo the Great (A.D. 390–461): "Davidic psalms are sung everywhere in the Church with all piety." In his *Confessions*, Augustine declares that "verily they be already sung all over the world . . . the psalms of David, these faithful songs, these sounds of devotion."

Clergy, laymen, even children, took part in a custom that was "sweet for every age and suitable for either sex." St. Ambrose pointed to the "great bond of unity when all the people raise their voices in one chorus." John Chrysostom observed in a passage that curiously recalls the biblical mention of "one sound" made by the chorus of Levites at the dedication of Solomon's Temple:

Though men and women, young and old, are different,
when they sing hymns their voices are influenced by the Spirit
in such a way that the melody sounds as if sung by one voice.

Among the early Christians, psalms came to hold the place that
popular songs would hold in later centuries. The tunes were simple
and the sentiments general, a combination that gave them widespread currency. Many "were known to nearly everyone by heart,
and were sung daily in the evening assembly by young and old."
Married couples were admonished "to emulate one another in
singing hymns and psalms, not only in the congregation but in
the home." Psalms were customarily sung before retiring, and children were made to learn them as morally instructive.

Where the social customs of Hellenism continued strong, as in
Egypt, Christians sang hymns responsively at banquets while drinking one another's health. As early as the second century, however,
Clement of Alexandria had indicated the deep cleavage between
"the burlesque singing, the instrumental music, choirs and dances"
at Roman revels, and the more seemly practices of the Christians:

> Teach and admonish one another in all wisdom, in psalms,
> hymns, and spiritual songs, singing to God with grace in the
> heart . . . and even if you wish to sing and play the harp or
> the lyre, there is no blame. Thou shalt imitate the righteous
> Hebrew king in his thanksgiving to God.

But although Clement defended the private playing of the lyre as
the sacred instrument of David, the use of musical instruments in
the Church was bitterly attacked, and by Clement as well. There
was reason for this. Like the Jews three centuries before, so now
the early Church found it imperative to repudiate a pagan music
that at the beginning of the Common Era had degenerated into a
pretext for obscenity and voluptuousness. By the end of the fourth
century no instrument was used in any Christian service. Greek
music was abolished not only from religious but from secular life,
and with the addition of a few simple sentences of common prayers, the Book of Psalms became the standard prayer book in the
Church.

For laymen, psalm-singing was a matter of spontaneous feeling. For the clergy and other servants of the new religion it soon became a religious duty. In a letter to the monk Rusticus, St. Jerome counsels, "Thou must learn the psalms word for word, by heart." Commending the nuns of St. Paula's convent in Jerusalem, he nonetheless warns that "no sister may remain if she does not know the psalms."

Of Paula, that devoted abbess and his cherished friend, Jerome also reports that she came to Palestine because "she wanted to teach Hebrew and succeeded in it so notably that she could sing the psalms in Hebrew." Her daughter, Blaesilla, who died young, also "overcame the difficulties of the Hebrew language in order to teach and sing psalmody together with her mother."

Anastasius, in his ninth-century *History of the Roman Popes*, relates that St. Damasus "ordered psalms to be sung by day and by night in all the churches." According to John Cassian (A.D. 360–435), many Eastern monks sang thirty to forty each night. This appears to have been no hardship, in view of "the variety of psalmodic melodies and the delight of the brethren in them."

Sts. Paul and Stephen had instructed that their manner of singing "should always be with a sweet melody." From all we can gather, such melodies must have been quite attractive. In postapostolic times they were characterized as "angelic" and "sweet." The style of singing, however, varied with the locality. Thus Pambo, abbot of the Egyptian cloister of Nitria, reproached one of his monks for "listening to the magnificent chants at the monastery of St. Mark in Alexandria, with the purpose of introducing them into his own monastery," while Augustine in the same century could complain that the Bishop of Alexandria "caused the reader of the psalm to sound it forth with so little warbling of the voice that it was nearer to speaking than singing," meanwhile praising the old (Jewish) usage of singing in the Church, when the psalms were set off "with a clear voice and a suitable modulation."

That the tremolo common to Eastern singing was frequently used we know from the notational Church signs of the Middle Ages called *neumes*, two of which, *quilisma* and *pressus*, symbolized note clusters that, like the corresponding Hebrew *shalshelet*, were to be sung in a tremulous voice. In both cases a vertical wavy line stood for the trembling movement of the hand by which the ancient Temple chorus masters and early Christian presbyters alike had elicited this particular effect. Curt Sachs, in *The Orient and Western Music*, would interpret the wrinkles around the nose and mouth of the angels on the Ghent altarpiece as evidence that the nasal style of the East still obtained in fifteeth-century Europe. The word for the neumes was itself a Judaic legacy, coming from the Hebrew word *neima* (tune, sweetness), designating the rendering of the lesson. Transformed into Greek as *neuma* (nod, sign), the neumes furnished the Latin Church from the eighth to fourteenth centuries with graphic symbols of the ancient Hebrew hand signs.

The earliest Church neumes of which we have record are found in the Book of Lamentations, which for the Jews now constituted an essential part of the liturgy commemorating the destruction of their Temple. For the early Christians, who were enduring similar persecution by the Romans, the words of the ancient prophet also furnished comfort, so it was only natural that the Lamentations of Jeremiah should be among the first Old Testament Scriptures they would adopt, to become an integral part of the Church liturgy for Holy Saturday.

The language of David and the prophets was venerated in the first centuries of the new era, although few Latin fathers and even fewer laymen knew biblical Hebrew, which by the second century had become virtually a dead language used only by scholars and synagogue functionaries. The early Church musicians were not aware that the ancient Hebrews had customarily used the letters of their alphabet to number certain Old Testament canticles. Thus the first verse of Lamentations was numbered with *aleph*, the first letter of the Hebrew alphabet, the second verse with *beth*, and so on acrostically until all twenty-two letters of the Hebrew alphabet had been used, after which a new chapter was begun, starting again with *aleph*.

When they came to setting the Latin text of Lamentations to music the early fathers must have been mystified by the presence of such words as *aleph*, *gimel*, and *phe* at the beginning of the scriptural verses, but they were reluctant to slight any word, however puzzling, of the venerated Hebrew tongue. Giving them a melismatic flourish, they confidently sang the ancient letter-numbers as part of the regular text until as late as the eighth century:

LAMENTATIONS 1:1   GREGORIAN

A - leph quo mo - do se - det so - la ci - vi - tas ple - na po - pu - lo,

fac - ta est qua - si vi - dua do - mi - na Gen - ti - um.

LAMENTATIONS 4:16   GREGORIAN

Phe _____ Fa - ci - es Do - mi - ni di - vi - sit e - o

But although the sacred text was much respected, emotions among the singers occasionally soared so high that words became superfluous. In their religious fervor soloists sometimes dropped the consonants, with esoteric implications thoroughly in keeping with early Church attitudes. These were the songs of which Augustine says, "He who rejoices needs no words, for the song of delight is without words."

The most prominent of such wordless utterances was the alleluia respond of the Mass, in which melismatic singing would reach its highest peak of floridity. Its affinity with the Hallel psalms of the Jewish synagogue is well attested; as the simple exclamation of praise, hallelujah, it had been an integral part of the Psalter, whose Hebrew title, we recall, meant itself a "book of praises." But in the synagogue as in the Church the hallelujah expanded its original role to develop, particularly in the latter, as an independent expression of spiritual joy, entirely free and disembodied. Its mystical implications led in time to the consonants being omitted and only the vowels sung: A E U I A. Later these would be superseded by those of the doxology, *Seculorum amen*: E U O U A E.

In the Church ritual the alleluia was sung by the soloist, repeated by the choir, and extended by a long vocalization, called the *Jubilus*, on the final A. This in itself formed a song of praise prompted by a boundless exaltation, and best characterized in the words of Jerome:

Jubilus is that which cannot be expressed or understood either in words or in syllables, or in letters, or in other utterance.

Jerome also mentions that the Jews did not make as free use of the formula as the Christians:

> Up to this day it is the custom of the Jews not to add an Alleluia to any psalm, unless it is prescribed as belonging to that very psalm. We, however, are accustomed to use Alleluias quite indifferently in the psalms, be they now of historical content, or sigh with penitent tears, or demand victory over the enemy, or pray for delivery from anxiety.

The Church's melismatic extension of the text, however, had its roots in the ornately prolonged psalm and prayer endings of Jewish holy days.

For more than two centuries the rhythmical plainsong of Ambrose brightened the service of the Western Church. But its very popularity was its undoing. The lively hymns and chants became corrupted by secular texts that tarnished the dignity of the sacred offices. When in 590 Pope Gregory came to the papal chair he instituted immediate and sweeping reforms in Church music, weeding out all secular features and gathering the acceptable remainder into two great collections, one of which formed the music of the Mass; the other, music for the daily Hours of Divine Service.

Hymns were no longer encouraged. A purist, Gregory went directly to the Scriptures and their ancient form of utterance. Psalms now came back into their own. As Gregorian chant, they were sung in unison, without harmonic support, and in an inflected monotone that followed the natural prose rhythms of the text. But the short, effervescent notes of earlier psalmody were sobered now into graver ones of more equal length, which lent their chanting a measured dignity that could not be entrusted to an untrained congregation. Qualified choirs were needed, and for these a *Schola Cantorum*, or singing school, was founded in Rome to standardize the training of singers and teachers throughout the Christian world. The course required nine years and all the chants were memorized. Within a decade the new tradition had spread throughout Europe and would remain its universal musical language until the eleventh century.

With the Renaissance the rise of polyphony, along with the

secular influence of folksong and madrigal and the popularity of many new musical instruments, undermined the power of plainsong. The sober, ecclesiastical beauty of the psalms was defaced by wanton changes and the mutilating shears of Renaissance musicians, and by the late-sixteenth century most of the plainchants had been discarded as "too simple and barbaric." As a result, Christian psalmody increasingly lost its Oriental Jewish characteristics, and by a slow assimilation to the new liturgical style, gradually forfeited its ancient identity.

At this stage our first fork of the ancient Jewish musical stream, its Hebrew beginnings utterly forgotten, drops from sight for centuries. Only in the last fifty years has it reemerged—its affinity with the Christian liturgy now dramatically established.

The second fork that branched from the parent stream of ancient Hebrew music flowed for the most part eastward, to remain so well hidden from Western sight that it was believed the song of the biblical era lay forever buried beneath the ancient ruins of Jerusalem. As late as fifty years ago a reputable scholar confidently voiced the general opinion:

> Both the secular and temple music of ancient Israel have long since died out in silence. Not one tone has remained alive, not one of her melodies do we hear.

This belief was conclusively shattered in the 1920's by the monumental research done by the late Abraham Zvi Idelsohn, who over a period of years collected and recorded the songs and chants of a number of Oriental Jewish tribes living in various countries of the Near and Middle East. Uprooted from their native Palestine by one or another circumstance over many centuries, they had settled into small separate communities scattered at remote intervals from the Tigris valley to Inner Morocco, and from the Caspian Sea to the southernmost tip of Arabia.

In Transcaucasia, Persia, Babylon, Yemen, and other localities, they had each maintained their own settlements, culturally isolated from one another, for a span of generations that conceivably reached far back into Old Testament history. During the unsettled times of the early kings many Hebrews, as we have seen, had been carried off captive to eastern countries. The destruction of the First Temple had dispersed many more throughout the ancient world, as the start of a general pattern of relocation that would be known as the Diaspora, or Dispersion. In Babylonia, where after the captivity many Jews had remained by choice, a stronghold of Hebrew tradition untouched by Hellenism arose, which would welcome and absorb later kinsmen fleeing the tyranny of first Greece and then Rome.

Commerce also fed the gradual migration. In other Near Eastern centers Hebrews from the time of Solomon to the Caesars had established autonomous local communities, where, aided by the Orient's inbred resistance to change, they had succeeded in maintaining their own national and religious characteristics untouched by the historical factors that affected European Jewry.

This was especially true of the Jews of Yemen, in southern Arabia, who prior to the British occupation of that country in World War I had lived for many centuries completely isolated from the rest of the world, forgotten even by their kindred. According to their own tradition, they had migrated into Arabia after the destruction of Solomon's Temple and had remained there despite appeals by Ezra to return to their homeland. After the rise of Islam in the seventh century A.D., they had endured fierce religious and social persecution from the Arabs, who had driven them to the extreme southern part of Arabia and had further intensified their cultural solidarity. For centuries prior to this, they had been forbidden by the Arabs to leave Yemen, but after the war of 1914 many of them resettled in Palestine, where Idelsohn made an intensive study of their folksongs and their sacred music.

Over the ages, particularly during the seventeenth century, their folk poets had produced a large oral literature of popular songs, many of which were adapted from Oriental tunes already existing. Although they showed a preference for melodies based upon makams that were related to their own synagogue modes, their folk music, Idelsohn found, showed strong Arabian characteristics, their village songs particularly being influenced by close contact with the native Arab population.

Quite a different picture, however, was presented by the chants of the Jewish synagogue services. Here, apparently, no popular Arabian influences had been able to penetrate. Among the Jews

of Yemen, Idelsohn found no sacred songs built on the most typi-
cally Oriental scale, the chromatic *Hedjaz*, nor did their various
liturgical expressions show any similarity to those of their Islamic
neighbors.

Even more surprising was the fact that the synagogal music of
the Yemenite Jews, as chanted for centuries at the southernmost
corner of the Red Sea, showed a startling similarity in its basic
style to the songs and synagogal chants of the Georgian Jews of
Transcaucasia, more than a thousand miles to the north, as well as
to the synagogal music of the even older Babylonian and Persian
communities.

Although they do not always apply them to identical portions of
the liturgy, all of the tribes would appear to have preserved the
same modes for their biblical chants, and all use essentially the
same melody motives. Their tunes are tetrachordal, rhythmically
free, and based upon three of the four basic scales of the Semitic
Orient (the unused one being the *Hedjaz*).

The first of these is used for chanting the Prophets and corre-
sponds, according to Idelsohn, to the ancient Greek Phrygian mode.
(We can approximate this on the white keys of the piano starting
with D, bearing in mind that tone steps in the Orient differ from
ours and thus to us never sound quite on pitch.) To this scale there
is sometimes added a B-flat, in which form it is used for most Jewish folksongs, and in the liturgy, for such emotionally charged
texts as Lamentations and certain portions of the Psalms. Tender,
it can even be joyous, though to us its minor character makes it
seem sad.

Both Yemenite and Persian Jews use this mode for chanting the
Pentateuch as well, although the rest chant it in a mode founded
upon the second basic Oriental scale, corresponding to the Greek
Dorian (and found on our white piano keys starting with E). Various modes used for the Psalms include one based on the third scale,
which resembles the Greek Lydian (white keys starting with C),
but with the addition of a B-flat. The choice of mode for the
psalms depends on the occasion; a psalm providing an interlude
between prayers, for example, is sung in the mode used for them.

All of the modes, of which the Yemenites themselves differentiate
fifteen for their various synagogal chants, consist of two to four
basic motives, and their purposes and manner of singing are strictly

observed. The prayers chanted in the Pentateuch mode are recited in the same way throughout the year, except during the High Holidays, when a special mode is used. The Psalms also have a special mode for the Sabbath and holy days.

Since the songs are not made up of fixed melodies they vary somewhat in the various synagogues, but always retain their basic similarity of scale and motive. Males of all ages participate in the chant, but women are allowed no part in religious music. Prayers are chanted in unison by the congregation, after which the precentor intones the service, which the worshipers softly repeat after him, raising their voices only in Amen. The *Kedusha* and the priestly blessing they sing at full voice.

Their chanting is very smooth and all keep together in the strictest unison, proving that their attitude is neither perfunctory nor indifferent. On the contrary, they show great intensity of feeling. It is not unusual for the precentor to work himself into a state of ecstasy in which he increasingly sharpens his tones toward the end of a song, driving them up to as high as his voice can reach. Many songs thus end in a considerably higher register than they begin. Singing, however, is supposed to be from the chest, since head tones, or falsetto, are thought to lack the proper emotional warmth.

No deviation from tradition is tolerated, the congregation being less concerned with a precentor's artistry than with his fidelity to the spirit and letter of the liturgy. Like the high priest of the Jerusalem Temple, the Yemenite precentor bears a direct responsibility to God and his slightest mistake in uttering a prayer, if not immediately corrected, will, they believe, cause the mass prayer of the worshipers to be rejected. No one therefore assumes the post lightly, for personal misfortune is construed as divine punishment for any smallest infraction of the ritual. Of one precentor who tragically lost all of his children it was held that the liberties he took with the liturgy had brought the calamity upon him.

Idelsohn's research uncovered in the Yemenite Jewish chants what would appear to be the best preserved and most authentic tradition of biblical cantillation. From its similarities to that of the other long-isolated communities only one conclusion seems possible. Here, preserved after nearly 3,000 years, is a living tradition of a music the world had believed lost forever. In the chants and cantillation of Eastern Jewry may well be found a direct link to the psalms of ancient Israel as the Levites sang them in the Temple of Solomon, and even, through these, to folksongs that echoed across the hills of Judah when David was a shepherd lad.

Corollary to this discovery, another and equally arresting fact was returned to light after centuries of obscurity. Criticism of the Renaissance edition of Gregorian chant, which had despoiled the somber beauty of the ancient Church songs, culminated in the last century in a movement to restore these to the Latin ritual. Ancient manuscripts in various countries were examined for clues to correctly interpreting the rhythmically free, unison chants of the early Christian centuries, and after years of patient effort, chiefly by the Benedictine monks of Solesmes, France, much of the authentic Gregorian style was recovered. At the beginning of this century Pope Pius X ordered a return to the old tradition of Gregorian chant, which is now officially embodied in the Vatican Gradual.

Scrutinizing examples of these restored chants of early Christian psalmody, Idelsohn was among the first to see the striking parallels between them and certain of the synagogue chants he had set down in modern notation in his ten-volume *Thesaurus of Oriental Hebrew Melodies:*

Example 1.

Compare with Idelsohn, Thesaurus, Vol. I:

NO. 19 (PSALM 29:1)

Mi - z - mor le - da - vid ___ ho - vu la - do - nay be - ne e - lim

etc.

ho - vu la - do - nay ___ ko - vod vo - oz ___

The similarities between Jewish and Gregorian psalmodies were confirmed by others, notably by Peter Wagner, an outstanding scholar in the field of Gregorian plainsong, who holds that "the Yemenite Pentateuch tune . . . used also for certain psalms, could very well constitute a Gregorian psalm-chant with its *Initium*, its *Tenor*, its *Mediante* and *Finalis*":

Example 2.   After Peter Wagner

Initium   Tenor   Mediante   Initium   Tenor   Finalis

Compare with Idelsohn, *Thesaurus*, Vol. I:

NO. 1

A - don ho - o - lo - mim, ba - al ho - ra - ha - mim

go - dol ho - e - zoh   dar - ko - na - a - ro - zoh   etc,

NO. 2

A - lo - hay ___   ha - ne - sho - moh shan - no - tat - to bi ta - ho - roh   etc.

The same holds true for the Sabbath psalmody, which is sung by the entire congregation standing:

Example 3.

Compare with Idelsohn, *Thesaurus*, Vol. I:

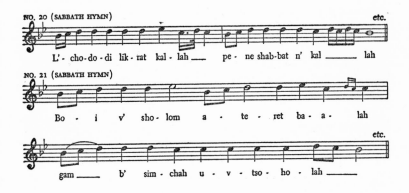

Similarities between the following Gregorian chant and the Jewish priestly blessing are self-evident:

Example 4.

Further examples:

From the abundance of such and similar evidence biblical scholars and musical historians alike were startled into new perception
of a fact that during the Middle Ages had been lost sight of: the
debt that Christian liturgical music owes to ancient Hebrew psalmody. This debt, never denied by the Church but only lately known
to the general public, is now leading to a new reassessment of the
ancient inheritance by which modern man, both Christian and Jew,
proclaims his confidence in his Creator.

From the tradition of the Jerusalem Temple the Church derived the principle of an inflected chant capable of adjusting to a

variety of liturgical needs, from a monotonic recitation in the ancient tones of the Lessons, Gospels, and Epistles, to the free melodic soaring of the Alleluia responds of the Mass. Set to the natural prose rhythms of human utterance, this inflected chant provided a vehicle of grave and noble dignity for the expression of Christian worship, no less than of Hebrew. Thus from the psalms and canticles rehearsed in the ancient Temple of Solomon there stemmed a tradition of musical worship that would foliate through the centuries into the towering tonal cathedrals of Palestrina, the foursquare fortress of the Lutheran chorale, and the tectonic grandeur of Sebastian Bach.

But whatever the formal contribution of Temple to Church, the essential wellspring of Christian musical liturgy must be traced, not to the priestly ritual in the high-girt sanctuary, but to the humble devotions in the many Jewish houses of prayer, where the primitive Christian faith first took root and drew its early strength from the psalms and prayer tunes of Judea. Preserved against incalculable odds through twenty centuries, enough traces of these survive in the folk tradition of Eastern Jewry to furnish living evidence of their ancient role during the desperate days when both Christian and Jew made common cause against the tyranny of pagan gods.

Music's universality has never been better demonstrated than by its dramatic evidence that the two great faiths of Western man drew spiritual sustenance from a common fund. Countless sources had enriched this, from the first chanted records of tribal history to the sublime conceptions of the Hebrew poets. Into it a score of early nations had poured the folk vigor of their songs and disappeared, leaving a musical legacy at once anonymous and incalculable.

Out of this amalgam the Hebrews early created a musical expression that would be strengthened and transfigured by the ordeal of twenty centuries. In the song of the Hebrew prophets was born a social conscience that would raise mankind a little above the level of tooth and claw. In the song of the Hebrew poets was first contained the adoration of a godhead that imposed no boundaries on the human spirit.

This is the great legacy that the music of ancient Israel transmitted as a common heritage. It is not so important that we know the exact tones in which its songs were sung. The tremendous thing is that they *were* sung and that their exultant message can still irradiate the heart.

The quest for the soul's integrity has been a long pilgrimage, and man still has far to go. Whatever reassures him that the journey is not a lone one takes its place among the noblest expressions of the human spirit. The Hebrew psalms, with their unfailing burden of faith and hope, became for countless generations a sacred token that their prayers were not despised, their joy not unregarded, their grief not singular. By their very universality they made the base of humanity itself more broad.

Yet these were the songs of a simple people who never achieved anything like the impressive civilization of their more powerful neighbors. We may ask: why did their songs endure, while those of Egypt and Greece and Rome faded into silence? The reason lies in their candid acknowledgment of the human condition. Every emotion common to the heart of man found its way into the songs of ancient Israel, because every hazard to which humankind is subject became parcel of its history.

This totality of feeling, kindling into a deep spiritual passion in the psalms, furnished a sympathetic bond between Jew and Christian in the early centuries which did honor to both. After intervening ages this recognition of essential kinship, not only between Jew and Christian but among all peoples, forms the great social and spiritual achievement of our time. In the chants of Christendom and Jewry alike the music of ancient Israel lives on to confirm their common heritage.

Meanwhile in modern Israel the vitality that informed its ancient songs is today creating a new music as expressive of its own time as was the music of its early flowering. This cannot recover the past, but it is a confident guarantee of the future.

Bibliography

Arnold, William R. "The Rhythms of the Ancient Hebrews" in *Old Testament and Semitic Studies, in memory of William Rainey Harper*. Vol. I, pp. 165-204. Chicago, 1908.

Bailey, Albert Edward. *Daily Life in Bible Times*. New York: Charles Scribner's Sons, 1943.

Baron, Salo W. *The Jewish Community*. Philadelphia: The Jewish Publishing Society of America, 1942.

Bertholet, Alfred. *A History of Hebrew Civilization*. Trans. by A. K. Dallas. London: G. G. Harrap & Co., Ltd., 1926.

Breasted, James Henry. *The Dawn of Conscience*. New York and London: Charles Scribner's Sons, 1933.

Briggs, Charles A. and Emilie Grace. *A Critical and Exegetical Commentary on the Book of Psalms*. New York: Charles Scribner's Sons, 1906-07.

Burrows, Millar. *The Dead Sea Scrolls*. New York: The Viking Press, Inc., 1955.

Champdor, Albert. *Babylon*. Trans. by Elsa Coult. London: Elek Books, Ltd., 1958; New York: G. P. Putnam's Sons, Inc., 1959.

Cheyne, T. K. *The Origins and Religious Contents of the Psalter*. New York: T. Whittaker, 1895.

Cornill, Carl H. *Music in the Old Testament*. Trans. by Lydia G. Robinson. Chicago: Open Court Publishing Co., 1909.

———. *The Culture of Ancient Israel*. Chicago: Open Court Publishing Co., 1914.

Cumming, Charles Gordon. *The Assyrian and Hebrew Hymns of Praise*. New York: Columbia University Press, 1934.

Delitzsch, Franz. *A Biblical Commentary on the Psalms*. Trans. by Francis Bolton. 3 vols. Edinburgh: Clark's Foreign Theological Library, 1871.

Douglas, Charles Winfred. *Church Music in History and Practice*. New York: Charles Scribner's Sons, 1937.

Dupont-Sommer, A. *The Jewish Sect of Qumran and the Essenes*. Trans. by R. D. Barnett. New York: The Macmillan Company, 1955.

Edersheim, Alfred. *Sketches of Jewish Life in the Days of Christ*. London: Religious Tract Society, 1876; New York: Hodder & Stoughton, 1910.

Engel, Carl. *The Music of the Most Ancient Nations*. London: W. Reeves, 1909.

Ewald, Heinrich A. *The Antiquities of Israel.* Trans. by Henry Shaen Solly. London: Williams and Norgate, 1876.

Finesinger, Sol Baruch. "Musical Instruments in the Old Testament," in *Hebrew Union College Annual.* Vol. III. Cincinnati: Hebrew Union College, 1926.

————. "The Shofar," in *Hebrew Union College Annual.* Vols. VIII and IX. Cincinnati: Hebrew Union College, 1931–32.

Galpin, Francis William. *The Music of the Sumerians and Their Immediate Successors, the Babylonians and Assyrians.* New York: The Macmillan Company; Cambridge: Cambridge University Press, 1937.

Gaster, Theodor H. *The Dead Sea Scriptures.* Garden City, N. Y.: Doubleday & Company, Inc., 1956.

Geiringer, Karl. *Musical Instruments: Their History in Western Culture from the Stone Age to the Present.* Trans. by Bernard Miall. London: George Allen and Unwin, Ltd., 1943.

Gradenwitz, Peter. *The Music of Israel.* New York: W. W. Norton & Company, Inc., 1949.

Grant, Frederick C. *Ancient Judaism and the New Testament.* New York: The Macmillan Company, 1959.

Harris, Charles W. *The Hebrew Heritage; A Study of Israel's Cultural and Spiritual Origins.* New York: The Abingdon Press, 1935.

Hastings, James. *A Dictionary of the Bible.* 5 vols. New York: Charles Scribner's Sons, 1899–1904.

Herder, Johann G. *The Spirit of Hebrew Poetry.* Trans. by James March. 2 vols. Burlington, Vermont: E. Smith, 1833.

Hollis, Frederick J. *The Archeology of Herod's Temple.* London: J. M. Dent and Sons, Ltd., 1934.

Idelsohn, A. Z. *Jewish Music in its Historical Development.* New York: Henry Holt and Company, 1929.

————.*Thesaurus of Oriental Hebrew Melodies.* Vol. I. Leipzig: Breitkopf und Härtel, 1914. Vols. II and III. Berlin: B. Harz, 1922.

Jahn, Johann, *Biblical Archaeology.* Trans. by Thomas C. Upham. New York: M. H. Newman & Co., 1853.

James, M. R. *The Apocryphal New Testament.* Oxford: Oxford University Press, 1924.

Jastrow, Morris, Jr. *Hebrew and Babylonian Traditions.* New York: Charles Scribner's Sons, 1914.

————. *The Song of Songs.* Philadelphia: J. B. Lippincott Co., 1921.

Jeremias, Alfred. *The Old Testament in the Light of the Ancient East.* Trans. by C. L. Beaumont. 2 vols. London: Williams and Norgate, 1911.

Join-Lambert, Michel. *Jerusalem*. Trans. by Charlotte Haldane. New York: G. P. Putnam's Sons, Inc., London: Elek Books Ltd., 1958.

Josephus, Flavius. *Antiquities of the Jews; Wars of the Jews; Against Apion*. Trans. by William Whiston. London: W. Bowyer, 1737.

Keller, Werner. *The Bible as History*. Trans. by William Neil. New York: William Morrow & Co., Inc., 1956.

Kenyon, Kathleen. *Archeology in the Holy Land*. New York: Frederick A. Praeger, Inc., 1960.

Kirkpatrick, A. F. *The Book of Psalms*. 3 vols. Cambridge: The University Press, 1892–1901.

Kohler, Kaufmann. *The Origins of the Synagogue and the Church*. N. Y., 1929.

Kramer, Samuel N. *From the Tablets of Sumer*. Indian Hill, Colorado: Falcon's Wing Press, 1956.

Langdon, Stephen H. *Babylonian Liturgies*. Paris: P. Geuthner, 1913.

Miller, Madeleine S. and J. Lane. *Encyclopedia of Bible Life*. New York and London: Harper & Brothers, 1941.

Oesterley, W. O. E. *The Jews and Judaism During the Greek Period*. London: Society for Promoting Christian Knowledge; New York: The Macmillan Company, 1941.

————. *The Psalms in the Jewish Church*. London: Skeffington & Son, 1910.

————. *A Fresh Approach to the Psalms*. New York: Charles Scribner's Sons, 1937.

Pfeiffer, Robert H. *Introduction to the Old Testament*. New York and London: Harper & Brothers, 1941.

Philo, Judaeus. "About the Life of Moses; About the Contemplative Life," in *Loeb Classical Library*. Trans. by F. H. Colson and G. H. Whitaker. Cambridge: Harvard University Press, 1929–62.

Rackham, Richard B. *The Acts of the Apostles*. 4th ed. London, 1909.

Rawlinson, G. *The Five Great Monarchies of the Ancient Eastern World*. New York: Scribner, Welford and Co., 1873.

Ryden, E. E. *The Story of Christian Hymnody*. Rock Island, Illinois: Augustana Book Concern, 1951.

Sachs, Curt. *The History of Musical Instruments*. New York: W. W. Norton & Company, Inc., 1940.

————. *Rhythm and Tempo*. New York: W. W. Norton & Company, Inc., 1953.

————. *The Rise of Music in the Ancient World, East and West*. New York: W. W. Norton & Company, Inc., 1943.

———. *World History of the Dance*. Trans. by Bessie Schönberg. New York: W. W. Norton & Company, Inc., 1937.

Saminsky, Lazare. *Music of the Ghetto and the Bible*. New York: Bloch Publishing Company, 1934.

Scramuzza, Vincent M. and P. L. MacKendrick. *The Ancient World*. New York: Henry Holt and Company, 1958.

Sendrey, Alfred. *Bibliography of Jewish Music*. New York: Columbia University Press, 1951.

Sheed, F. J., trans. *The Confessions of St. Augustine*. New York: Sheed & Ward, Ltd., 1943.

Smith, W. Robertson. *Lectures on the Religion of the Semites*. Edinburgh: A. & C. Black, 1889.

———. *The Old Testament in the Jewish Church*. New York: D. Appleton & Company, 1881.

Stainer, John. *The Music of the Bible*. New ed. London: Novello & Co., Ltd., 1914.

Tcherikover, Avigdor. *Hellenistic Civilization and the Jews*. Trans. by S. Applebaum. Philadelphia: Jewish Publishing Society of America, 1959.

Thirtle, James William. *Old Testament Problems*. London: Henry Frowde, 1916.

———. *The Titles of the Psalms*. London: Henry Frowde, 1904.

Trachtenberg, Joshua. *Jewish Magic and Superstition*. New York: Behrman's Jewish Book House, 1939.

Unger, Merrill F. *Archeology and the Old Testament*. Grand Rapids, Michigan: Zondervan Publishing House, 1954.

Weinman, Karl. *History of Church Music*. Ratisbon, New York: F. Pustet, 1910.

Werner, Eric. *The Sacred Bridge*. New York: Columbia University Press, 1959.

Wilkinson, Gardner. *The Manners and Customs of the Ancient Egyptians*. 3 vols. London: T. Murray, 1878.

Woolley, Charles Leonard. *Ur of the Chaldees*. London: E. Benn, Ltd., 1929.

Zeitlin, Solomon. "The Dead Sea Scrolls and Modern Scholarship," *Jewish Quarterly Review*. Fall, 1956.